YWAIN AND GAWAIN

EARLY ENGLISH TEXT SOCIETY

Original Series 254

1964 (for 1963), reprinted 1982

¶ Sir Gawayn answerd als curtays
þou sal noght do sir als þou sais
wit honowr sal noght be myne
bot sorro it aw wele at be þine
þis is þe lief wyth owten hone
& grawntes þat I am vndone
Sone þat light so sais þe boke
togeder oþer in armes toke
& kissed so ful fele syþe
þan war þai both glad & blithe
in armes so þai stode togeder
vnto þe king com pusand reder
& fast he cowart forto here
of þir knightes what þai were
& whi þai made so mekil gamyn
Sen þai has so foghten samyn
¶ Ful hendli þan asked þe king
whilk has so sone made saghtling
bitwix þam þat has bene so wrath
& aiþer haues done oþer scath
he said I went ȝe wals ful fain
aiþer of ȝow haue oþer slayn
& now ȝe er so frendes der
sir king said Gawain ȝe sal her
for enkrasing & hard grace
þus haue we foghten in þis place
I am Gawayn ȝowr awin neuow
& he ywayn faght with me now
when we war neer wen I wis
in name he frayned & I his
when we war knawen sone gan we sese

YWAIN AND GAWAIN

EDITED BY

ALBERT B. FRIEDMAN

AND

NORMAN T. HARRINGTON

Published for

THE EARLY ENGLISH TEXT SOCIETY

by the

OXFORD UNIVERSITY PRESS

LONDON   NEW YORK   TORONTO

1964

Oxford University Press, Walton Street, Oxford OX2 6DP

London Glasgow New York Toronto
Delhi Bombay Calcutta Madras Karachi
Kuala Lumpur Singapore Hong Kong Tokyo
Nairobi Dar es Salaam Cape Town
Melbourne Auckland
and associate companies in
Beirut Berlin Ibadan Mexico City

Published in the United States by
Oxford University Press, New York

Printed in Great Britain
at the University Press, Oxford
by Eric Buckley
Printer to the University

PREFACE

THE editors are grateful to the Trustees of the British Museum for permission to print the unique copy of *Ywain and Gawain* and to reproduce in facsimile a page of the manuscript as the frontispiece to the present edition. From Professors B. J. Whiting and F. P. Magoun we received many useful suggestions, and the editorial consultants of the Early English Text Society offered much good advice on the style and proportions of the Introduction and Commentary. Although our debt to Joseph Ritson and Gustav Schleich, the previous editors of the romance, is specified at many points in the textual notes and apparatus, we should be remiss if we did not also acknowledge here that their editions smoothed our way considerably.

A. B. F.
N. T. H.

Claremont, California
7 *June* 1962

CONTENTS

INTRODUCTION

I. The Manuscript and Editions

THE unique copy of *Ywain and Gawain* is preserved in the Cotton collection of the British Museum, specifically in MS. Cotton Galba E. IX, a large folio (320×220 mm.) on parchment. The text of the romance runs to 4032 lines and is complete. In addition to *Ywain and Gawain* (*YG* hereafter), which occupies ff. 4–25, the codex contains the following items:

(i) An inscription: *Chaucer exemplar emendate scriptum*, f. 1ᵛ. It was this inscription that first caught Tyrwhitt's attention and led to the discovery of these poems. The recto is blank.

(ii) A leaf inserted from a handsome book of hours, f. 2.

(iii) A faded seven-line fragment from a poem on the siege of Calais, f. 3. The full version of this poem (in the same hand) appears at the end of the manuscript, f. 113ᵛ. Below this is an inventory of linen, in two parts (7 and 5 lines), added in a different fifteenth-century hand and cancelled. The verso is blank.

(iv) *The Seven Sages of Rome*, ff. 25ᵛ–48ᵛ. See Brown and Robbins, *The Index of Middle English Verse*, 3187.

(v) Poem on the transitoriness of the world, ff. 48ᵛ–49. Begins: *Al es bot a fantum þat [we] with ffare.*

(vi) *The Prophecies of Merlin*, ff. 49–50ᵛ. Begins: *Herkenes speches of manikyn thinges / Of gret ferlys*, &c. See *Index*, 1112.

(vii) *Narratio de domino denario [Sir Peny]*, ff. 50ᵛ–51. See *Index*, 1480.

(viii) A Rood Poem, f. 51ᵛ. The heading has: *Vos qui transitis: si crimina flere uelitis. / Per me transite: quoniam sum ianua uite.* Begins: *Bides a while and haldes ʒoure pais / and heres what god him seluen sais / hingand on þe rode.* At the end a modern hand has added: *de domino denario / mani thinges not to / be reiected*, &c. (referring to the whole gathering, not just this item).

(ix) Poems of Laurence Minot, ff. 52–57ᵛ.

(x) *The Gospel of Nicodemus*, ff. 57ᵛ–66ᵛ. See *Index*, 512.

(xi) A verse treatise on the Seven Deadly Sins found also in several manuscripts of the *Cursor Mundi*, ff. 67–69. Begins: *Here will I tell a schort tretice | Made of þe seuyn dedly vice*, &c.

(xii) An incomplete version of the 'Book of Penance' which is added to the *Cursor Mundi* in several manuscripts, ff. 69–73ᵛ. Begins: *Als witty men ful wele has talde, | Schrift aw to be thrinfalde*, &c. See *Index*, 694.

(xiii) A *Pater Noster* followed by a metrical exposition, found also in some manuscripts of the *Cursor Mundi*, ff. 73ᵛ–75. F. 75ᵛ is blank.

(xiv) *The Pricke of Conscience*, ff. 76–113. See *Index*, 3428.

(xv) On the fly-leaf are some notes on the points of a horse, beginning: *The horss hath xxv properties, þat ys to say: He hath iiii off a lyon, iiii of an ox, iiii off an asse, iiii off an hare, and iiii of a fox, and v off a woman*. Also the same hand has added a poem on the siege of Calais in 1400, ff. 113ᵛ–114ᵛ (cf. item iii). Begins: *In Juyl whan the sone schon | Tres levys and herbis grene*, &c. See *Index*, 1497.

(xvi) On f. 114ᵛ appears the name Richard Chawfer, elaborately lettered in capitals three times in a modern hand.

The complete manuscript has three fly-leaves (ff. 1–3) and 111 leaves, arranged in gatherings of twelve leaves each.[1] The seventh gathering, however, is short of one leaf, and the last gathering contains only four leaves. The end of most gatherings is marked by a catchword.[2] At the beginning of each gathering, moreover, there is a signature (A to L) in large, clear, modern majuscules. Hulme, who made a careful study of the chirography of the manuscript, distinguished six separate hands at work in the composition of its various portions (pp. xxii f.). All the hands except two, however, present the same general characteristics and belong roughly to the same period. The first hand extends to f. 48ᵛ; the second hand extends eight lines into the first column of f. 50. The third hand, notable for its awkwardness and lack of care, extends to f. 51ᵛ;

[1] We refer throughout to the modern foliation of Galba E. ix. To obtain the older foliation, subtract three from the new.

[2] There are not, however, catchwords at the end of every gathering as W. H. Hulme states in his edition of *The Harrowing of Hell and Gospel of Nicodemus*, E.E.T.S., E.S. 100 (1907), p. xxii. Catchwords are missing appropriately at ff. 51ᵛ and 75ᵛ, both of which are final pages of poems. Also there is no catchword at the bottom of f. 110ᵛ. There are catchwords in the hand of the scribe responsible for *YG* at the bottom of ff. 15ᵛ, 27ᵛ, and 39ᵛ.

the fourth hand to f. 76; the fifth to f. 113; and the sixth hand, altogether different from any of the preceding, extends through the last three pages (ff. 113ᵛ–114ᵛ). Of these hands the first is responsible for *YG* and for *The Seven Sages of Rome*. It is a hand belonging to the first quarter of the fifteenth century.

The pages of *YG* are divided by horizontal and vertical rulings into two columns of forty-seven lines each. The condition of the parchment is generally good, although the early part of the manuscript (ff. 4–10 particularly) seems to have suffered from water damage during the fire of 1731 which destroyed part of the Cotton collection. As a result there is a certain amount of shrinkage and discoloration, especially at the inner corners of the early folios where the top four or five lines are shrivelled and difficult to read. Apart from this and a small tear at the top of ff. 4 and 5, the manuscript is remarkably clean and legible. There are three red rubrics in the same hand. The first, *Here begyns Ywaine and Gawain*, occurs at the beginning of the poem at the head of the first column. On f. 16ᵛ, between l. 2428 and l. 2429, is the rubric *Here es þe myddes of þis boke*. Since this remark occurs 412 lines past the middle of the romance as we have it, it means, if taken literally, that some 800 lines are missing from the second half of the poem—an interpretation which we reject (see note to ll. 2428–9). Immediately beneath the last column of the poem the final rubric reads: *Ywain and Gawayn þus makes endyng, | God grant us al hys dere blyssing. Amen.* The ink of the manuscript is easily legible although fading slightly to medium brown in many places.

At the beginning of the poem there is a large, ornate blue capital, picked out in red, which extends downward for four lines. Besides this there are forty smaller capitals throughout the text, alternately red and blue, each extending through two lines. Delicate flourishes from these capitals often extend upward and downward in the margins for sixteen or seventeen lines. Poems copied by the fourth hand (ff. 52–76) contain capitals ornamented in black and yellow, the flourishes of which are cunningly contrived to reveal the faces of angels and demons, or the leaves and blossoms of flowers. The ornamentation of the capitals of *YG*, however, though meticulous, is non-representational. By modern standards these capitals do not always mark natural divisions in the text, and on three occasions (ll. 1551, 2353, and 3681) we have not thought it necessary to indent a line beginning with a red or blue capital.

Throughout the text there are also numerous paragraph marks, with decoration in red and blue extending downwards in the margin. Compared with modern practice the paragraphing is exceedingly capricious and in many instances has not been followed in this edition.[1] The line opposite a paragraph mark begins with a capital letter in the ink of the text emphasized with a dab of yellow or red. Other lines begin with a minuscule letter. Interior capitalization is uneven, and when the difference between a majuscule and a minuscule is simply one of size, it is impossible to tell whether a capital is intended or not. There is no regularity in the capitalization of proper names. Gawain and Lunet are usually capitalized, but the name of the hero of the poem is spelt throughout with a small *y*. Moreover, no regular system of punctuation is discernible. A light dash is used from time to time to designate a short pause, and very infrequently there is a full stop, but these marks are so rare and so careless that the manuscript may be said to be virtually unpunctuated.

The handwriting is large, round, and very legible. There are the inevitable small erasures and a few cancellations, but on the whole it is a careful, craftsmanlike piece of work. Occasional insertions above the line have been made by the scribe and by one, or possibly two, later hands. Usually the scribe is careful to distinguish between *n* and *u*, although combinations of *m*, *n*, and *u* frequently present difficulty. As is common in manuscripts of this period *y* and *þ* are indistinguishable, but, fortunately, the context in every case makes clear which letter was intended and no controversial readings arise from this confusion.

Of the provenance and early history of this manuscript nothing is known until it reached the hands of the noted antiquarian Sir Robert Bruce Cotton (1571–1631), whose collection of manuscripts passed to the British Museum in 1753. In 1781 Thomas Warton published liberal excerpts from the first half of *YG* in his *History of English Poetry* along with the remark that it had 'some great outlines of Gothic painting, and appears to have been written in the reign of king Henry the sixth' (iii. 107–34). The first edition of the poem was undertaken by Joseph Ritson, who in 1802 included it in his *Ancient Engleish Metrical Romanceës*, together with a general introduction, notes, and glossary (i. 1–169; iii. 225–42). The last notable contributions to scholarship on *YG* were made by Gustav

---

[1] For the paragraphing see p. lxi.

Schleich, who edited the poem (Oppeln and Leipzig, 1887), and two years later produced his study on its relationship to Chrétien de Troyes.[1] The edition is still of value, particularly for its linguistic commentary. A long extract from *YG* (ll. 1–1448) was published in an American textbook selection of romances in 1930,[2] but none of the readings and only an occasional note is of independent value.

II. ANALYSIS OF THE STRUCTURE

Unlike most romances of adventure, the structure of *YG* is remarkably tight and logical, a virtue due mainly to the fact that it is essentially an abridged free translation of *Yvain*, or *Le Chevalier au Lion*, perhaps the most mature and carefully constructed work of Chrétien de Troyes. The strongly developed central story deals with the wooing and winning of a lady by a knight, a crisis in their relations which ends in estrangement, a series of adventures in which the moral regeneration of the knight is accomplished, and a final scene of forgiveness and reconciliation. Into this story are introduced two long episodes: a preliminary episode (ll. 7–564) which sets the stage and introduces the hero, and an almost self-contained episode (ll. 2743–3828) which displays the hero's prowess and leads ultimately to the climax of the work—a combat between the hero of the romance and that paragon of all chivalry, Sir Gawain. The structure of the romance may be analysed as follows:

I. (ll. 7–564) At Arthur's court Colgrevance tells of his encounter with a Hospitable Host, a Giant Herdsman, and a Storm-Knight at a marvellous well where he has been discomfited in battle and then has returned on foot to the court. On hearing the story King Arthur determines to see the well, but Sir Ywain vows to avenge his cousin and have the adventure for himself.

II. (ll. 565–1656) Ywain journeys to the well, mortally wounds its defender, and subsequently wins, with the help of Lunet, the hand of the dead knight's widow, the beautiful Alundyne. When Arthur appears at the well with his knights, he is feasted for a week,

[1] *Über das Verhältnis der mittelenglischen Romanze* Ywain and Gawain *zu ihrer altfranzösischen Quelle* (Berlin, 1889).
[2] *Middle English Metrical Romances*, ed. W. H. French and C. B. Hale (New York, 1930), pp. 485–527.

at the end of which Gawain persuades Ywain to accompany him on a tour of the tournaments. At the end of a year Ywain neglects the term which his wife has set, and after she repudiates their love, he runs mad in the forest.

III. (ll. 1657–3828) Ywain is cured of his madness by a lady and her maidens. When he has recovered, Ywain undertakes a series of adventures by means of which, through a combination of bravery and selflessness, he is able to accomplish his redemption. In rapid succession there follow his defeat of Sir Alers (ll. 1869–1974), his rescue of a lion from a dragon (ll. 1975–2016), and his successful fights against Harpin of the Mountain (ll. 2207–2506) and a wicked steward and his two brothers (ll. 2507–2645). At this point is interpolated the story of a younger daughter of a rich lord who dies without a male heir. The two sisters disagree about the disposition of the land, and the younger daughter is dispossessed of her inheritance by her sister. Eventually the younger sister secures Ywain as her champion, and after another adventure in which Ywain kills two monsters and liberates a bevy of captured damsels, he meets Gawain in a long and inconclusive combat to determine the justice of the rival sisters' claims (ll. 2743–3828).

IV. (ll. 3829–4032) At the conclusion of this last adventure Ywain returns to the marvellous well, where, with the aid of the faithful and astute Lunet, he is reunited with Alundyne.

From the foregoing analysis it can be seen that a little over half of *YG* (ll. 1656–3828) is devoted to a series of episodes designed to display the valour of the hero and to show the steps by which his redemption is accomplished. In the course of the romance we watch Ywain come to the rescue of various ladies in distress, the performance of which involves him in a succession of increasingly desperate fights against mounting odds. In rapid order Ywain does battle against a plundering baron, a dragon, a giant, three wicked knights, two half-human monsters, and finally, Sir Gawain, the most redoubtable opponent of them all. These episodes are almost wholly unrelated to each other, the only common element being the appearance in each of Ywain and his lion. None of the episodes, moreover, is associated with either the historical or the legendary Ywain. Rather they seem to have been chosen from a common stock of Arthurian adventures which could be attached at will to any of the knights of the Round Table. As a result many of the episodes in this section have seemed to some scholars to be disconnected and pointless—a series of adventures which could have been expanded or contracted at the whim of the author without harming the unity of the romance. A. C. L. Brown, commenting on Chrétien's *Yvain*, said of the multiplication of adventures that 'a probable explanation of Chrétien's extensive insertions and additions towards the end of the romance is that he desired to bring his piece up to the length of his *Erec*, *Cliges*, and *Lancelot*'.[1] Even so wholehearted an admirer of Chrétien's artistry as Gustave Cohen objects to the excessive spinning out of adventures in *Yvain*: 'Ce qu'on peut objecter encore à ces aventures accessoires greffées sur la principale, c'est qu'elles sont toujours déterminées par le hasard, conduit par la fantaisie du conteur, et que rarement elles sont amenées par le caractère du protagoniste.'[2] Of recen years several scholars have attempted to show that what at first seems like a miscellaneous string of adventures is actually a carefully contrived set of opportunities for Yvain to redeem himself from the sin of Pride.[3]

It should perhaps be added here that *YG* is but one of several medieval translations or redactions of *Yvain*. The earliest extant is the Middle High German *Iwein* (before 1204), by Hartmann von Aue. The Welsh *Owein*, or *Chwedyll Iarlles y Ffynnawn* (The Tale of the Lady of the Fountain), which is in Lady Charlotte Guest's *Mabinogion*, may include traditions anterior to and independent of *Yvain*.[4] It is dated *c*. 1350. The Norse prose *Ívens saga* ascribes itself to the reign of Hákon IV (1217–63); the Swedish *Herr Iwan, Lejon-Riddaren*, which imitates Chrétien's metre as well as his matter, is dated internally 1303. The Swedish work was early translated into Danish.[5]

---

[1] 'Iwain: A Study in the Origins of Arthurian Romance', (*Harvard*) *Studies in Phil. and Lit.* vii (Boston, 1903), 133. For the belief that Chrétien added developments and episodes for the joy of story-telling, see Gaston Paris, *Mélanges de littérature française du moyen âge* (Paris, 1912), pp. 244–6.

[2] *Chrétien de Troyes et son œuvre* (Paris, 1931), p. 354.

[3] See A. Adler, 'Sovereignty in Chrétien's *Yvain*', *PMLA*. lxii (1947), 281–305, and J. Harris, 'The Role of the Lion in Chrétien de Troyes' *Yvain*', *PMLA*. lxiv (1949), 1143–63.

[4] See A. C. L. Brown, 'On the Independent Character of the Welsh *Owein*', *Romanic Rev.* iii (1912), 143–72, and R. S. Loomis, *Arthurian Tradition and Chrétien de Troyes* (New York, 1949), pp. 278 ff.

[5] On the Scandinavian versions, see *Riddarasögur*, ed. E. Kölbing (Strassburg, 1872), pp. xii ff., and *Germania*, xx (1875), 396 f. The Welsh, German, and Scandinavian versions are also discussed in *Arthurian Literature in the Middle Ages*, ed. R. S. Loomis (Oxford, 1959), pp. 196–9, 434–8, 441 f., 465–7.

III. Relation to Chrétien's *Yvain, le Chevalier au Lion*

That the English poet (E) worked directly from a manuscript of *Yvain* (composed between 1166 and 1181[1]) is established beyond doubt by the almost identical conduct of the narrative, by striking similarities in descriptive detail, and by the many passages of word-for-word translation. Nowhere in the romance, however, does the poet mention Chrétien (Ch. in line references hereafter) by name. Rather we have such conventional locutions as *als sayes þe buke* (9), *als it telles in þe boke* (3209), *so sais þe boke* (3671), *Of þam na mare have I herd tell | Nowþer in rumance ne in spell* (4027 f.). The poet also omits Chrétien's closing lines, in which he names and signs the poem (Ch. 6814 f.):

> DEL CHEVALIER AU LYON fine
> CHRESTIIENS son romanz einsi.[2]

Of the surviving manuscripts of *Yvain* none furnishes a completely satisfactory source for the English poem.[3] Schleich, who has made the most exhaustive textual comparison of YG with the surviving French manuscripts, demonstrates that the English poem has close affinities with the group of manuscripts which Foerster designated PH, but that there are a number of variant readings not consistent with this classification. Schleich goes on to suggest that the French source of YG was closer to Chrétien's original than any of the manuscripts existing today (*Verhältnis*, pp. 18–19).

The English poem is by no means a slavish translation of *Yvain*. The poet does not hesitate to trim, eliminate, correct, or add when it suits his purpose. Whole episodes are lopped off, while others are

---

[1] The latest proposed date is 1177–81 (A. Fourrier, *Bull. bibl. de la soc. int. Arthurienne*, ii (1950), 81–88. Earlier proposals: Foerster, before 1173; G. Paris, 1173–4; F. E. Guyer, 1166–7; U. T. Holmes, 1169; P. A. Becker, after 1166— see U. T. Holmes, *Crit. Bibl. of French Lit.*, i (1952), 106 f.

[2] The citations of Chrétien are from *Der Löwenritter* (*Yvain*), ed. Wendelin Foerster (4th edn., Halle, 1912).

[3] The existing manuscripts of *Yvain* are listed and classed in Wendelin Foerster's edition (Halle, 1887), pp. vii ff., an account criticized and corrected by A. Micha, *La Tradition manuscrite des romans de Chrétien de Troyes* (Paris, 1939), pp. 146–66 and *passim*, and by P. Jonin, *Prolégomènes à une édition d'Yvain* (Aix-en-Provence, 1958), pp. 15–123. The Modena fragment is described in G. Bertoni, 'Fragment d'un manuscrit du "Chevalier au Lion"', *Romania*, xliii (1914), 427–9; 'Chrestien de Troyes: le manuscrit d'Annonay', ed. A. Pauphilet (Paris, 1934), reproduces the fragment at Annonay.

telescoped into a few lines. As a result, the 6,818 lines of Chrétien's poem are reduced to 4,032 lines in the English version. For the most part the redaction has been carried out with controlled skill, the modifications following a coherent pattern. The poem is clearly the work of a minstrel catering for the sober, realistic audience of a provincial baron's hall, an audience whose sensibilities and sympathies were not adjusted to Chrétien's elaborate and subtle representations of courtly love or to high-flown chivalric sentiment. The elegant and dilatory court romance of Chrétien has become in the hands of the English minstrel a rapid-paced story of love and gallant adventure. As Jessie L. Weston has said, it is Chrétien's matter, not his manner, that tempted the English translator.[1]

A. *Excision of courtly love and chivalric refinements.* Evidence of the sterner temperament and more strenuous preoccupations of the English poet occur at the very beginning of *YG*. After Arthur's Whitsunday feast, the knights and ladies withdraw from the banquet tables and amuse each other by talking and telling stories. In Chrétien's version they speak of the *angoisses*, the *dolors*, and the *granz biens* of love, and then proceed to bemoan the low estate to which love had then fallen (18–28):

> Mes ore i a mout po des suens;
> Que a bien pres l'ont tuit leissiee,
> S'an est amors mout abeissiee;
> Car cil, qui soloient amer,
> Se feisoient cortois clamer
> Et preu et large et enorable.
> Ore est amors tornee a fable
> Por ce que cil, qui rien n'an santent
> Dïent qu'il aimment, mes il mantent,
> Et cil fable et mançonge an font,
> Qui s'an vantent, et droit n'i ont.

In *YG*, however, the guests prefer accounts of *dedes of armes and of veneri* to idle banter about *amor* (E 25–36):

> Fast þai carped and curtaysly
> Of dedes of armes and of veneri
> And of gude knightes þat lyfed þen,
> And how men might þam kyndeli ken
> By doghtines of þaire gude dede
> On ilka syde, wharesum þai 3ede,

> For þai war stif in ilka stowre,
> And þarfore gat þai grete honowre.
> þai tald of more trewth þam bitw[e]ne
> þan now omang men here es sene,
> For trowth and luf es al bylaft;
> Men uses now anoþer craft.

From the very outset we are led to expect a tale of *doghtines* and *dedes of armes*. The bias of the English poet against elaborate dissections of the human heart results in the excision of one of the great purple passages of Chrétien's romance, the description of how Yvain was smitten with love after he had seen Laudine (E—Alundyne) mourning the death of her husband, whom he had slain. In an extended passage of 239 lines (1302–1541), Chrétien describes in Ovidian terms[1] how Yvain is wounded by Love, despairs of winning the heart of Laudine, yet decides to submit to the rule of Love and remain in the castle. Throughout, the scene is developed in the traditional rhetoric of love. In addition the passage is characterized by continual and subtle word-play. Much is made, for example, of the double sense in which Laudine is Yvain's 'enemy' and of the way in which Yvain is both literally and figuratively a 'prisoner of Love'.

The passage is significant for yet another reason. Chrétien is careful to pose explicitly the moral problem involved in the love of a knight for a lady whose husband he has just killed. With what propriety, in other words, can Laudine encourage the attentions of Yvain? It is essentially a dramatic question, and Chrétien poses it with full consciousness of the irony of Yvain's position (1360–1):

> Son cuer an mainne s'anemie,
> S'aimme la rien, qui plus le het.

Understandably Yvain frets over his awkward situation, but consoles himself with the sudden reflection that *fame a plus de mil corages*. Thematically this notion serves a double purpose: it induces Yvain to remain in Laudine's castle as her servant in Love, and it provides at least a rudimentary explanation for the widow Laudine's subsequent change of heart and the easy consolation she finds in her new husband, Yvain.

---

[1] On Chrétien's debt to Ovid, see F. E. Guyer, *Romance in the Making* (New York, 1954), pp. 85–101, 181–219.

In the hands of the English poet the passage fares badly. He cuts
Chrétien's 239 lines to 39 (869–908)—one of the major reductions
of the poem. Only enough detail is kept to make the action credible
and clear. As a result, E gives only the barest essentials of Yvain's
infatuation, considering it sufficient to say, quite simply, that
Ywain fell in love with Alundyne while looking at her through the
window.

Everywhere Chrétien's elaborate figures are either radically cur-
tailed or omitted. One of the more notable omissions (5374–96) is
a graceful tribute in the manner of Ovid to the daughter of the lord
of the *Chastel de Pesme Avanture*. So great was her beauty, says
Chrétien, that if the God of Love had seen her he would have cast
off his deity, become a man, and wounded himself with one of his
own arrows. Also omitted is an extended passage (2639–71) in
which Chrétien plays somewhat tediously on the theme that a knight
in love resembles a body without a heart, a biological phenomenon
that is only explained by the fact that the lover, wonderfully enough,
grows a new 'heart of hope', a heart which is, alas, more often than
not false and treacherous. Still another major omission takes place
at that point in Chrétien's narrative (2722–41) where the damsel
bearing Laudine's message of repudiation to her errant husband
draws a detailed distinction between the false lover, who steals
hearts treacherously, and the true lover, who, wherever he goes,
cherishes the heart of his lady and takes care to restore it to its
proper place.

The English poet is also notably unsympathetic to Chrétien's
lively interest in the fine points of chivalric behaviour—an interest
which reflects the tastes and preoccupations of the cultivated circle,
presided over by Marie de Champagne, for which Chrétien wrote.[1]
We have already remarked how explicitly Chrétien develops the
moral dilemma which faces Laudine when Lunete presses the suit
of the slayer of Esclados le Ros. As a practical woman she knows
she must have a knight-protector to defend the fountain, and Yvain
comes ready to hand with the highest recommendation. Ideally,
however, the idea of marrying the slayer of her husband is repugnant to her, and even later, when she has reconciled herself to the
marriage, she is still concerned with what the world will think of

---

[1] For a discussion of the relationship between Marie de Champagne and
Chrétien, see T. P. Cross and W. A. Nitze, *Lancelot and Guenevere* (Chicago,
1930), pp. 67–69.

her action. As Laudine warns Lunete, Yvain will have to act so that nobody can say (1809–10),

> C'est cele, qui prist
> Celui, qui son seignor ocist.

The important point at issue in the whole dilemma is whether or not, according to the social code of the time, Yvain has become the lady's mortal enemy by killing her husband. This dilemma the lady solves very neatly by an adroit piece of logic-chopping (Ch. 1760–75) in which she proves that, because Yvain acted out of self-defence, he cannot be considered guilty of the death of Esclados. According to all the dictates of *droit, san et reison* therefore, she is not obliged to hate Yvain, and is free, if she so desires, to marry him. This piece of casuistry, which reflects the characteristic delight of the age in the art of subtle disputation, is cast in the form of a dialogue which Laudine imagines taking place between herself and Yvain. The same dialogue with minor changes actually takes place several hundred lines later (Ch. 1995–2004), when Lunete presents Yvain to his mistress for the first time. In E, however, the subtly reasoned dialogue is not represented in either place. Alundyne, in fact, makes no attempt to justify her sudden decision to marry Ywain on any grounds other than sternest necessity. Her lands and her fountain must be defended, and, as the steward says with hard-headed practicality (E 1221–4):

> wemen may maintene no stowre,
> þai most nedes have a governowre.
> þarfor mi lady most nede
> Be weded hastily for drede.

Another example of Chrétien's interest in social punctilio which E fails to reproduce concerns what must have been a practical and familiar problem of courtly behaviour. In the midst of his description of the festivities which Yvain holds for Arthur and his knights, Chrétien pauses a moment (2452–65) to consider the delicate line separating the courteous and legitimate attentions a hostess may pay to her guests from over-familiarity and indiscretion. Some fools, Chrétien remarks, may mistake the attentions, embraces, and *bele parole* of a hostess for love. Such behaviour, however, far from being reprehensible, is the perfect example of courtesy, and Laudine is commended by Chrétien for the gracious manner in which she honours her guests *chascun par soi et toz ansamble*.

Chrétien also treats in some detail the rival claims of marriage and chivalry, and the conflicting demands each makes on the married knight.[1] Chrétien had already occupied himself with this theme in *Erec et Enide*, where Erec's uxoriousness causes his valour to be called in question, thus providing the dramatic situation from which spring the series of adventures that form the bulk of that romance.[2] In *Yvain* Chrétien returns to this theme once again.

This time the problem is raised by Gauvain, who, in a long elaborate speech (2486–2538), urges Yvain to leave his bride and to accompany him on a round of tournaments, lest, by forsaking chivalry, Yvain lose the love of Laudine and the esteem of his fellows. As Gauvain says (2484–92):

> 'Comant? Seroiz vos or de çaus . . .
> Qui por lor fames valent mains?
> Honiz soit de sainte Marie,
> Qui por anpirier se marie!
> Amander doit de bele dame,
> Qui l'a a amie ou a fame,
> Si n'est puis droiz, que ele l'aint,
> Que ses pris et ses los remaint.'

To this argument Gauvain adds a rhetorical appeal to the memory of old friendship, a reminder of the sweetness of deferred pleasures, and a warning against the enervating effects of bad habits generally. It is little wonder that Yvain is lured away from the comforts of Laudine to a life of high chivalric activity. The demands of honour have been clearly and explicitly opposed to those of conjugal love, and honour, for the time being at least, has triumphed.

The Englishman's handling of Gawain's speech (1455–78) is much more perfunctory. Once again he has been content to keep only the essential details before the reader. Although the exigencies of the plot force him to reproduce Gawain's injunction against sloth and degeneracy, the speech as a whole is about half as long, it lacks the high, passionate tone of Gauvain's warning, and, above

---

[1] Cross and Nitze point out (*Lancelot and Guenevere*, p. 67) that Chrétien upholds the ideal of married love in all his romances with the single, notable exception of the *Charrete*. Whether or not the notion of adulterous love developed in that romance was repugnant to him, it is certain that in his next work, *Yvain*, Chrétien quite pointedly stresses the sanctity of married love. As Professor Nitze says: 'Chrétien, poet of the *courtois* world, remains at heart a *bon bourgeois*.' It is perhaps not without significance that of all Chrétien's surviving romances, only *Yvain*, the most moral and the most eventful, was adopted by the English.

[2] See especially ll. 2437–2583 of *Erec et Enide*, ed. W. Foerster (Halle, 1909).

all, fails to reproduce the rhetorical heightening by which Chrétien emphasizes the importance of the scene. Here, as in almost every other instance where his source includes a discussion of courtly love or etiquette, E shows himself stubbornly indifferent.

B. *Omissions and condensations.* The English poet emphasizes the narrative movement of the poem by a continual process of elimination and reduction. Cumulatively these changes tell us a great deal about the poet, his method, and the tastes of his audience. The cleaner, tidier story that results has been achieved, unfortunately, by sacrificing many of Chrétien's best-calculated effects, to say nothing of his subtler nuances. Within our scope it is possible only to offer selected illustrations; other instances are recorded in the commentary.

1. Chrétien's management of suspense in the plotting of *Yvain* is perhaps the strongest mark of his skill as a narrator. Yvain's reconciliation with Laudine hangs in suspense during his adventures with the lion; and while disguised as the Knight of the Lion, he comes within an ace of abandoning the niece and nephews of Gauvain to an ugly fate because of a prior commitment to act as the champion of the slandered Lunete. These arcs of suspense are integral to the design of the plot and remain in E, but E often suppresses Chrétien's local suspense. For example, as Yvain approaches the *Chastel de Pesme Avanture* he is warned against lodging there not only by the outcries of a series of villagers but also, and passionately, by an aged lady of station (Ch. 5143 ff.— E 2931 ff.). E, for economy's sake doubtless, drops the lady's speech as redundant, though it vitally contributes to the foreboding atmosphere. Again, just before Yvain and Gauvain, each unrecognized by the other, begin their Sohrab and Rustum combat, Chrétien suspends the action for an allegorical disquisition on *Amor* and *Haïne*, developing at length the ironic possibilities of the situation and prolonging his audience's anxiety as to the outcome of a battle between invincible heroes (5998–6107). E apparently found the digression too fanciful—and indeed Chrétien has overdone a good thing here. Always eager to get on with the story, E cuts the passage from 109 to 11 lines (3513–24), incidentally dissipating the suspense. And on occasion E positively undercuts the suspense inherent in the situation, as when he makes Lunet assure the trembling Ywain, while conducting him to his first interview with her mistress, that (E 1142)

Sho loves þe wele withouten lite.

2. E regularly omits details of ceremony, dress, and other circumstantial particulars. When Yvain greets Lunete (Ch. 6694),

Les iauz li beise et puis le vis;

Ywain merely 'thanked hir ful fele sith' (E 3943). In E, Chrétien's squires lose the crane falcons they wear on their wrists. Costume is usually given short shrift: Chrétien describes the dress of the younger sister on her appearance at King Arthur's court in some detail (4738 ff.); E spares it not a word. E says the contending sisters are daughters of 'a grete lord' (2746); Chrétien names him as 'li sire de la Noire Espine' (4705). Perhaps the most striking contrast is the passage in Chrétien where the court ladies at Lunete's trial lament her fate, particularizing their obligations to her (4361–79). E reproduces laconically their general lament only (2539–42).

3. The descriptions of combat are always more circumstantial in Chrétien (cf. Ch. 3152 ff.—E 1875 ff.), E taking special care to excise gory particulars (cf. Ch. 4194 ff.—E 2441 ff.). The same sensitivity accounts for E's toning down scenes of intense emotional display, such as Alundyne's (Laudine's) grief at her husband's funeral (Ch. 1144 ff.—E 817 ff.). One especially misses in E the sharp bickering among Keu, Calogrenant, and Yvain that initiates the heroic action.

4. Chrétien's topical allusions, literary references, and French place-names are omitted by way of naturalizing and modernizing the romance, and also perhaps to correct the Frenchman's geography, for Chrétien's characters move from Arthur's various British courts to the Breton forest of Broceliande (where much of the action takes place) without the slightest mention of a channel crossing.[1] E deletes mention of Broceliande (Ch. 189, 697) as well as references to le bois d'Argone (Ch. 3228) and les rives de Sainne (Ch. 5980–1). Chrétien's allusions to the Chanson de Roland (3235–6) and to Forré, the Arab doctor in the Narbonnais branch of the cycle de Guillaume (597), are also rejected, perhaps on the grounds that they would not be recognized by a fourteenth-century English audience. So, too, E fails to reproduce topical references to

---

[1] The geographical vagaries of Chrétien's poem are probably traceable to slavish or unimaginative imitation of his source. See R. S. Loomis, *Arthurian Tradition and Chrétien de Troyes* (New York, 1949), pp. 290–3.

li dus d'Osteriche (Ch. 1042), to *l'anpererriz de Rome* (Ch. 2064), and to *Noradin*, i.e. Nureddin Mahmud (Ch. 596).

5. Either because of artistic inability or lack of interest, E passes over Chrétien's ironical touches, such as those in Yvain's speech against Keu (Ch. 630 ff.—cf. E 499 ff.) or the dramatic irony that occurs after Lunete's ordeal when the disguised Yvain tells Laudine that he cannot linger at her court until his lady ceases to be angry with him, and Laudine replies, unaware that she herself is the angry lady (Ch. 4593–5),

> 'Certes,' fet ele, 'ce me poise.
> Ne taing mie por tres cortoise
> La dame, qui mal cuer vos porte.'

The witty teasing of Yvain by Lunete is also lost (Ch. 1541 ff.—cf. E 909 ff.), as are most of Chrétien's decorative similes. Few substitute graces take their place. Perhaps the only arresting figure contributed by E is the homely one in which the lion is described as carrying a recently killed deer across his back as though it were a 'mele-sek' (2032). Of the remarkably rich animal imagery in the first episode of *Yvain*, almost none is reproduced in E. The exception is the description of the Giant Herdsman, some of whose features—in Chrétien, most—are likened to those of various animals (E 247 ff.—Ch. 288 ff.). Chrétien's Calogrenant describes the defender of the well approaching (487–8)

> plus tost qu'uns alerions,
> Fiers par sanblant come lions.

Keu chides Yvain's vowing to revenge Calogrenant with the remark (594)

> L'an dit que chaz saous s'anvoise.

In his retort, Yvain refuses to behave like the watchdog that stiffens and growls when another dog snarls at him (646 ff.). When the defender comes towards Yvain, he makes (813–14)

> si grant bruit,
> Con s'il chaçast un cerf de ruit;

the English version has him coming on (630)

> Als fast so þe fowl in flight,

a lame line repeated (1304) to describe Ywain's appearance as defender against King Arthur. Perhaps the most apt animal simile in the French romance is that used to dramatize Yvain's pursuit of the mortally wounded Esclados le Ros (880 ff.). Yvain spurs after Esclados like a gerfalcon swooping upon a crane. The falcon approaches so closely that it seems about to seize its prey, and yet it fails to strike. E abbreviates the passage to (664–5)

> And fast folow[d] Syr Ywayne,
> Bot he ne might him overtake . . .

6. E omits Chrétien's psychologizing, perhaps out of choice, deeming it excrescent, but more likely because, trained in a different tradition of story-telling, he is unable to cope with the dramatic dialogue and the interior dialogue which Chrétien employs to project his insights. Thus the brilliant stichomythic repartee of Yvain's crucial first interview with Laudine (1972 ff.) becomes in E (1148 ff.) three set speeches; and the subtle conversation in which Lunete persuades her mistress to accept Yvain (Ch. 1598 ff.) is rendered by a long speech in which Lunet states her case, followed by a summary of Alundyne's reactions (E 940 ff.). To be sure, Alundyne's final capitulation to her *confidante* in E closely imitates Chrétien's dialogue style (E 959 ff.). What goes on in the minds of the characters as they experience fear or disappointment or other emotions seems not to interest E. Neither Calogrenant's trepidation as he prepares to pour water on the magic stone (Ch. 432–8) nor Yvain's disappointment in his failure to capture Esclados (Ch. 891–9) is reported. And where Chrétien constructs a clever interior dialogue in which Laudine convinces herself that Lunete's motives are disinterested and her counsel wise (1738 ff.), and carries on a hypothetical interview with her husband's slayer as though he were present (1760 ff.), E records (1040 ff.) merely the conclusion reached in these ruminations.

C. *Lacunae.* Schleich in his edition of *YG* (pp. xl–xliv) argues that a number of omissions (after ll. 836, 870, 1429, 1689, 1732, 2504, 2827, 3732, and 4273) do not represent the intention of the poet but are the result rather of faulty copying. We find the omissions, however, to be just the sort of extraneous matter that E habitually sacrifices in order to get on with the story, even though in these particular retrenchments the English poet has sometimes omitted a vital fact or confused the trend of the narrative. The more cogent of Schleich's arguments are countered at the appropriate places in the commentary.

D. *Additions.* E very occasionally introduces material not found in his source. He prefixes the narrative with the standard minstrel *incipit*, naturally lacking in Chrétien, and concludes with a prayer, which is also conventional minstrel procedure. In the account of Salados's (Esclados's) funeral procession (E 829–32),

> Bifore þe cors rade a knyght
> On his stede þat was ful wight,
> In his armurs wele arayd
> With spere and target gudely grayd.

If the *his* of ll. 830 and 831 refers to the dead Salados rather than the anonymous knight, we have a reference to the custom of giving the horse and weapons of the deceased a place of honour in the procession (cf. Arcite's funeral in Chaucer's *Knight's Tale*, i (A), 2889 ff.)—a detail not found in any of the extant versions of Chrétien's poem, nor in the analogues. More noteworthy is an addition which occurs after the climactic fight between Ywain and Gawain. The trial by champion having ended in a draw, Arthur orders the elder sister to partition the land she has inherited and to give half to her younger sister, who in return must make *fewte* to her elder sister and acknowledge her *als hir lady*. Thus far E follows his source, but suddenly he steps forward in his own person and volunteers the following information (3767–72):

> þis land was first, I understand,
> þat ever was parted in Ingland.
> þan said þe King, withow[t]en fail,
> For þe luf of þat batayl
> Al sisters þat sold efter bene
> Sold part þe landes þam bitwene.

These lines are clearly inserted to inflate the importance of King Arthur's decision by making it an historical precedent for the laws of partible and impartible lands. The insertion is historical fiction (see commentary), but taken together with other legal interpolations (cf. ll. 1253, 3759–65) implies that the poet had somewhat unusual legalistic interests. A final touch of independence comes at the very end of the poem. Whereas Chrétien is satisfied to reunite Yvain and Laudine, and to show Lunete sharing in their happiness, E assures his less sophisticated audience that the major characters lived happily ever afterward. Nor is the lion forgotten. He continues to thrive, and Ywain, Alundyne, Lunet, and the lion remain together until—and it is the finest line in the poem in its chill finality—*þat ded haves dreven þam down.*

E. *Improvements*. We have already noted E's deletion of Broceliande in order to keep the action logically in Britain (above, B 4).
He also felt himself to be correcting Chrétien's geography by locat-
ing the opening scene *At Kerdyf þat es in Wales* (E 17) instead of
at Carduel (Carlisle), which Chrétien—drawing doubtless upon
traditions recalling that Carlisle had been a fortress of the Strathclyde Welsh—situates in Wales (see commentary on l. 17). E's
most important improvement is his clarification of the one badly
confused and incredible episode in *Yvain*.

The passage in question (Ch. 907 ff.) has to do with the physical
details of Yvain's captivity between the two portcullises, the description of his passageway-prison, and the mysterious appearance
of Lunete from her own room. E's dissatisfaction with Chrétien's
account is understandable. To begin with, Chrétien tells us that
Yvain has been trapped between two falling gates or portcullises
that have fallen at each end of the narrow entrance-way to the
castle. Apart from the cunningly contrived mechanisms of the trap,
it seems in all other respects like an ordinary castle gate—a narrow,
fortified, and public means of entrance into the stronghold. It soon
appears, however, that this is no common means of entrance and
egress. By a curious piece of dream logic the passageway has suddenly
become an elegant chamber

> Qui tote estoit celee a clos
> Dorez, et paintes les meisieres
> Du buene oevre et de colors chieres.[1] (Ch. 964–6)

[1] It is curious that this description of the chamber-prison coincides in a
number of significant details with the description of Lunet's room in the Welsh
Owein. In this poem Lunet hides Owein in her upper chamber, where 'there was
not . . . a nail which was not coloured with priceless colour, nor was there a panel
without gilded carvings of divers designs upon it' (*Mabinogion*, ii. 43). It is
also noteworthy that of all the versions of Ywain's captivity and release that of
Owein is the most rational and convincing. Here Lunet appears to Owein on the
outside of the portcullis, and hands him through the ironwork a ring which will
make him invisible. Her instructions are that when the retainers of the black
knight come in search of him, he is to slip out of the passageway and to come
to a place where she will be waiting. This Owein does, and Lunet leads him to
her upper chamber, where she feeds him and provides for his comfort. It is from
a window of this chamber that Owein looks out and sees the procession and
the widow passing in the street below. Clearly this is the easiest, most natural
account of the episode that has come down to us. For an extended discussion
of the Welsh and French versions, see Brown, *Romanic Rev.* iii (1912), 143–72.
This passage and a few slight details in which *YG* and *Owein* agree with one
another against *Yvain* have prompted certain scholars to argue that the Welsh
and English poets drew on popular traditions as well as Chrétien—see, in addition
to Brown, J. L. Weston, *Modern Quarterly*, i (1898), 201–2.

Not only is the chamber cunningly decorated, but as we find out subsequently it is perfectly appointed with couches, quilts, and seats. Into this chamber steps Lunete. She has come from an adjoining room (*chanbrete*) through a small door which Chrétien describes as *estroit*, but which also must have been invisible, for none of the retainers knows of the door, nor are they able to find it despite a minute search of the chamber.[1] She gives Yvain the magic ring, seats him on a couch, and returns to her own room to fetch him food and drink. Later she leaves him again when the crowd of retainers arrives in search of the murderer. They find the dead horse (at the end of the elegant *sale!*), but despite their best efforts are unable to locate Yvain, who remains invisible on the couch during the search. It is at this point that Laudine enters the chamber, and with her the funeral procession and the bier. Laudine and the corpse are, therefore, in the same room with Yvain. The wounds of the corpse break open and begin to bleed in the presence of the murderer, and before passing out of the castle the retainers once more renew their search for Yvain who, they are now certain, is in the room. When the funeral procession has passed through the room, Lunete returns and directs Yvain to a little window where he can watch the fair lady as she marches in the procession. Later, after the burial, Lunete leads Yvain to her own room, where he remains until she has successfully interceded with Laudine on his behalf.

Such an account poses a number of problems, all of which E recognized and tried to remedy. In the first place, the mysterious transformation of the passageway from the normal means of entry into an elaborately decorated chamber is strangely maladroit, particularly when it continues to serve as an exit from the castle during the funeral scene. One also wonders why, if Lunete's room adjoining the passageway is really as secret as it seems to be, she does not hide Yvain there immediately instead of making him submit to the search. Also, just why does Yvain have to look out of a window at Laudine when each end of the passageway is barred only by the iron lattice-work of a portcullis? Why, in any case, should Yvain make such a point of seeing the lady when, in fact, she

---

[1] Throughout this section Chrétien distinguishes carefully between the chamber and Lunete's own room. The well-appointed chamber he calls *la sale anclos* (964) and *la sale* (1587). Lunete's room, on the other hand, is *une chanbrete* (970), *sa chanbre* (1047), *la petite chanbrete* (1579).

has just been in the same room with him a minute before? Plainly Chrétien's version of this episode is highly contaminated; there are too many loose ends and awkward situations for even the crudest story-teller. One can only speculate that Chrétien either did not understand his source or was so intent on working up the melodramatic scene with the murderer and the bleeding corpse that he was willing to sacrifice all credibility and realism. The success of this scene, of course, demands that Yvain should remain in the passageway for the confrontation with the corpse, even though logic demands that Lunete should spirit him off to her own room as she does later in the poem. The episode is highly unsatisfactory.

To remedy this situation, E conducts the scene in a different fashion. Lunet appears to Ywain in the plain, unadorned, unfurnished passageway (*stall*). She has appeared from a door in the wall of the passageway, which, apparently as in Chrétien, connects with her room. When she has given him the magic ring, she leads Ywain through the door into her room (E 749), where she bids him *sit opon hir bed*. We now see why E omitted the scene with the corpse and the bleeding wounds. The funeral cortège must pass outside the room in the passageway. Thus it is impossible to arrange a confrontation between the murderer and the corpse. E's version of the story also has the advantage of making Ywain's request to look out of the window perfectly natural. He has heard the cries of the lady (833) as she passed next to Lunet's room, but he has not yet seen her. He asks Lunet, therefore, if there is *sum hole or sum window* from which he can catch a glimpse of the lady. E's version is clearly superior. With the initial exception of the door between the passageway and Lunet's room, all the details of the scene are carefully thought out. The result is a clear gain in credibility.

F. *Confusions in the English version.* E's habit of pruning and economizing is occasionally responsible for confusion and loss of necessary background material. The clumsy plotting of the quest of the younger sister for Ywain has already been examined (above, C. 6). E also fails to explain Lunet's fall from favour and to indicate the steward's motive in persecuting her. Chrétien takes some pains to tell how and why Lunete finds herself in her predicament, but E (2159–66) foreshortens this background to the point of distortion, leaving the motive for the steward's enmity obscure and arbitrary. E is helped, to be sure, by the fact that stewards in the romances are, as a type, deceitful and wicked.

Another episode that suffers from over-condensation is the account (1759–1868) of the magic ointment used to cure Ywain's madness, the deliberate loss of the box, and the falsehood the maiden tells her mistress. E has so pruned Chrétien's carefully detailed background for the loss of the empty box of ointment that when in the English version the maiden suddenly casts it into the water we are scarcely aware of her reasons for doing so. In fact E's handling of this whole episode is exceedingly perfunctory, almost as if he were following his source mechanically without fully understanding the springs of the action.

There is a whole class of obfuscations in E which can only be explained as due to carelessness. Such a case is found in l. 441, where *his lady bryght* seems to refer to the wife of the Hospitable Knight rather than to his daughter as Chrétien is careful to point out. Even more confusing is the mention of *þe chapel* in l. 603, where clearly the keep of the Hospitable Knight is meant. This slip occurs, undoubtedly, because E in the lines immediately before has been referring to *þe wel and þe fayre tre*, objects with which the chapel is closely associated. The context makes it clear, however, that the *bretise* (163) or *halde* (170) is indicated. E's reference to *þe riche lady* in l. 2645 is also disturbing. The confusion stems partly from the fact that E refers to Alundyne by the unfamiliar epithet *riche*, partly from the fact that Alundyne appears in this scene for the first time without her previous presence having been established. E has forgotten that slightly more than 100 lines earlier in the same scene (2530) he deliberately eliminated the episode in Chrétien where Yvain sees Laudine (Ch. 4344–51) standing with a crowd of people around the unfortunate Lunete. A later reference to Laudine is therefore perfectly prepared for in Chrétien, but when E duplicates this line by alluding to *þe riche lady* in his text, her presence can only seem mysterious.

E must surely have perplexed his hearers by his too perfunctory allusions to the abduction of Guenevere by Meleagant (E 2181–6; 2203–6). It is because Gawain is busy seeking to recover the Queen that he cannot serve as Lunet's champion—he pledged her his service earlier in the poem—or redeem his nephews and save his niece from Harpin of the Mountain. These adventures fall to Ywain by default. When the elder sister appears at court to contract for a champion, Chrétien is careful to mention that the Queen has been recovered and Gawain is again available for duty. E says nothing of the return of the Queen. It is Chrétien who might have alluded to the abduction the more lightly, for his hearers would be expected to know of the incident from his extended treatment of it in his *Lancelot*.

Another instance where E momentarily nods occurs in ll. 2793–4. Here E has so far forgotten himself that he permits the younger daughter to know that Gawain has agreed to act as champion for her elder sister, knowledge which she clearly cannot and must not have if the climactic battle between Ywain and Gawain is to be fought incognito. Another instance of imprecision occurs in E's account of the adventures in *þe Castel of þe Hevy Sorow*. Here E fails to make clear the exact relationship between the *ful fayre may* of l.3086 and the *lady* of the following line. The role of the *lady*, in fact, remains shadowy throughout, and the scene as a whole must be considered one of the most unsatisfactory renderings of Chrétien in the English version. Also confusing is E's version of the movements of Ywain and the younger daughter just before the encounter with Gawain. In Chrétien Yvain and the damsel leave the *Chastel de Pesme Avanture* and journey together towards the town where Arthur has been holding court for two months. The night before the duel they spend just outside the town in a modest inn, getting up at dawn in order to be on hand for the trial. In E, however, Ywain and the damsel ride directly to Arthur's temporary seat, spend the night secretly in *þe town* (3404) and then at dawn *wan þam wightly out of toun* (3412) to Arthur's court. Apparently, though he does not make it clear, E envisaged the combat between Ywain and Gawain as taking place in a field outside the ramparts of the town, for when the lion appears on the scene (3786)

> þe folk fast to toun gan fle.

A final discrepancy in E occurs at l. 3838, where Ywain is described as returning to the well where, henceforward, *he thinkes forto dwell*. A few lines later, however, he casts water upon the magic stone, bringing on the customary storm and precipitating the dénouement of the tale. Such an action is plainly unexpected in a man who had come to the well to live, presumably, in solitude and contrition. In Chrétien Yvain returns to the fountain with the avowed intention of fighting (*guerroiier*), in order to force the hand of Laudine and thereby win her back. His action, therefore, in bringing on the storm is perfectly consistent with his motives.

G. *Characterization.* E's major characters are much less finely drawn than Chrétien's; indeed, they come perilously close to being mere puppets. This insufficiency of characterization is mainly attributable to the altered tone of the English romance. E has muted the vivacity and passion of Chrétien: the fits of emotion, the high flights of rhetoric, the ardent involvement in conversation, battle, and love are toned down and muffled. The sharp, angry exchanges between Keu and Guenievre at the beginning of Chrétien's poem are a case in point. These exchanges, which serve to display the seneschal's chronic ill-humour, on the one hand, and the quick temper of the Queen, on the other, lose much of their sting in E. Kay is less malicious; the Queen less angry and outspoken. When she retorts to one of Kay's more sarcastic speeches, it is with *milde mode*, whereas in Chrétien she curses and damns him scathingly. Her attitude in E is more conciliatory, and the effect is to lower the emotional intensity of the scene and, incidentally, to blunt the sharpness of the characterization.

Of the three main figures, Lunete is least changed in the transfer to English. She remains sly, shrewd, and serviceable. Yet even Lunete is a flatter character in E than in Chrétien. E slights her earlier embassy to Arthur's court when, despite her discourtesy and lack of tact (Ch. 1005–8), she was befriended by Yvain. We are also deprived by E of the symbolic encounter between Gauvain and Lunete (the Sun and the Moon) and their amorous dalliance on the occasion of Arthur's visit to Laudine's castle. Obviously Lunete leads a richer life than E hints at. And she is a far more engaging person in Chrétien, for E has excised the lines in which Lunete playfully teases the hero before his first encounter with her mistress. In E, Lunet is always brisk and businesslike, too busy for playfulness and too ingenuous for deceit, even so slender a deceit as the white lie her French counterpart uses to tantalize the anxious knight.

The character of Laudine undergoes a much more profound change. By turns passionate and suspicious, imperious and coy, she is a strange and complex creature, and even Chrétien, with all his psychological penetration, has trouble in making credible the precipitancy with which she marries the slayer of her husband and the obduracy with which she later resists a reconciliation with him. Chrétien makes much of her frenzied grief over the corpse of her husband: she claws her hair and clothes, faints at every step, and then makes an attempt at suicide. Finally she gives way to an outburst of hysteria in which she comes dangerously close to blasphemy. Such emotional violence was apparently distasteful to E, for one hears nothing in the English poem of the attempt at suicide, and her hysterical outburst is cut entirely. As a result Laudine's heroic stature is diminished.

Chrétien's Laudine is above all a sophisticated woman, fond of authority, accomplished in court etiquette and in the dialectics of love. Haughty, strong-minded, and proud, she is, nevertheless, capable of almost adolescent fickleness and curiosity. It is her inconsistency, in fact, that proves to be her strongest characteristic. *Fame a plus de mil corages* (1436), and Laudine is more fickle than most of her sex. This quality prepares us for her amazing volte-face towards the slayer of her husband, just as Criseyde's tendency to be 'slydinge of corage' prepares us for her capitulation to Diomede. Chrétien shows considerable skill in making Laudine's change of heart believable; we are able to observe Laudine, in the words of Gustave Cohen, 'glissant de la douleur à la curiosité, et de la curiosité à l'amour' (*Chrétien de Troyes*, p. 360). Alundyne's conversion, on the other hand, is managed arbitrarily. We learn nothing of the traits of character that prompt her decision to forgive Ywain. She goes to bed detesting the slayer of Salados and arises the next morning determined to have him as her husband. She accepts Ywain because she needs a knight to defend the fountain. There is little mention of love.

The transformation of Yvain to Ywain is from a *cavaliere servente* to a bluff fighting man whose virtues are those of the typical romance hero—courage, skill at arms, steadfastness, and generosity. Not an accomplished courtier or lover, Ywain cannot 'mince it in love' like his French original. If his suit prospers it is because he has proposed an alliance as much as a love-match. Yvain's eloquence, refinement, and love of indirection are beyond Ywain. The English hero eschews irony in his response to Kay's attack (E 499–508); he is as incapable of the thrust and parry of courtly dialogue (Ch. 1975–2036) as he is of spinning out the elaborate conceits (Ch. 1428–1506) expected of a courtly lover. A man of sentiment and feeling, Chrétien's hero is frequently on the brink of tears and occasionally weeps (2579, 2615). He is capable of overwrought soliloquies in his despair that bring him to attempt suicide. That such a man could lapse into madness as a result of guilt and disappointment in love is altogether probable. Madness comes upon the restrained, phlegmatic English hero as though it were a sudden physiological disorder. And if Ywain is the more sober, he is also completely without guile. Whereas the French hero does not scruple at petty deceit in promising the lord of the *Chastel de Pesme Avanture* that he will return to wed his daughter, a promise which he makes in bad faith, Ywain prefers to outface the importunate lord with plain, blunt honesty. More than any other single factor, it is the conception of the hero which sets the English romance apart from its source.

IV. SOURCES

The origins of *Yvain* are obscure and controversial. Commentators fall into two groups: those who trace the sources for the major episodes to Celtic mythology and those who prefer to believe that Chrétien elaborated a few folk-themes independently.[1] Among those who have upheld the latter theory, the chief spokesman has been Foerster, who derives the basic theme from a widely known *Märchen* of a maiden who is first captured by a giant and later liberated by a young hero.[2] On to this folk-motif Chrétien grafted the theme of the storm-making spring, which Wace had recently treated in the *Roman de Rou*,[3] and the theme of the easily consoled widow drawn from the *Roman de Thèbes*.[4] For W. A. Nitze, how-

---

[1] For bibliographies and summaries of the prolonged discussion of the sources, see W. Foerster, *Kristian von Troyes: Wörterbuch zu seinen sämtlichen Werken* (Halle, 1914), p. 107; R. Zenker, *Forschungen zur Artusepik: Ivainstudien* (Halle, 1921), pp. xxi–xxviii, 3–176; J. D. Bruce, *The Evolution of Arthurian Romance* (Göttingen, 1923), ii. 75–82; J. R. Reinhard, 'Chrétien de Troyes: A Bibliographical Essay', *Essays and Studies in Engl. and Comp. Lit.* (Ann Arbor, 1932), pp. 195–231. Later articles are cited below.

[2] Foerster, *Wörterbuch*, pp. 109 ff.

[3] Ed. H. Andresen (Heilbronn, 1879), ii. 283 f., ll. 6399–6408. Cf. Giraldus Cambrensis, *Topographia Hibernica*, ed. J. Demock, *Opera* (1867), v, 89 f. For studies of this and other rain-making springs, see L. B. Morgan, 'The Source of the Fountain Story in *Yvain*', *MP.* vi (1909), 331 ff.; G. L. Hamilton, 'Storm-making Springs: Studies on the Sources of the *Yvain*', *Romanic Rev.* ii (1911), 355 ff.

[4] Foerster builds on the work of A. Hilka, *Die direkte Rede als stilistisches Kunstmittel in den Romanen des Kristian von Troyes* (Halle, 1903), p. 128, n. 1, who first noted the similarity. Foerster was influenced by Hilka to reject his former theory that the story of the Widow of Ephesus was the source of the relationship between Yvain and Laudine. Zenker, however, disputes the direct influence of *Thèbes* in *Z. f. franz. Spr. u. Lit.* xli (1913), 140–8. F. Guyer, *MP.* xxvi (1929), 273–6, argues that it is *Thèbes* that is indebted to Chrétien.

ever, the core of the romance is the defence of the fountain with the victorious assailant succeeding the defender. Chrétien, Nitze maintains, drew upon a French or Breton version of the Arician myth of Diana Nemorensis, which happens to be the starting-point for Frazer's *Golden Bough*. Just as Diana's grove is protected against intruders by a succession of armed defenders, so Laudine's fountain is protected by Salados, then by his conqueror Yvain.[1]

The Celtic theory is sustained most elaborately by A. C. L. Brown, who contends that *Yvain* is a partly rationalized fairy mistress tale of the type preserved in the Irish sagas *Serglige Conculaind* and *Tochmarc Emere*.[2] The first of these tales closely parallels the central action of *Yvain*: the Irish hero Cuchulainn is lured to an Other-World region by Liban, a fay and sister to the beautiful Fand who has fallen in love with Cuchulainn. There Cuchulainn fights successful battles against three hostile warriors and as a result wins possession of Fand. Later he loses Fand by disobeying her command, goes mad, and wanders in the mountains until cured of his madness by druidical charms and a magic drink of forgetfulness. To his theory that Yvain is derived from Celtic legend, Brown adds as corroborative evidence a number of Celtic parallels to situations and characters in Chrétien's romance.

Brown's much criticized views[3] have been reinforced in recent years by the speculations of R. S. Loomis. The adventures of Calogrenant and Yvain at the fountain Loomis derives from Irish legends having to do with Curoi's testing of the Ulster warriors and with the slaying of Curoi by Cuchulainn. He accepts Brown's provenance for Yvain's winning of Laudine, adding to Brown's 'evidence' the legendary association of Yvain and his father Urien with the fountain-fay Morgain.[4] According to Loomis the story of Calogrenant's humiliation also owes much to the theme of the Combat at the Ford, a Welsh tradition preserved in the mabinogi

---

[1] See 'A New Source of the *Yvain*', *MP*. iii (1905), 267 ff., 'The Fountain Defended', *MP*. vii (1909), 145 ff., and '*Yvain* and the Myth of the Fountain', *Speculum*, xxx (1955), 170 ff.

[2] 'Iwain: A Study of the Origins of Arthurian Romance', (*Harvard*) *Studies in Phil. and Lit.* vii (Boston, 1903). For Brown's criticism of Nitze, see 'Chrétien's *Yvain*', *MP*. ix (1911), 2 f.

[3] See Bruce, *Evolution of Arthurian Romance*, i. 96–99, ii. 75–82; Cohen, *Chrétien de Troyes*, p. 352; C. B. Lewis, *Classical Mythology and Arthurian Romance* (Oxford, 1932), pp. 4–7, 297.

[4] *Arthurian Tradition and Chrétien de Troyes* (New York, 1949), pp. 130 ff., 274 ff.

of Pwyll. The Pwyll legend not only furnished the adventures of Calogrenant and Yvain with the Hospitable Host and with the Storm-Knight but also supplied the mythic background for Gawain's sojourn at the castle of Bercilak and his experience at the Green Chapel in *Sir Gawain and the Green Knight*.[1]

The motif of the grateful lion, which gives Chrétien's romance its name, ultimately reaches back to Apion's story of Androcles and the Lion.[2] Chrétien had the story from the *Epistles* of Petrus Damianus (d. 1072), where, for the first time in the history of the motif, the cause of the lion's distress is a serpent and not, as in earlier forms, a thorn in the paw or a bone caught in the teeth. There are two other twelfth-century treatments of the lion–serpent version beside *Yvain*, one in Alexander Neckam's *De Naturis Rerum*, the other in the legend of Golfier de Lastours from the *Chronicle* of Jaufré de Vigeois (1184). Brown's attempt to show Celtic sources for the episode of the lion and the serpent[3] has been criticized by Brodeur for not differentiating between guiding or helpful beasts and grateful beasts.[4] More recently, Brodeur's objections have been unconvincingly answered by T. M. Chotzen,[5] who points to similarities between the actions of the lion in *Yvain* and those of a helpful animal in the eighth-century Irish tale of the fight to the death between Conall, the foster-brother of Cuchulainn, and Lugaid son of Curoi.

V. Language

As the phonological analysis and accidence below will demonstrate, the dialect of *YG* is Northern with some admixture of North-East Midland forms. Since the sporadic Midland forms are fully attested by the rhymes, they cannot be discounted as scribal alterations;

---

[1] See *JEGP*. xliii (1943), 170 ff., and *Wales and the Arthurian Legend* (Cardiff, 1956), pp. 85 ff. Loomis is contradicted by A. B. Friedman, 'Morgan le Fay in *Sir Gawain and the Green Knight*', *Speculum*, xxxv (1960), 273 ff.

[2] See Foerster, *Wörterbuch*, pp. 99, 121 f.; G. Baist, 'Der dankbare Löwe', *Roman. Forsch.* xxix (1910), 317; O. M. Johnston, 'The Episode of Yvain, the Lion and the Serpent', *Z. f. franz. Spr. u. Lit.* xxxi (1907), 157 ff. (Oriental provenance); A. G. Brodeur, 'The Grateful Lion', *PMLA*. xxxix (1924), 485–524.

[3] 'The Knight and the Lion', *PMLA*. xx (1905), 673–706.

[4] Op. cit., pp. 515–22.

[5] 'Le lion d'Owein (*Yvain*) et ses prototypes celtiques', *Neophilologus*, xviii (1933), 131–6.

indeed, the evidence, slight as it is, is on the side of the scribe's being more distinctly Northern than the poet.[1]

A. *Spellings and sounds*

Vowels

1. OE. *ā > a*. The retention of the unrounded vowel is the prime discriminant of the Northern dialect (see Luick, § 369, Moore, § 106, Wyld, § 157).[2] The spelling *ai/ay* usual in Barbour's *Bruce* and later Scottish texts—the *i/y* being a graphic sign of length rather than vowel quality (Jordan, § 19, Wright, § 121)— is never encountered in *YG*. Examples: *brade* 259, *hate* (OE. *hāt*) 378, *lath* 135, *lathly* 247, *na* 2984, *sari* 2068, *fra* 205, *swa* 3503, *smate* 419, *wate* 423, *rade* 154, *rase* 77, *gase* 146, *snaw* 375, *stane* 361, *wa* 3016, *tane* (Northern pp. from ON. *taka*) rhymes with *ane* 1175, 1553, *ilkane* 1083, 1937, 3349, *onane* 175, *nane* 1535, 3431, *gane* 2925, *stane* 1447. OE. *ā* rhymes with *ā* in French loan-words (*wate*:*debate* 3889) and with *ā* derived from the lengthening of *ă* in EME.: *lathe* (OE. *lāð*):*bathe* (OE. *baðian*) 1863; *skath* (ON. *skaði*):*bath* (OE. *bāþā*) 1859; *wrath* (OE. *wrāð*):*skath* 3684; *mare* (OE. *māra*):*schare* (OE. *scear*, Anglian *scær*) 683; *sare* (OE. *sār*): *care* (OE. *caru*) 2999.

2. OE. *ā > o*. The rounded vowel [ɔ:], typical of the Midland and Southern dialects, occurs sporadically in *YG*: (i) Before *n*— *gone*:*Jon* 1511, *pareon*:*onone* 679, :*none* 751, *none*:*opone* 2907. (ii) Before *r*—*sore*:*bifore* 1040, *more*:*fore* 3419, *more*:*byfore* 1265. (iii) When final—*also*:*unto* 1489, *so*:*do* 3149, *do*:*go* 2503. Rounding occurs only once before *s*—*lose* (OF. *los*):*gose* 1573. In adjacent lines we find *pore* (56) and *pare* (57). Similarly, random variation of *mare/more* and *nane/none* occurs throughout *YG*. *lord*:*acorde* 1183 and *loverd* 1908 are probably due to literary influence from the South (cf. Luick, § 369. 6). Alongside *oght* and *noght* no forms

---

[1] Cf. Hall, *Minot*, p. xviii; B. von Lindheim, *Wiener Beiträge z. engl. Phil.* lix (1937), 65–71.

[2] The following manuals of phonology are referred to by short titles throughout this section: E. J. Dobson, *English Pronunciation 1500–1700* (Oxford, 1957); R. Jordan, *Handbuch der mittelenglischen Grammatik* (Heidelberg, 1934); K. Luick, *Historische Grammatik der englischen Sprache* (Leipzig, 1921–40); S. Moore, *Historical Outlines of English Sounds and Inflections* (Ann Arbor, Mich. 1951); L. Morsbach, *Mittelenglische Grammatik* (Halle, 1896); J. and E. M. Wright, *An Elementary Middle English Grammar* (Oxford, 1928); H. C. Wyld, *A Short History of English* (Oxford, 1927).

in *a* or *au* occur in *YG*, indicating that derivation was from OE. (*n*)*ōht* shortened to (*n*)*oht*, not from (*n*)*āwiht*.

3. OE. *ā+ld* or *ng* > *a*. LOE. *ā* which was the result of the lengthening of *ă* before *ld* or *ng* remains *a*: *ald* 3130, *hald*:*cald* 2931, *halde*:*balde* 289, *balde*:*talde* 1123, *gang* 2915, *omang* 34, *lang* 2385. Midland variants intrude rarely: *boldly* 1220 (cf. *baldely* 1047, *balde* 1123, 1285) is the only instance of *o+ld* in the interior of a verse; *strong* 1300, 2453, but *strang* 300, 2386, 3200, &c.

4. OE. *ā+w* or *g* [ɣ] > *aw*: *knawen* (OE. *cnāwan*) 3148, :*awyn* 2817, *aw* (OE. *āgan*) 122, 3668 (cf. *aght* 723), *awin*, adj. (OE. *āgen*) 2672, 3754. Cf. *aw* (ON. *agi*) 92, 2411 (where it rhymes with *thraw* from OE. *þrāg*). Rounded forms: *lowe* (ON. *logi*):*knowe* 343, *throw* (OE. *þrāg*):*window* 849, :*sadelbow* 2461.

5. OF. *a* > *au* before nasal + labial or dental: *chaumber* 2730, 3115 (but *chamber* 48, 52, &c.), *haunt* 1467, 1496 (but *hante* 1470, :*grante* 1503—note also *grant* 3282), *baundoun* 1944, *lawnd* 245.

6. OE. *ă+n* > *a/o*. *a* is the preferred spelling, though there is some hesitation. Note *many* 792, 814, 828, &c., beside the much less frequent *mony* 159, 598, 607, &c.; *gan* 405, 408, 2009, &c., beside *gon* 393, 1511. The characteristic West Midland *mon* is never encountered in this text; indeed, the rhyme *man*:*on* (prep.) 2283 and the alteration of *lemon* to *leman* 1474 show the scribe deliberately avoiding *mon*. This rhyme and alteration may also be taken as hints that the text being copied contained *mon* and *lemon*.

7. OE. *æ* > *e*. The spelling *e* represents both *ę̄* for the *æ* which resulted from the fronting of WGmc. *ā* (*ǣ¹*) and *ę̄* for *æ* from the *i*-umlaut of OE. *ā* < WGmc. *ai* (*ǣ²*). The short vowels are the result of shortening in LOE. and EME. Examples: (i) *ǣ¹*—*drede*: *nede* 1140, 1224, 2289, :*spede* 891, :*stede* 1917, :*rede* 2154; *adred*: *sted(e)* 772, 3195; *bere*:*chere* 818; *were*:*chere* 2537, 3002, &c., :*dere* (OE. *dēore*) 1355, :*here* 1343, 3678, &c., :*infere* 3331, 3713. *Strete* rhymes with *mete* (OE. *mētan*) 552, 611, and with *bihete* (reformed on OE. *behēt*, pt. of *behātan*) 157, 1393. (ii) *ǣ²*—*cled*:*led* 201, 2231, 2383; *clene* 758, &c.; *dele* 516, 960; *ever* 1588, 3437, &c.; *heled* 1721; *left* 882, :*eft* 1038; *lene* 1527, 2676; *leste*:*beste* 1663; *leve* 1458, 2289; *reche* 330, *se* 3657, *wreth* 995. In *wele*:*dele* 515, 1363 we have OE. *ę̄* rhyming with OE. *ǣ²*, a rhyme which Dobson (ii. 612, § 107 and references) would attribute to the marked instability of *ę̄* and its tendency to fall together with *ę̄* in the Northern dialects of Middle English.

8. OE. $\bar{æ} > a$. *war(e)* (OE. *wǣron, wǣre, wǣren*) is the regular form in *YG* (5, 24, 31, 53, &c.); *were* occurs only as a rhyme word (1044, 1343, 1356, and ten other instances). The *a*-spelling represents both $\bar{æ}^1$ (*ware*:*bare* 3161, *hare*:*mare* 253) and $\bar{æ}^2$ (*laft*:*craft* 35, 801, 2735, and the numerous appearances of *ani*; *eni* is unknown). Note the hesitation shown by *adred*:*sted(e)* 772, 3195, *adrad*:*stad* 718. Schleich (p. vii; cf. Luick, § 362. 2) properly suggests that certain words usually treated under $\bar{æ} > a$ actually derive from LOE. $\bar{a}$: *pare* (from OE. *pār* rather than its parallel form *pǣr*), *whare* (both alone and in compounds with prepositions), *ani, anes, maste*, all in numerous instances. Derivation from $\bar{a}$ is further indicated by the occasional $\bar{o}$ (rounded from $\bar{a}$) in words in which *e* or *a* is expected: *wore*:*pore* 2737, *whore* 1652, 2548, *moste* 1608, 1890, 2160, *or* 550, 1078, 1236. *Are* (cf. *arly* 2692) rhymes with *fare* 461, *pare* 609, 845, *mare* 1029, 3946, and *ware* 3562. To explain *are*/*or* Jordan (§ 48. 4) posits the rivalry of forms from OE. *ǣr* with those from an OE. **ār* or ON. *ár*. In *YG are* and *or* are differentiated in function: *are* is the adv., *or* the prep. or conj.

9. OE. $\breve{æ} > a$. Examples: *was* 12, 13, 19, and throughout; *brac* 420, *sat* 54, 56, 219, :*pat* 244, 809, :*what* 431, *spak* 277, 1712, :*lac* 1134, :*brak* 3777, *bad* 409, 418, &c., :*glad* 1097, *forgat* 1623, *stak*: *spak* 699, *brast* 644, 821, *glad*:*had* 1351, 2050. The use of *e* for *a* in certain words is due to ON. rather than Southern influences (see R. E. Zachrisson, *Pronunciation of English Vowels, 1400–1700* (Göteborg, 1913), p. 61): *sek*:*nek* 2032, *gres* 2705, *efter* 860, 1079, 2161, &c. (*after* is unknown in *YG*). OE. *hwonne*/*hwanne*/*hwænne* appears in *YG* only as *when* (213, 475, &c.); *ponne*/*panne*/*pænne*, however, is represented by both *pen* and *pan*. Differences in spelling, and presumably pronunciation, regularly mark differences in meaning. The form *pen* is exclusively temporal (*pen*:*ken* 2883, :*men* 1333, 2523); *pan* is both temporal (112, 117, 125, 162, &c.) and the conj. of comparison (34, 94, 95, &c.); *fast* is the adj. or adv. (*fast*:*kast* 2511, :*last* 2603, 2897, :*agast* 3178), *fest* the verb only (*fest*:*kest* 1989, :*rest* 3831).

10. EME. *ai > a*. This peculiarly Northern development (1300–50) of the ME. diphthong which evolved from OE. *ĕg* or *ĕg* or from ON. *ei* or OF. *ai*/*ei* (cf. Moore, § 111; Jordan, § 132) occurs so rarely in *YG* as to be of dubious significance. Schleich lists *sertan*/*-ly* (OF. *certain*/*certein*) 858, 1691, 2623, &c. beside

sertayne/-ly 1621, 1725, 2089, &c.; *sertayne* also rhymes four times with *Ywayne*. *Ordand* (OF. *ordeiner*) 1399, 1867, 2731, &c., appears beside *ordain(d)* 1546, 3386. *slane* 794, rhyming with *ilkane* 1296, :*stane* 2082, :*tane* 3042, :*gane* 3239, presumably has the vowel of ON. *slá*, beside *slayne* (OE. *slægen*): *laine* (ON. *leyna*) 703, :*bayn* (ON. *beinn*) 765, :*Ywaine* 1147; :*maine* 1006, 3699, :*ogayn* 3485, :*fain* 3686. *Faire/fayre* (OE. *fæger*) appears only once as *fare* (3094), though rhyming there with *ayre*; *vetale* (OF. *vitaile*):*asayle* 1873 is noteworthy since, as we see from the examples in the next paragraph, the *ai*-spelling tended to be preserved before *l* in words of French origin (see Jordan, § 233).

11. OF. *ai* > *e*, both in stressed and unstressed syllables. Examples in stressed syllables: *eger* 1894, *debonere*:*here* 1160, *pese* 1170, 3285, &c., *rese* (OE. *ræs*) 3245, :*sese* (OF. *cesser*) 3591, :*dese* (OF. *deis*) 1207. In unstressed syllables: *tráveld* 3360, *bátel* 656, 1084, &c., but also *bátayl* 2172, 2300 and *trávail* 3059, 3948.

12. OE. *ĕa*. (i) OE. *ēa* > *e* (*ę̄*): *brede* 758, *eres* 257, *grete* 251, 467, &c., *leve* 880, 2289, &c., *nete* 252. Rhymes with *ę̄* from *ǣ*[1], however, are not uncommon: *rede*:*ded(e)* 662, 713, 2075, 3029, &c., :*brede* 758. (ii) *ēa*+palatal *g* or *h* > *igh/egh*, developing through LOE. *ē*: *high* 597, 807, *hegh* 1239, 2200; *yghen* 900, *eghen* 1014; *hight*:*syght* 1812, *heght* 363. (iii) The parallel forms of the noun *meaht* (Anglian *mæht*)/*miht* produce in our text *maght* (:*laght* 3621) beside *might* (:*upright* 1799). The pt. of OE. **magan* appears as *might* usually (:*bryght* 441, :*right* 1243, :*night* 1064), rarely as *moght* (:*soght* 226, :*thoght* 1216). Similarly *neaht* (*næht*)/*niht* produce *naght*:*saght* 3897 beside the usual *night* (cf. Jordan, § 64). (iv) *seah* (pt. of *sēon*) is represented by three forms in *YG*: (*a*) the Southern *se* (:*me* 196); (*b*) *sagh* (271, :*lagh* 152, 3931), doubtless from Anglian *sæh*; (*c*) normally *saw*. The last form, Jordan (§ 63. 1, following Luick), derives from a pl. *saʒen* > *sawen*, newly formed, perhaps first in the North, from *sah*; but it could have developed directly from *sauh*—cf. § 29 below.

13. OE. *ēo* > *e* and rhymes with *e* from *ǣ*[1]:*be*, *tre*, and *thre* throughout; *ferth*:*erth* 1881, *held*:*feld* 3202, *ʒede*:*hede* 1715, :*dede* 1778, :*stede* 1880, :*spede* 2998, *wex* (pt.) 369, 385, 623. The variation of *ʒede* with *ʒode* (2390, 2977) shows development from double forms, one a falling diphthong (*ge-ĕode* > *ʒede*), the other rising (*ge-eóde* > *ʒode*). Similarly, *trewth* 33 beside *trowth* 35, 40, &c.

Schleich (p. xii) points out that *trow* in *YG* is the verb (981, 2591, 2843, &c.) and that *trew* is exclusively adjectival (40, 145, 209, &c.). *ȝing* 722, 2643, 4015 continues the common Northumbrian *ging* (see A. Campbell, *OE. Grammar* (Oxford, 1959), § 176), though the comp. is *ȝonger* 3453, 3461. *Yrel(s)* 3065 is probably not a scribal error for the usual *eryl*: the *e* is to be explained as a parasitic glide vowel before a liquid—as is the *y* in *eryl*; the raising of *e* before *r* is not infrequent in Northern texts (see Jordan, §§ 34 and 66).

14. OE. *e* > *i/y*. Raising before *nd* or *ng*, a characteristic of the North and North-East Midlands (see Luick, § 379; Jordan, § 34), occurs commonly: *hinde* 700 beside *hende* 1418, *:wende* 1829; *Ingland* 3768, *Yngland* 7; *hinges* (ON. *hengja*) 327, *hingand* 1036.

15. OE. *e* > *i/y* in end syllables, beside the normal *e*: *dedis* 3802, *dedys* 2248, *lepis* 2472, *helpid* 1442, 2643, &c., *helpyd* 2154, *knawin* 3695, *awin* 3754, *owyn* 521, *gamyn* 1440, *litil* 3450, *nobil* 3563, *evyr* 3207, *sertis* 3588.

16. OE. *ō* > *o/u*, the *o*-forms being the more common. The *u*-spelling reflects the raising of *ǭ* to *ü* [y:] in the Northern dialects about 1300. In *YG* *u* and *o* are frequently matched in rhymes: *gude:blode* 3547, *blude:wode* 2071, *luke:toke* 1161. *gude* and *luke* occur frequently in the interior of lines; *uper* once (634) replaces *oper*; *buke:luke* 9 is the only instance of *u:u* (OE. *ō:ō*). *love* (OE. *lufu*):*glove* (OE. *glōf*) 3525 illustrates OE. *u* in an open syllable rhyming with a derivative of OE. *ō*. In the rhyme *love:obove* 1539, *love* is altered by the scribe from *luve*.

17. OE. *ō*+medial *g* or final guttural *h* becomes *ow* or *ogh*. The late Northern development of *ō*+*g* into *ew* [ɪʊ] is not encountered in *YG* (see Moore, § 111. 5 and § 61. 5). Examples: *bowes* (OE. *bōgas*) 2037, *bogh:slogh* 2040 (cf. also *bogh* 392); *drow* (OE. *drōh*) 3537 beside *drogh* 639, 1983, &c.; *swow(n)yng* 868, 2064 beside *swogh* 824. *Ynogh* (OE. *genōh*) appears only in this form, as does *logh* (OE. *hlōh*).

18. OE. *ŏ* before lengthening groups (*rd, rth, ld*) > *u/o*. Note *burde* 186 and *bord* 189 in close proximity, *furth* 595, 1140 beside *forth* 120, 2582, and elsewhere, *hulde:gulde* 887.

19. OF. *o/ou* > *o/u/ou*. (i) In accented syllables *ou* (*ow*) is the rule: *nevow:now* 3691, *traytowre:dishonowre* 494, *honowre* 3667, *:stoure* 3137, *:emparoure* 3143, 3311, *champiowns:barouns* 3065, *lioun:doun* 2721, *:toun* 2804, 3412, *:boun* 3787, *socoure:stoure* 3205. (ii) In unaccented syllables *o* or *u* is the rule: *hónore* 720, *hónord*

4015, 4019, *lévore* 2386, *sócore* 1988, 2288, 2363 beside *sócure* 1876, 2318, *chámpion* 3146, *lýon* 2521, *tráytur* 1626. The following exceptions to Schleich's rules (p. xi) may be noted: *lyón* 3839, *traytúre*: *losenjoúre* 1601, *tresóre* 3796, *tresúre* 1858, *savóre* 2019, *líoun* 2346, 2656, and elsewhere. The irregularities in the following examples are obviously caused by the unequal length of the rhymed words: *champion*:*son* (OE. *sunu*) 2690, 3017, 3156, *procession*:*son* 827.

20. OE. *ū* > *ou* (*ow*). Examples: *oure* 108, *ȝowre* 137, *now*:*ȝow* 3293, *stownd*:*wownd* (*wound*) 383, 2653. *us* and *but* are invariably exceptions because of the shortening of the vowel due to lack of stress.

21. OF. *ü* > *u*. Examples: *misaventure*:*creature* 2413, *armure* 1932, 2439, *aventure* 3013, 3448. *doure* (OF. *durer*):*stoure* 2634 is an exception to the usual practice in *YG*.

22. OE. *ȳ* > *i*. The unrounding of OE. *y*, a Northern and East Midland trait (see Morsbach, § 127; Wyld, § 158; Jordan, § 39. 2) is implied by the following examples in which the *y* resulting from *i*-umlaut of OE. *u* rhymes with original *i* or is itself spelt *i*: *kyn*:*him* 559, :*blin* 1048, *gylt*:*spilt* 2539, *dyn*:*in* 779, *kys*:*þis* 3921, *kynde*: *fynde* 1051, *unkinde*:*finde* 3573, *fulfill*:*untill* 137, *pride*:*biside* 2131, 2249, *kith*:*sith* 3944. The anomalous *come* (OE. *cyme*) 447, :*dome* 85 is explained by *MED.* as a product of the early introduction of the vowel of inf. *cōmen*.

23. OE. *y/i* > *e*, representing lowering. Rhymes with words having authentic *e*: *þeder*:*togeder* 3675, *unshet*:*set* 63, :*weket* (OF. *wiket*) 853. Also *reches* 2120, *evyl* 1649, *leþir* 599. See Morsbach, § 115. 4, where *YG* is cited.

24. Apparently parasitic vowels appear in spelling in words from both OE. and OF.: *cherel* 612, *eryl* 1871, 1877, &c., *yrels* 3065, *chameber* 1020, 1190, 2231, *simepel* 2107. The extra syllable in each instance is metrically superfluous.

Consonants

25. OE. *c* is spelt *c*, *k*, *ch*. (i) Before back vowels *c* and *k*, both for [k], are interchangeable: *castel* 1837, *kastel* 1435; *cum* 1518, *kum* 1690; *cumly* 2874, *kumly* 2886. Cf. *covenant* 2302 beside *kownand* 3894 (both from OF. *convenant*); *carped* 25, *karped* 498 (both from ON. *karpa*). (ii) In combinations, *k* appears before *n*, *c* before *r*, and both *c* and *k* with *l*: *knawen* 2671, *knight* 1200, &c., *Crist* 2874, *craft* 36, *kled* 2383, *cled* 2232, *klub* 3159, *clubbes* 3200.

(iii) Initially, before front vowels that resulted from mutation, OE. *c* [k] appears as *k*: *king* 1194, &c., *kene* 127, 374. (iv) Palatal *c* [tʃ] appears as *ch* when initial: *choll* 1994, *chaf* 1684; cf. *chere* (OF. *chere*) 631. The appearance of *karl* 559 beside *cherle* 268, 612 is doubtless due to different etymologies: ON. *karl* / OE. *ceorl*; similarly *kyrk* 777, 2844 is from ON. *kirkja*. (v) Palatal *c* in medial positions is represented by *ch* (*dreche* 480, *reche* 330, *teche* 318, *towche* 115); *cch* and *tch* are unknown. The variation of *ch* and *k* medially is used in *YG*, as in most texts of the period, to differentiate grammatical function: *speche* is the noun (1964, 3619, &c.), *speke* the verb (2006, :*wreke* < OE. *wrecan* 3045, 3269); *riche*, adj. 2992, 3907, adv. 2731; *rike*, the noun, rhymes with *slike* 141, *byswike* 2335. *Mekyl*, everywhere in *YG*, is due to Scandinavian influence, as is the second element in *stowtlyk* 667, the only occurrence in *YG* of the older form of the adverbial suffix.

26. OE. *f*. (i) Medial *f* is normally spelt *v* or *u* and was presumably voiced: *lefe* (OE. *lēaf*) 392, pl. *leves* 355; *self* 3181, &c., *selven* 344, 3277, &c. No forms with *u* will be found in the present text because we have normalized the haphazard scribal variation of *u* and *v*, which were in many cases, especially when medial, indistinguishable. Occasionally *f* and *v* (*u*) occur medially in the same words: *shiferd* 3539, *cheverd* 637, 3553; *rifen* 3539, *reven* 653, 3632. All forms of the verbs *gifen* and *lifen* are written with *f*, but the noun from OE. *lif* appears both as *life* (1624, 2292, &c.) and as *live(s)* (908, 3233, 3982). Note also *bilive* 1102 and *olive* 307, 901, &c. The various forms of OE. *lufian*, such as *luf* 894, *lufes* 2292 (but *loves* 1142), *lufed* 1164, along with those from *gifen* and *lifen* above—if it could be proved that the spellings were indeed phonetic —would illustrate the unvoiced labio-dental typical of the Northern and North Midland dialects (cf. Jordan, § 217). (ii) Initial *v* is found only in words of French origin. (iii) Final *v* does not occur: *wive* 907, 3324, &c., *love*:*obove* 1539, :*glove* 3525. (iv) The loss of *f* between *l* and a labial occurs in *twelmoth* 1507, 1514, 1570 (cf. Jordan, § 216. 1, where *YG* is cited).

27. OE. *g*. (i) Initial palatal *g* remains a spirant and is spelt ȝ or *y*. Forms with guttural *g* like *gif* 3002, 3293, *forgif* 1145, *gaf* 1619, and *geten* 3019, 3501 derive from Scandinavian cognates. *Gan* once dubiously appears as *yane* (881). The OE. prefix *ge-* appears as *y-* or *i-*: *ynogh* 706, *inogh* 1469, 3463, *iwis* 2963, 3693. (ii) For medial *g*, see *ā*+*g*, *ĕa*+*g* and *ō*+*g*. Note also *bow* (OE. *boga*) 1659, 2462

and the rhymes *sawes* (OE. *sagu*) : *felawes* (ON. *félagi*) 83, 131, 3793 and *dawes* (OE. *dagas*):*felawes* 3811. (iii) In the group *æ*+palatal *g*, the *g* is vocalized, the group becoming *ai/ay*: beside *daw*:*law* 3130 appear *day*:*Kay* 91, *day*:*say* 3873, and beside *fawnyng* 2002, *fain*:*Gawayn* 2288, *fayn* 3250, *fayne*: *Ywayne* 748, 1346. (iv) The plosive pronunciation of *g* occurs regularly in *bryg* 167, 1849, 2215 and *ryg* 1833.

28. OF. *g* for [dʒ] is spelt both *g* and *j*: Schleich cites *jermayne* 458, *germayne* 1273, *wajed* 2172, *waged* 2570, *jujement* 3720, *juge-ment* 2642.

29. OE. *h*. (i) Final *h*, the guttural or palatal spirant, appears in *YG* as *gh* or *w*: *aw* 3668, *drogh* (OE. *drōh*) 639, 1135, &c., *drow* (OE. *drōh*) 3537, *flegh* 642, *high* 597, 807, &c., *logh* 1136, 3464, *sagh* 152, 271, &c., *saw* 165, 625, &c., *wogh* 895. (ii) Initial aspirate *h* is lost in *oste* 222, 235, 440, &c., *ostell* 702, *umage* (OF. *homage*) 1952. An initial *h* intrudes in *haby* 1610, *habide* 2524, 2935, &c. (iii) Initial OE. *hw* (and ON. *hv*) appear as *wh*, but *wo* (OE. *hwā*) 145, 504, *wen* (OE. *hwænne*) 2071. Note also *whyf(e)* 3297, 4011 (OE. *wif*) and the etymologically false *h* in *whideware* (OE. *wide*+ *hwær*) 3782, which is the result either of confusion with *whederward* or of mis-spelling *widewhere*. The *quh* spelling characteristic of Scottish texts is not found in *YG*; the variant *qu*, however, appears in *quyn* 159, a word of Scandinavian origin (cf. Swedish *hven*, Norwegian *hvine*).

30. OE. *sc*. In our text *sc* normally becomes *sh*, but *sch* occurs several times, notably in *scho* (64, 114, 116, and 5 others). Beside *schilde* 2 appears *shilde* 3234, 3354; similarly *schaft* 420, *shaftes* 637. Note also *schare* 683, *schrive* 2545. *Scill* 3273 is from ON. *skil*, *scyn* 2446 from ON. *skinn*. *Cheverd* (cf. *shiferd* 3539, 3553, *shever* 3234) is probably an error, but *fless* 1665, 2052, and twice again (cf. *flesh* 1698) is obviously a genuine form (cf. Jordan, § 183 n.). The dropping of *c* of *sc* before the preterite of the weak past tense, which occurs in *blist* (OE. *blyscan*) 3163, is also Northern (Jordan, ibid.). Cf. also *warist* 2654 from an OF. inchoative verb. The characteristically Northern *sal* and *suld/sold* are ubiquitous.

31. OE. *þ/ð*. (i) The scribe regularly writes *þ* for the OE. voiced interdental spirant when initial, *th* for the OE. voiceless sound, a practice observable in the article *þe* and in *þat*, *þis*, *þai*, *þaire*, *þan*, *þeder*, *þus*, &c., compared with *the* (OE. *þeon*) 1015, 3141, *thoner* 370, *thole* 383, 425, &c. (ii) Medially *þ* and *th* are found in the same

words: *breþer* 460, *brether* 2494; *clopes* 2233, *klothes* 1132; *hepin* 925, *hethin* 3310; *sepin* 2232, *sethen* 3814; *tiþand* 3937, *tithand* 140, 2774, *wheþer* 2921, *whether* 3987. (iii) þ is never final, *siþe: blyth* 1092 illustrating the scribe's scruples on this point. As Schleich suggests, pairs like *worth* 1548—*worthy* 1391 and *myrth* 3098— *mirthes* 1261 imply that the spelling does not accurately reflect change in articulation. (iv) OE. ð appears as *d* when final in *ded* (OE. *dēað*) 425, 1089, 1262, &c., and in *quod* (OE. *cwæð*) 1341.

B. *Accidence*

Nouns

For the most part the nouns conform to the strong masc. type and have the following endings:

> Sg. Nom. Acc. ——, Poss. -(*e*)*s*, Dat. (-*e*)
> Pl. -*es* (-*iş*, -*s*)

The variant endings in the pl. are without etymological significance. There is also random variation in the same word: *dedes* 1504, 1575, and elsewhere, but *dedys* 2248, *dedis* 3802; *aventurs* 155, *aventures* 225, 237, 3013; *arms* 1485, *armes* 1504; *knyghtes* usually, but *knightis* 2256.

Possessives without inflexional endings: *fader* 522, *lord* 816, *moder* 828, 2689 (both in the phrase *moder son*), *king* 732, 1194, 1238, 3644 (all in the phrase *king son*; *kinges* 529, 944, 2336, &c.), *Sir Kay* 1329, *twelmoth* 1514, *lady* 1628, *ermite* 1695, *hors* 1833, *lioun* 1995, *dragon* 1998, *Ywayn* 2351, *Gawayn* 2779, *devil* (*þe devil sons*) 3018, *oþer* 3947.

Plurals without -*s*: *breþer* 460, 2165, 2494 and *maiden* 3251; *shilling* 3058, *ȝere* 153, 1707, *span* 256 (after numerals); *face* 2971; *hend* (ON. *hendr*) 3822, cf. *handes* 715, 2773 and *te hend* 207; *eghen/yghen* 900, 1014, &c.

Adjectives

No distinction is made between the sg. and the pl., or between the weak and strong forms of the adj. The -*e* of the adj. is sounded in *þat gude man* 177 and *þat wode man* 1678, &c., for metrical rather than grammatical reasons.

Pronouns

(*a*) The 3rd fem. sg. is usually *sho*, occasionally *scho* 64, 114, 116, 202, 207, 823, 2181, 2913. The acc. form is *hir*; the poss. is sometimes *hir* 208, sometimes *her* 937.

(*b*) The 2nd sg. sometimes assimilates *þ* to *t* after monosyllabic verbs: *ertow* 484, 1409, 2987, 3655; *saltou* 3289; *wiltou* 2990; *hasto* 911.

(*c*) The forms of the 3rd pl. are *þai* (:*may* 3360, 3364), *þam* 3, *þaire* 29 (*þare* 3162).

(*d*) The form of the demonstrative pl. 'those' is *þa*; *þase* occurs only once (3525). For 'these' *þir* or its variant *þire* are normal; *þise* is found once (2991).

(*e*) Interrogative pronouns (functioning on occasion as relative or indefinite pronouns) appear as *wha* 1080, 1317, &c., *who* 2541, 2690, &c., and *wo* 145, 504. In the poss. *whas* 2841 appears; in the acc. *wham* 3090.

Verbs

(*a*) Infinitive. Verbs whose stems end in either a vowel or -*r* sometimes show an ending in -*n*(*e*): *bene* (:*bytwene* 460), *gane* (:*nane* 800), *undertane* (:*ilkane* 1084), *sayn* (:*ogayn* 1501), *forfarn* (:*barn* 976). But the following forms without ending are certified by rhymes: *be* 3289, *ta* 1771, *say* 429, *sla* 1001.

(*b*) Indicative, Present. Sg.: 1. ——; 2. -*s*, -*es*; 3. -*e*, -*es*. Pl.: —— (usual), -*s*, -*es*.

Examples: 1st sg.: *grante* 1503, *tell* 3321, *pray*: *say* 2835. 2nd sg.: *sais* (:*curtays* 3666), *wenes* 73, *dose* 283. 3rd sg.: *says* 1419, *tase* (:*was* 1979), *mase* (:*was* 2683). 1st pl.: *have we* 1734, *we lyf* 2252; 2nd pl.: *ȝe knaw* (:*thraw* 2362); 3rd pl.: *þai dwell* (:*omell* 1435), *þai cum* 311, *bical* 2157. In *we . . . suffers* 3044, *ȝe . . . thinkes* 1530, the verb and pronoun are separated; in *men uses* 36 the *men* may well be the indefinite pronoun.

The ending -*es* is found only twice in the 1st sg. (*grantes* 3670, *lufes* 3657), both separated from the pronoun. The 3rd sg. of *haten* is always *hat* 1053, 2145, &c.

(*c*) Preterite-present Verbs. The 2nd sg. is usually without ending: *þou sal* 736, *will* 577, *may* 734, *dar* 1169. See, however, *salt* 3913, *saltou* 3289, and *wiltou* 2990.

(*d*) Indicative Past. With rare exception, the Indicative Past is without inflexions to distinguish number or person. The following instances are certified by rhyme: *þou com(e)* 2562, *slogh* 705, *did* 3659, *þai said* 3346. In the interior of the line note *þou did* 729, *said* 3811; *we dyd* 78, *wist* 86; *ȝe hight* 1016; *þai gat* 32, *blew* 373. The ending *-en* is found once in the pl.: *þai riden* 3528. The suffix for the past tense of weak verbs is usually *-ed*, but *-d*, *-de*, *-id*, *-t*, and *-et* are not uncommon: *answerd* 483, *folowd* 669, 672, &c., *herd* 696, 833, *hungerd* 2018, *opend* 697, 2997, *spird* 2829, *sufferd* 489, 2999, *delt* 640, *enoynt* 1779. Note *hopid* 539, 3393 beside *hoped* 892, 1675, 3079, *karpet* 467 beside *carped* 25, *karped* 498, *stird* 1883 beside *stirt* 1661, 3247. *helpid* 1442, 2643, &c., never appears otherwise, nor does *kepid* 2720, &c.

(*e*) Imperative. Sg.: ——. Examples: *tel* 293, *folow* 323, *sai* 2660, *arme* 471. Pl.: *-es*, ——. Examples: *understandes*:*tithandes* 139, :*landes* 1519, *say*:*may* 3003. Within the line the following examples appear: *pray* 89, *wit* 3910, *listens* 6, 3731; *takes* 88, 3178, 3296, &c.

(*f*) Present Participle. *-and*: *standand* (:*land* 363), *syttand* (:*hand* 638), *lyfand* 670, *dweland* 883, &c.

(*g*) Past Participle. Strong verbs show *-en* or *-n(e)* after a vowel or *r*: *done* (:*þe none* 2307), *knawen* (:*awyn* 2817), *knawin* 3695, *farn* 911, *sene* (:*bitwene* 2534), *tane* 2985. See the forms *bun* 3179 and *fun* 3936 for *bunden* (which appears at 2511) and *funden* (1734).

(*h*) Verbal Noun. *-ing*: *myslyking* (:*kyng* 537), *askyng* (:*ring* 738), &c.

(*i*) The Verb 'to be'. The infinitive is both *be* and *bene*: *be* (:*cuntre* 3289), *bene* (:*bytwene* 460, 3771).

Pres. Indic. 1st sg. usually *am*, but *be* 1586. 2nd sg. usually *ert*; once *es* (:*trowthles* 1625). 3rd sg. normally *es*, but *bese* twice (3062, 3864) and *ys* once in a rhyming position (:*wis* 2844). Pres. Indic. pl.: usually *er* in all persons (1176, 2525, 3516, &c.) but occasionally *are* (:*ware* 2991) and *bene* (:*quene* 985) in the 3rd pl., though in the latter instance the construction is complex. Once the sg. *es* is used (3590), but again the construction is ambiguous. Past Indic. sg.: *was* appears in the following cases: *I was* (:*I pas* 2109), *was I* 846, and *none was* 12. The form *wase* (1436) seems to have been changed from *ware*.

C. *Vocabulary*

Typically Northern or North-Midland words are common throughout: *boun*, *bus* pr. and *bud* pt. of *byhove*, *fra*, *ger*, *graid*, *hepin*, *ilka*, *ma* ('make'), *mikel/mekyl*, *sen*, *slike*, *skill*, *ta* ('take'), *pusgate.* Also: *at* with inf. 812, 2271, 2344, &c., *are* ('formerly') 374, 610, *ʒing* 722, 2643, *hilles* (OE. *haldan*) 741, *mon/mun* ('must', 'shall') 703, 2136, 2258, *tithand* 140, 2808, *traystes* 2908, *werr* ('worse') 436. Among the rarer Scandinavian words are *bayn* (ON. *beinn*) 766, 2097, *bir* (ON. *byr-r*) 1661, *dang* (ON. *dengja*) 3167, *fang* (ON. *fanga*) 299, 2642, *fraisted* (ON. *freista*) 3253, *layt* (ON. *leita*) 237 and *tint* (ON. *tyna*) 2599. The less usual French words in *YG* are *abayst* (OF. *abaissier*) 846, *actoune* (OF. *aqueton*) 2616, *baundoun* (OF. *bandon*) 1944, *gilry* (OF. *gillerie*) 1604, *jewyse* (OF. *juise*) 2127, *quisteroun* (OF. *quistron*) 2400, *stoure* (AF. *estur*) 31, 61, and *warisowne* (AF. *warison*) 918, 3586.

D. *Rhyme*

Vowels of different length are not uncommonly linked in rhyme, such as *man:nane* 279, *woman:tane* 2557, *line:yn* 269, *opon:stone* 561. Schleich (p. xxxiii) points out that (*I*) *hade:*(*I*) *made* 249, 1431, 1723 is probably not an unequal quantity, the *a* of *hade* having very likely been lengthened. Certain rhymes in *YG* were clearly suggested by Chrétien's rhymes. The following are instructive: *aventurs:armurs* 155, *aventures:armeures* Ch. 175; *payn:playn* 161, *plainne:painne* Ch. 181; *creature:mesure* 247, *desmesure:criature* Ch. 287; *kownsayle:mervayle* 317, *consoille:mervoille* Ch. 363; *mervayl:kounsayl* 2275, *mervoil:consoil* Ch. 3897; *velany:curtaysly* 497, *vilenie:corteisie* Ch. 633; *voice:croyce* 825, *voiz:croiz* Ch. 1163; *presowne:warisowne* 917, *prison:garison* Ch. 1569; *tresown:presown* 2133, *prison:traison* Ch. 3595; *place:manace* 3171, *place:menace* Ch. 5529; *mischance:conisance* 3649, *mescheance:mesconoissance* Ch. 6267.

VI. Metre and Alliteration

The metre of *YG* is the regular short (octosyllabic) rhymed couplet, the popularity of which in the fourteenth century is shown by its use in such diverse works as *Richard Coer de Lion*, *The House of Fame*, *The Pricke of Conscience*, and the *Confessio Amantis*. Unlike the polished octosyllabics of Gower, however, *YG* displays some of the more usual licences and irregularities of traditional English accentual verse. Thus the number of syllables varies between six and ten according to the presence or absence of anacrusis, and whether the verse ending is masculine or feminine. Pronunciation of the final *e* is also uncertain. As a general rule it has become silent, but from time to time, according to the needs of the verse, it may be sounded. Overfull lines and wrenched accents occur infrequently, but generally the author's ear is sound. To a certain degree this smoothness and variety is traceable to the author's adroitness in shifting the caesura back and forth in his poetic line,[1] and to his frequent use of the run-on line. Habitually he carries the sense over from one couplet to the next, running sometimes to eleven lines of verse. In addition, he often closes his sentence at the end of the first line of the couplet in the modern manner.[2] The result is verse of a very high order for the period—quickly paced, various, and smooth.

Like most Northern poets, E greatly prizes metrical regularity. A high proportion of the verses scan easily and correctly, and those that do not can usually be corrected by a knowledge of the author's use of elision, syncopation, and the final *-e*. Schleich's examination of the metrics of *YG* disclosed the following major characteristics (pp. xxv–xxxi):

(1) Final *e*, though usually suppressed, is sometimes sounded for the sake of the metre. Cases in which final *e* is sounded are: *mete* (47, 2045), *tale* (62, 120), *hende* (112, 173), *kene* (127), *þat gude man* (177), *swete* (212, 2691), *þou teche* (318), *large* (255, 2568), *more* (258), *face* (259), *solde* (436), *dore* (749), *here* (773), *stede* (795), *grace* (863), *speke we* (870), *wide* (1574, 2929), *þat wode man* (1678), *mele* (2032), *sone* (2168), *we have* (2246), *byforehand* (2879), *leve frend* (2990), *þai saide* (3289), *felle* (3478, 3811), and *terme* (3998). In addition, the following words probably add a final *e*: *werld* (46), *hight* (59), *hert* (144, 3831), *amerawd* (361), *luf* (1166), *wald* (543), *wil* (583), *went* (585), *pass* (600), *fast* (630), *long* (652), *stif* (654), *he met* (670), *said* (719), *tel* (987), *hight ȝe* (1016), *erth* (1325), *all kynges* (1411), *mirth* (1428), *bow* (1674), *boyst* (1850), *his best rede* (1910), *bourd* (1912), *walk* (3511), and *al* (3956).

---

[1] An examination of 500 verses (ll. 1001–1500) showed a caesural pause after the fourth syllable in 117 instances, after the second syllable in 50 instances, after the third in 47, after the fifth in 45, after the first in 18, after the sixth in 5, and after the seventh in 1.

[2] Our examination of 1,000 lines of verse shows that the poet prefers generally to close the sense at the end of a couplet. In 271 instances the sense is stopped at the end of a couplet; in 45 instances it is stopped at the end of the first line of the couplet. We counted 168 run-on lines in the same 1,000 verses (ll. 1001–1500, 3501–4000).

(2) The *e* in *ne* is frequently dropped when this word occurs after a personal pronoun. In such cases the pronoun unites with the following *n* to form one word. See, for example, *I ne sal* (916), *he ne sal* (3146), *þai ne sal* (713), *he ne sold* (309), *I ne most* (1475), *I ne may* (2673), *sho ne myght* (2755).

(3) The vowel of the definite article is sometimes elided, as in *þe assemble* (19), *þe eres* (146), *þe evyn* (1512), *þe assyse* (3445). The *e* of *ne* is also sometimes dropped and the *n* attaches itself to the following word (instead of to the preceding, as in (2) above) to form one syllable, as in: *ne was* (532), *ne wald* (1151), *ne wate* (1821, 3857, 3868), *ne war* (3250). Also we find that the vowel of *me, þe*, and *so* elides occasionally before words beginning with vowels or *h*: *me asayle* (1999), *þe here* (3669), *so es* (1420). Elision is shown in the spelling of *savese* (723) for *so avyse* (113).

(4) Final *i/y* is frequently lost before a following initial vowel: *ani of* (66), *moni a* (598, 828), *many and* (2517), *lady and* (1481), *lady his* (1957), *foly I* (3997).

(5) Synizesis occurs chiefly in French vowel combinations beginning with *i/y*: *regyowne* (858), *specially* (2160), *gracious* (3094). It can also be found in the comparative and superlative of certain adjectives: *sarier* (2126), *merier* (3001), and *sariest* (2111).

(6) Syncopation is very common, occurring frequently in inflexions ending with a consonant and in adverbs with endings in *es*: *tales þat he* (2498), *hinder-arsown* (681), *thinkes on me* (1530), *hailsed him kindly* (171), *broken þe term* (1616), *ʒolden to þe* (3653), *said anis with* (1161), *unnethes þow sal* (344), *sertes in al* (2278), *say nedes bus* (1085), *inmiddes þe brest* (2442). Syncopation is sometimes already indicated by the spelling: *weders wekend* (411), *sporrs sho sparid* (2892), *wemens will* (967), *maydens hall* (806), *governs alkin* (3469), *cums sho noght* (3430), *opend it* (2997), *past with mekyl* (161), *farn þis day* (911), *ogayns him so* (3604), *ogayns þam thre* (2532). *Sithes* (868, 1419, 2087, 2854) is to be pronounced as if it were written *siths*, as is clearly indicated by the rhythm. Similarly, the demands of the metre indicate that the genitive ending in *kinges son Uriene* (2149) is to be syncopated, as if by analogy with *king son Uriene* (732).

(7) Vowels occurring between accented syllables are syncopated, as in: *mine avenant* (3174, 3765, 3885), *als covenand* (3969), *jugement sal* (2642), *unement dere* (1752, 1898), *reverence þam* (1322), *of veneri* (26), *charite I* (2835), *surete in* (3032), *damysel aght* (724),

covering of (3000), *levening smate* (377), *semely syght* (365), *nobilly þat* (2787), *hastily hies* (2877), *kyndeli ken* (28), *me mildeli* (172), *ful lufely* (332), *baldely or* (1047, 3194), *halely gane* (881). Syncopation is sometimes revealed in the spellings: *kownand* (3894), *kindly* (171, 174), *hendly* (198, 2850, 3376).

(8) End syllables concluding with a liquid are also sometimes syncopated: *saghtel þe knyght* (3917), *bourewemen alswa* (1711), *wapen þat man* (3233), *oþer of his* (2325), *nowþer of þam* (3613), *under þe fairest* (325), *efter hir* (1099), *water þe boyst* (1835), *sowl Uterpendragowne* (522), *maister had eten* (2046, also 2607, 3822), *chamber to sir* (1020), *þover atire* (2968), *kastel þe way* (1377), *dragon in at* (1991), *lyown out of* (3778), *lyoun sho was* (2346, also 2571, 2895), *porter no word* (2959).

(9) Syncopation takes place in such words as *owyn* (1230, 1647, 3014, 3691, &c.), *knawin* (3695), *mayden* (1807, 2856), *withowten* (345, 3057), and *yren* (2038, 2386). One can also expect syncopated forms for *never* (3206), *ever* (3437, 4011), *aventure* (180, 237, 3448), *misaventur* (2413), *aventerous* (3399), *hevyd* (1036), *lavedy* (2828), *wheþer* (3748), *seþin* (1103, 2799). That syncopation takes place in such verb forms as *taken* (2858), *funden* (3714, 3919), *makes* (3172, 3987), *takes* (3054, 3072), *haves* (3319, 3477), *haved* (3684), *byhoves* (3022), is indicated both by the metre and by the existence of such shortened forms as *tane* (691), *fun* (3936), *mase* (692), *tase* (841), *has* (1147), *hade* (250), *bus* (2504, 2763, 3023, 3131, 3881; also see *bud*, 3029). In addition, *over* (3452, 765, 3137, 1132) and *sevenight* (3360, 3395) undoubtedly syncopate.

(10) Schleich assumes that the zeal of E for metrical regularity led him on many occasions to shift the accent awkwardly to un-accented syllables, e.g. *askés* (2790), *knyghtés* (3587), *maný* (3012), *softlý* (2722), *undér* (3084), &c., but it is perhaps wiser to recognize that E was not so zealous about metrical regularity and that the words were accented normally and produced hobbling lines.

Especially noticeable in *YG* is a marked tendency to alliteration: of the 4,032 verses, 1,426 show some degree of alliteration. Certain passages, particularly, are heavily alliterated, as, for example, the description of the combat between the hero and Sir Gawain (ll. 3537–44):

> þai drow swerdes and swang obout,
> To dele dyntes had þai no dout.
> þaire sheldes war shiferd and helms rifen,

Ful stalworth strakes war þare gifen.
Bath on bak and brestes þare
War bath wounded wonder-sare;
In many stedes might men ken
þe blode out of þaire bodies ren.

As can be seen from the above passage, alliteration is used to bind the accented syllables together, although in cases where more than four syllables alliterate in a line of verse, unaccented syllables perforce alliterate. Of the 1,426 lines which show alliteration, 1,110 of these alliterate two syllables and 232 alliterate three syllables. Twenty-three lines alliterate four syllables, as in

> Hir maners might no man amend; (208)

and

> At cum to court als knyght unknawyn. (3414)

Fifty lines alliterate two pairs of two syllables, as in:

> Fer and nere and findes him noght; (1656)

and

> Sum men þat myght his bales bete. (1806)

Nine lines show alliteration of one sound twice and another sound three times, as in:[1]

> He rynnes fast, with ful fell rese. (3245)

On two occasions one sound alliterates twice and another alliterates four times:

> Swilk als he had, swilk he him gaf; (1683)

and

> Sone when he had of hir had syght. (1811)

The frequent presence of alliterative phrases and tags in *YG* indicates the continued popularity of this traditional feature of English verse among the writers of the rhyming romances.[2] Most of the alliterative phrases, however, are such as can be found in almost any fourteenth-century text, many of them being mere tags as in the tautological expressions *might and mayne, robbed and reft, many and mekil,* and *fers and fell.*

---

[1] See ll. 927, 1053, 1620, 2595, 2697, 3517, 3611, 3695.
[2] See J. P. Oakden, *Alliterative Poetry in Middle English. A Survey of the Traditions* (Manchester, 1935), pp. 312–43.

Of the almost countless alliterating words and phrases in *YG*, the most important are: *bak and brest* (3541, 3611), *bel and boke* (3023), *bird bright* (3313), *bowsom and bayne* (3101), *curtayse cumpany* (43), *dintes doure* (2634), *doghtines of dede* (29), *done to dede* (2147, 2188, 2375), *doghty of dede* (866, 3802), *faire and fine* (203), *faire forest* (238, 295), *ferly fayne* (1346), *fers and fell* (2409), *forth to fare* (234), *for friend or fa* (3131), *frith and fell* (2711, 2795), *ful feloun* (2776), *Goddes grace* (3564, 4001), *grete and gay* (19), *gudely grayd* (832, 2968), *heled and hale* (1721), *hendely te hend* (207), *Herkens, hende* (149), *hevy herte* (1976), *hevyn on hight* (3339), *hide and hew* (886), *kene and calde* (1293), *kene karping* (127), *knave or knyght* (1594, 3565), *kumly knyght* (2886), *landes lays* (2792, 3740), *large and lang* (2385), *lely lire* (2510), *light of lepes* (72), *lordes and ladies* (20, 4018), *made his mane* (692, 1535, 2103, 2761), *main and mode* (1031), *man of main* (2793), *man of moder born* (185), *mani a moder son* (828), *many and mekil* (2517), *mar of main* (1005), *mayden meke* (557, 1769), *mekyl mayn* (58, 871), *mekyl more* (1265), *mekyl myght* (1799, 2118, 2279, 2715, 3133), *mekyl myrth* (1417, 1436, 1970, 3350, 3933), *might and mayne* (3, 2499), *milde mode* (483), *milde and meke* (1366), *maste of myght* (3068, 3505), *rathly red* (1177), *robbed and reft* (2253), *rope and rare* (242), *save and se* (3470), *by se and sand* (3657), *snaw and slete* (375), *soth to say* (15, 614, 1235, &c.), *spir and spy* (3013), *stalworth strakes* (3540), *stif in stowre* (31), *stif strakes* (654), *swier and swayne* (1549), *tale to tell* (90, 123, 2483, 2498, &c.), *toun and toure* (2365), *in toure ne town* (3817), *toure or toun* (2885), *towre and towne* (1576, 1949, 4019), *treson and trechery* (1609), *twa and twa* (2622, 3337), *war ne wise* (12, 21, 1241, 2904), *wele and wo* (2682), *weked wordes* (128), *wend my way* (236, 349, 430, 1561, &c.), *werld so wyde* (2278), *wilde and wode* (1650), *wode for wa* (822, 1650, 2406), *wide woundes* (2630), *wyde werld* (2278).

VII. RHETORIC

E manages to tell his story without the aid of Chrétien's conceits, rhetorical flourishes, and epic similes. He seems reluctant to hazard a figure of any kind, and when he does it is likely to be as popular and unimaginative as:

A lady folowd white so mylk (819)

or

Hir yghen clere als es cristall. (900)

Indeed, as Whiting has pointed out,[1] of Chrétien's twenty-eight formal comparisons, many of which are similes articulated through a number of lines in the epic manner, the English author adapted only five (E 251 f., 257, 260, 262, 629 f.). Of these, four are from Chrétien's graphic description of the Giant Herdsman (Ch. 295 ff.). To these he adds nine similes of his own, none of which has an ornamental function or shows any degree of inventiveness:

> His browes war like litel buskes; (E 261)

> Als þe bark hilles þe tre,
> Right so sal my ring do þe (E 741 f.)

> A lady folowd white so mylk; (E 819)

> Hir yghen clere als es cristall. (E 900)

> Him thoght þat he [the horse] was als lyght
> Als a fowl es to þe flyght; (E 1303)

> þe king said, 'Lady white so flowre'; (E 1421)

> þat da he kest þan in his nek
> Als it war a mele-sek; (E 2031 f.)

> Of riche cloth soft als þe sylk; (E 3105)

> And þarto white als any mylk. (E 3106)

The popular character of these figures is manifest.

The English poet, however, shows a fondness for proverbs and short, pithy sayings. Although there are six proverbs in *Yvain* which were not translated[2] there are three which were, and two more which the Englishman added. The proverbs translated from the French are:

> Toz jorz doit puïr li fumiers
> Et taons poindre et maloz bruire,
> Enuieus enuiier et nuire; (Ch. 116 ff.)

> It es ful semeli als me think,
> A brok omang men forto stynk; (E 97 f.)

> Plus a paroles an plain pot
> De vin, qu'an un mui de cervoise; (Ch. 592 f.)

> It is sene now es efter mete!
> Mare boste es in a pot of wyne
> þan in a karcas of Saynt Martyne; (E 468 f.)

---

[1] B. J. Whiting, 'Proverbs in Certain Middle English Romances in Relation to their French Sources', *(Harvard) Studies and Notes in Philol.* xv (1933), 116–18.

[2] Whiting (ibid., pp. 115 f.) lists the following: ll. 594, 595 ff., 1325 f., 1428 f., 1435 f., 2146 f.

Que cil ne fet pas la meslee
Qui fiert la premiere colee,
Ainz la fet cil, qui se revange; (Ch. 641)

And als, madame, men says sertayne
þat, wo so flites or turnes ogayne,
He bygins al þe melle. (E 503 ff.)

To these are added two English proverbs:

Bot ȝit a fole þat litel kan,
May wele cownsail anoþer man; (E 1477 f.)

For fole bolt es sone shot. (E 2168)

Chrétien's sententious remarks are handled by the English translator with notable freedom. He passes by six[1] and adopts only one:

'Nenil,' fet il; 'de reposer
Ne se puet nus hon aloser'; (Ch. 5095 f.)

He said, 'þat knyght þat idil lies,
Oft siþes winnes ful litel pries.' (E 2923 f.)

To these he adds five sententious remarks out of his own stock:

And in þe hert þare es þe horde
And knawing of ilk mans worde; (E 147 f.)

For best comforth of al thing
Es solace efter myslikeing; (E 387 f.)

To speke of lufe na time was þare,
For aiþer hated uþer ful sare; (E 633 f.)

Madame, it es oft wemens will
þam forto blame þat sais þam scill; (E 967 f.)

And said, 'Wha juges men with wrang,
þe same jugement sal þai fang.' (E 2641 f.)

Like most rhymed romances *YG* makes use of tags to fill out lines, to attest to historical veracity, and to overcome various metrical difficulties. Unlike many of his *confrères*, however, E is relatively restrained in his use of tags (only 59 clear-cut examples in 4032 lines). A number of E's tags assure the audience that what is being recited is not the minstrel's own invention but has been copied from a *boke*, the truth of which is unimpeachable: *als sayes*

---

[1] Whiting (ibid., p. 116) lists ll. 31 ff., 2464 f., 2515 ff., 2852 f., 3120 f., 3582 ff.

þe buke (9), *als it telles in* þe *boke* (3209), and *so sais* þe *boke* (3671).
Lest the reader or listener doubt the veracity of his story, the author
frequently interjects phrases like þe *soth to say* (15, 1605, 1847,
2022, 2211, 2658, 3997), *trewly to tell* (329), *es noght at layne* (703,
1127, 3979), *for soth to tell* (1267), and *if men wil luke* (10). Particularly characteristic are a number of phrases calling upon God,
most of which have four syllables and are convenient for filling the
second half of a line: *God do him* (þe) *mede* (181, 728, 2700, 2717,
3377, 3479), *by Goddes dome* (437), *so God me rede* (713, 2075, 2187),
so God me save (1191), *so God me glad* (1473, 1857, 2369, 3381),
so God me (þe) *mend* (1745, 2285, 2660, 3879), *God mot þe se* (1597),
for Goddes tre (1843), *by Goddes dome* (2561), *God mot ʒow spede*
(2998), *God mot ʒow se* (3355). Similarly, there are a number of
oaths, also of four syllables, which have the characteristics of tags.
Such are: *by Saint Symoun* (2661), *by swete Jhesus* (2887), *in Cristes
name* (3639), and the periphrastic expressions *thorgh his might þat
tholed wownd* (383), *by him me boght* (3154), *For hys luf þat lens us
life* (3483).
     In addition there are a number of tags drawn from the general
fund which the author calls on from time to time to stiffen a limping
verse. In this category are: *als me think* (97), *als ʒe sal here* (154),
I ʒow bihete (158, 2221), *þat be ʒe balde* (169, 1285, 2781), *on al wise*
(227, 1250, 1506, 1559, 3147, 3915, 3972), *by est and west* (338), *if
that I may* (465, 2527), *als* (so) *mot I ga* (2139), *and als* (so) *mot I the*
(3141, 3499).
     One final stylistic feature deserves mention. The author shows
a special fondness for beginning a line of verse with *and*, a characteristic which has hardened almost into an idiosyncrasy. In the
4032 lines of verse in *YG* there are 637 instances of initial *and*, or
a little more than one every six lines. The large number of initial
connectives is partly explained by the poet's predilection for run-
on lines, which he handles, according to one critic, as effectively
as Chaucer.[1]

VIII. Author and Date

All that can be learnt of the author of *YG* must be deduced from
the poem. Undoubtedly he was 'a minstrel of the North countree',

---

[1] R. W. Ackerman in *Arthurian Literature in the Middle Ages*, ed. R. S.
Loomis (Oxford, 1959), p. 509.

a member of the tribe which Percy and Scott glamourized and Ritson described more coolly. He holds to an aesthetic which places the eventful above the emotional and reflective; he is suspicious of artfulness, ornamentation, psychological probing, self-conscious subtleties; he tells a story with the straightforward vigour of the best English romances. Something may be made of his toning down or complete omission of cruel or bloody passages and his reticence in the handling of highly charged emotional scenes. On one or two occasions he displays a more than ordinary interest in the law, but this hardly means that he was a lawyer or cleric.

It is almost equally difficult to fix the date of composition with any precision. External evidence is lacking altogether, nor are there any topical references in the text itself which might help. Ritson thought that the poem was composed 'in the time of Richard II, or towards the close of the fourteenth century; and not, as appear'd to Warton, who knew nothing of the age of MSS. and probably never saw this, "in the reign of king Henry the sixth".'[1] Schleich, however, prefers an earlier date: 'Ich bin sogar geneigt die Hs. noch weiter in das vierzehnte Jahrhundert, womöglich bis in die erste Hälfte desselben, zurückzuverlegen.'[2] Other commentators are agreed only in placing the composition at some time in the fourteenth century.[3]

As mentioned in Section VI. 1, inflexional -e, though generally silent, is sometimes sounded in YG. There are in the 4032 lines of the poem some 33 words which probably pronounce final -e, and another 25 words which may add a final -e for the sake of the metre. These survivals give some support for a date prior to 1350. But the problem is not quite so simple. While final -e had probably become silent in the spoken language in the North by the middle of the fourteenth century, it is quite possible that the written language, always more conservative, tended to preserve inflexional -e

[1] Ritson, *Ancient Engleish Metrical Romanceës*, iii. 229.
[2] Schleich, *YG*, p. i.
[3] Bruce, *Evolution of Arthurian Romance*, i. 127 f., puts the poem in the fourteenth century without further specification. Wells, *Manual*, p. 5, follows Schleich in dating the poem 1300–50—as does R. W. Ackerman in *Arthurian Literature in the Middle Ages*, ed. R. S. Loomis (Oxford, 1959), p. 509—while French and Hale (p. 485) give 1350–1400 as the date of composition. For its citations from *YG*, *OED*. gives *c*. 1400, but this refers to the date of the manuscript. *MED*. dates its citations a(nte) 1425 for the manuscript and ? *c*. 1350 for the date of composition.

in a random fashion.[1] The poet's language, however, is markedly unambitious and colloquial, and may therefore be presumed to reflect spoken rather than formal usage. The date 1325–50 seems best to suit the facts.

This date is also implied by the male attire described in *YG*. Dorothy Everett has remarked on the romance-writers' tendency to bring 'up to date . . . their properties', to dress their characters in armour and clothing fashionable at the time of writing.[2] E is miserly with descriptions, as we have noted, but in both instances where he adds details of dress not in Chrétien (1402–4, 1770–2), he refers to the *ceinture* style that came into vogue, along with the *cote-hardie*, early in the reign of Edward III. The 'girdels al of gold ful fyne' (E 1404) that Alundyne's barons wore to greet King Arthur, are *ceintures d'or*, the elaborate, often richly jewelled belts worn diagonally across the upper thighs to hold the short skirt of the new tight-fitting coat in place. These belts were an innovation of the 1330's; presumably only in that period would a reference to them impress an English audience with the high fashion of Alundyne's entourage.[3] Certainly the mention of this accessory discredits any date before 1325.

IX. ABBREVIATIONS

The following abbreviations have been used in the Introduction and Commentary:

Arth. Trad.	R. S. Loomis, *Arthurian Tradition and Chrétien de Troyes*, New York, 1949.
Ch.	Chrétien de Troyes, *Yvain* (in line references only). All citations are from *Der Löwenritter* (*Yvain*), ed. Wendelin Foerster, 4th edn., Halle, 1912.
E	The author of *Ywain and Gawain*.
MED.	*Middle English Dictionary*, ed. Hans Kurath and S. M. Kuhn, Ann Arbor, 1952–.

---

[1] Luick, *Hist. Grammatik*, § 473.

[2] *Essays on Middle English Literature* (Oxford, 1955), pp. 5–6.

[3] See N. Bradfield, *Historical Costumes of England* (1958), p. 39; F. M. Kelly and R. Schwabe, *A Short History of Costume and Armour* (1931), pp. 20–21; cf. H. Eagleson, 'Costume in the Metrical Romances', *PMLA.* xlvii (1932), 339–45.

Morte d'Arthur	*The Works of Sir Thomas Malory,* ed. Eugène Vinaver, 3 vols., Oxford, 1947.
OED.	*The Oxford English Dictionary on Historical Principles,* ed. J. A. H. Murray *et al.,* Oxford, 1884–1933.
Ritson	Joseph Ritson, *Ancient Engleish Metrical Romanceës,* 3 vols., London, 1802. *Ywaine and Gawin:* Text, i. 1–169; Notes, iii. 225–42.
Schleich	*Ywain and Gawain,* ed. Gustav Schleich, Oppeln and Leipzig, 1887.
YG	*Ywain and Gawain.*
Periodicals:	
Engl. Stud.	*Englische Studien.*
JEGP.	*Journal of English and Germanic Philology.*
MLN.	*Modern Language Notes.*
MLR.	*Modern Language Review.*
MP.	*Modern Philology.*
PMLA.	*Publications of the Modern Language Association of America.*

The following works have been referred to by shortened titles at a distance from the initial (full) references:

Brown, A. C. L., 'Iwain: A Study in the Origins of Arthurian Romance', (*Harvard*) *Studies in Philology and Literature,* vol. viii, Boston, 1903.

—— 'On the Independent Character of the Welsh *Owein*', *Romanic Review,* iii (1912), 143–72.

Brown, Carleton, and Robbins, R. H., *The Index of Middle English Verse,* New York, 1943.

Bruce, J. D., *The Evolution of Arthurian Romance,* 2 vols., Göttingen, 1923.

Chaucer, *Works,* ed. F. N. Robinson, 2nd edn., Boston, 1957.

Chrétien de Troyes, *Erec et Enide,* ed. Wendelin Foerster, Halle, 1909.

Cohen, Gustave, *Chrétien de Troyes et son œuvre,* Paris, 1931.

Cross, T. P., and Nitze, W. A., *Lancelot and Guenevere,* Chicago, 1930.

Foerster, Wendelin, *Kristian von Troyes: Wörterbuch zu seinen sämtlichen Werken,* Halle, 1914.

French, W. H., and Hale, C. B., *Middle English Metrical Romances,* New York, 1930.

Hartmann von Aue, *Iwein,* ed. Fedor Bech, Leipzig, 1888.

Lewis, C. B., *Classical Mythology and Arthurian Romance,* Oxford, 1932.

Lister, Wilfrid, 'Notes on the Text of the Middle English Romance "Ywaine and Gawin" ', *MLR.* xxxv (1940), 56–58.

Mabinogion, tr. Thomas Ellis and John Lloyd, 2 vols., Oxford, 1929.

Minot, Laurence, *Poems,* ed. Joseph Hall, Oxford, 1887.

Nitze, W. A., and Jenkins, T. A., *Le Haut Livre du Graal: Perlesvaus,* 2 vols., Chicago, 1932–7.

Paton, Lucy A., *Studies in the Fairy Mythology of Arthurian Romance,* Boston, 1903.

Reid, T. B. W., *Yvain,* Manchester, 1942. (Foerster's text but with useful introduction and notes.)

Schleich, Gustav, *Über das Verhältnis der mittelenglischen Romanze* Ywain and Gawain *zu ihrer altfranzösischen Quelle,* Berlin, 1889.

The Seven Sages of Rome, ed. Killis Campbell, Boston, 1907.

The Vulgate Version of the Arthurian Romances, ed. H. O. Sommer, 8 vols., Washington, D.C., 1909–16.

Wells, J. E., *A Manual of the Writings in Middle English, 1050–1400,* New Haven, Conn., 1916 ff.

Weston, J. L., ' "Ywain and Gawain" and "Le Chevalier au Lion" ', *Modern Quarterly of Language and Literature,* i (1898), 98–107, 194–202.

X. The Present Edition

In this edition the spelling of the manuscript is retained, except for corrections of obvious scribal errors. Such emendations have been enclosed in square brackets. The footnotes give the manuscript forms as well as items of palaeographical interest.

Abbreviations are abundant throughout the manuscript. *And* is almost invariably abbreviated; *þat* and *with* much less often. A notable peculiarity is the frequent appearance of the curled *r,* a long upward flourish curling tightly to the left to end in a dot, which apparently had the value of *re* for the scribe. Almost always it is used terminally, but at least once (*pareate* 672) it is used medially. We have consistently expanded curled *r* to *re* (e.g. *here* 3669: see frontispiece). A curl with the value of *er* is also frequently used (e.g. *efter* 3727). Various other abbreviations involving *r* (*ra, ri, er, ar, ur*) are also frequent. A straight stroke over a letter is the usual mark of contraction to indicate omitted *m* or *n* (e.g. *welkum* 3717; *in* 3690: see frontispiece), although sometimes omission is indicated by a short wavy line. The customary flourish turned downward after a letter is used to indicate terminal *es* or *is*. A *p* with a loop crossing the downstroke is the special sign for *pro* (e.g. *prowess,* 3699: see frontispiece); *p* under a dash for *pre* (e.g. *prest*); and *p* with a dash through the downstroke for *per* or *par* (e.g. *part* 3746; *depart* 3752). Throughout the text these abbreviations and the common contractions have been silently expanded.

In view of the vagaries of medieval metrics, we have not emended the text on metrical grounds. We have altered the scribal use of capitals to conform with modern usage, and have modernized the punctuation. The letters *u* and *v* have been adjusted to modern practice (*envy, served, unto* for the frequent manuscript spellings *enuy, serued, vnto*). Similarly, we have printed *j* for *i* in accordance with modern usage (*jorne, jermayne* for *iorne, iermayne*). Words that stand divided in the manuscript (e.g. *no thing* 1457, *a noper* 400) have been joined without notice.

The following lines begin with a capital letter in the ink of the text and have a paragraph mark opposite them (cf. p. xii):

15, 41, 59, 71, 85, 105, 117, 125, 135, 157, 167, 181, 195, 213, 231, 235, 253, 267, 277, 285, 295, 319, 331, 349, 361, 371, 379, 389, 423, 431, 451, 471, 495, 525, 545, 555, 565, 603, 629, 639, 651, 661, 677, 691, 701, 713, 731, 747, 763, 787, 805, 817, 833, 847, 891, 899, 919, 931, 945, 973, 987, 999, 1011, 1021, 1033, 1035, 1053, 1073, 1085, 1097, 1109, 1119, 1131, 1149, 1161, 1177, 1207, 1221, 1227, 1245, 1261, 1271, 1281, 1301, 1311, 1337, 1347, 1383, 1401, 1413, 1421, 1435, 1457, 1473, 1489, 1499, 1515, 1531, 1545, 1561, 1567, 1577, 1593, 1603, 1619, 1645, 1657, 1671, 1687, 1697, 1727, 1741, 1759, 1775, 1799, 1817, 1829, 1833, 1849, 1883, 1897, 1909, 1923, 1931, 1947, 1955, 1971, 1993, 2009, 2017, 2025, 2037, 2053, 2071, 2087, 2103, 2117, 2129, 2145, 2159, 2165, 2181, 2193, 2203, 2209, 2225, 2239, 2249, 2259, 2273, 2285, 2297, 2309, 2323, 2339, 2349, 2367, 2379, 2391, 2397, 2413, 2441, 2447, 2463,

2481, 2491, 2503, 2543, 2555, 2571, 2585, 2597, 2631, 2649, 2661, 2675, 2697, 2711, 2715, 2725, 2759, 2777, 2789, 2807, 2821, 2835, 2855, 2871, 2887, 2899, 2913, 2949, 2965, 2977, 2995, 3009, 3027, 3047, 3057, 3073, 3095, 3101, 3115, 3141, 3153, 3175, 3191, 3195, 3211, 3235, 3261, 3279, 3293, 3315, 3339, 3357, 3377, 3385, 3415, 3467, 3481, 3499, 3509, 3529, 3545, 3561, 3593, 3619, 3633, 3655, 3665, 3701, 3715, 3731, 3751, 3759, 3797, 3811, 3829, 3841, 3855, 3877, 3907, 3921, 3935, 3967, 3983, 3997.

YWAIN AND GAWAIN

Almyghti God þat made mankyn,
He schilde his servandes out of syn
And mayntene þam with might and mayne,
þat herkens Ywayne and Gawayne;
þai war knightes of þe tabyl rownde,   5
þarfore listens a lytel stownde.

Arthure, þe Kyng of Yngland,
þat wan al Wales with his hand
And al Scotland, als sayes þe buke,
And mani mo, if men wil luke,   10
Of al knightes he bare þe pryse.
In werld was none so war ne wise;
Trew he was in alkyn thing.
Als it byfel to swilk a kyng,
He made a feste, þe soth to say,   15
Opon þe Witsononday
At Kerdyf þat [es] in Wales,
And efter mete þare in þe hales
Ful grete and gay was þe assemble
Of lordes and ladies of þat cuntre,   20
And als of knyghtes war and wyse
And damisels of mykel pryse.
Ilkane with oþer made grete gamin
And grete solace als þai war samin.
Fast þai carped and curtaysly   25
Of dedes of armes and of veneri
And of gude knightes þat lyfed þen,
And how men might þam kyndeli ken
By doghtines of þaire gude ded
On ilka syde, wharesum þai ȝede;   30

Here bigyns Ywaine and Gawain: *rubric in red above the line in the same hand*
1 *A large initial capital, extending to l. 4, decorated in red and blue.* þat *and* m
of made *illegible because of tear in MS.*   2 servandes: ervan *illegible because of*
tear   3 þam: þa *illegible*   4 Ywayne: Ywa *illegible*   5 þe: e *illegible*
17 es: *added over the line by another hand*

For þai war stif in ilka stowre,
And þarfore gat þai grete honowre.
þai tald of more trewth þam bitw[e]ne
þan now omang men here es sene,
For trowth and luf es al bylaft;   35
Men uses now anoþer craft.
With worde men makes it trew and stabil,
Bot in þaire faith es noght bot fabil;
With þe mowth men makes it hale,
Bot trew trowth es nane in þe tale.   40
þarfore hereof now wil I blyn,
Of þe Kyng Arthure I wil bygin
And of his curtayse cumpany;
þare was þe flowre of chevallry.
Swilk lose þai wan with speres-horde,   45
Over al þe werld went þe worde.

Ch. 42   After mete went þe kyng
Into chamber to slepeing,
And also went with him þe quene.
þat byheld þai al bydene,   50
For þai saw þam never so
On high dayes to chamber go.
Bot sone, when þai war went to [s]l[epe],
Knyghtes sat þe dor to kepe:
Sir Dedyne and Sir Segramore,   55
Sir Gawayn and Sir Kay sat þore,
And also sat þare Sir Ywaine
And Colgrevance of mekyl mayn.
þis knight þat hight Colgrevance,
Tald his felows of a chance   60
And of a stowre he had in bene,
And al his tale herd þe quene.
þe chamber dore sho has unshet,
And down omang þam scho hir set;
Sodainli sho sat downright,   65
Or ani of þam of hir had sight.
Bot Colgrevance rase up in hy,

---

33 bitwne MS.; R(itson)'s emendation   47 A red initial capital   kyng:
yn almost illegible because of tear   53 slepe: obliterated by a brown discoloration;
R.'s emendation   54 k of kepe is obscured   55 am of Segramore obscured

And þareof had Syr Kay envy,
For he was of his tong a skalde,
And forto boste was he ful balde.   70
'Ow Colgrevance,' said Sir Kay,
'Ful light of lepes has þou bene ay.
þou wenes now þat þe sal fall
Forto be hendest of us all.
And þe quene sal understand,   75
þat here es none so unkunand;
Al if þou rase and we sat styll,
We ne dyd it for none yll,
Ne for no manere of fayntise,
Ne us denyd noght forto rise,   80
þat we ne had resen had we hyr sene.'
'Sir Kay, I wote wele,' sayd þe quene,
'And it war gude þou left swilk sawes
And noght despise so þi felawes.'

Ch. 92   'Madame,' he said, 'by Goddes dome,   85
We ne wist nothing of þi come
And if we did noght curtaysly,
Takes to no velany.
Bot pray ȝe now þis gentil man
To tel þe tale þat he bygan.'   90
Colgrevance said to Sir Kay:
'Bi grete God þat aw þis day,
Na mare manes me þi flyt
f. 4ᵛ   þan it war a flies byt.
Ful oft wele better men þan I   95
Has þou desspised desspytusely.
It es ful semeli, als me think,
A brok omang men forto stynk.
So it fars by þe, Syr Kay;
Of weked wordes has þou bene ay.   100
And, sen þi wordes er wikked and fell,
þis time þarto na more I tell,
Bot of the thing þat I bygan.'

---

80 Ne for *MS.*; *superfluous* for *copied from preceding line*   84 despise *MS.*
and R; Schl(eich) emends to despised   94 flies: fl *unclear because of rip in MS.*
95 better: *first* e *unclear*   100–11 *A large brown discoloration obscures the*
beginning of these lines: 100 Of we; 101 And sen þi wor; 102 Þis ti; 103 Bot of

Ch. 124   And sone Sir Kay him answerd þan
                 And said ful tite unto þe quene: 105
                 'Madame, if ʒe had noght here bene,
                 We sold have herd a selly case;
                 Now let ʒe us of oure solace.
                 þarfore, madame, we wald ʒow pray,
                 þat ʒe cumand him to say   110
                 And tel forth, als he had tyght.'
                 þan answerd þat hende knight:
                 'Mi lady es so avyse,
                 þat scho wil noght cumand me
                 To tel þat towches me to ill;   115
                 Scho es noght of so weked will.'
                 Sir Kai said þan ful smertli:
                 'Madame, al hale þis cumpani
                 Praies ʒow hertly now omell,
                 þat he his tale forth might tell.   120
                 If ʒe wil noght for oure praying,
                 For faith ʒe aw unto þe kyng,
                 Cumandes him his tale to tell,
                 þat we mai here how it byfell.'
                 þan said þe quene, 'Sir Colgrevance,   125
                 I prai þe tak to no grevance
                 þis kene karping of Syr Kay;
                 Of weked wordes has he bene ay,
                 So þat none may him chastise.
                 þarfore I prai þe, on al wise,   130
                 þat þou let noght for his sawes
                 At tel to me and þi felawes
                 Al þi tale, how it bytid.
                 For my luf I þe pray and byd.'
Ch. 142   'Sertes, madame, þat es [me] lath,   135
                 Bot for I wil noght mak ʒow wrath,
                 ʒowre cumandment I sal fulfill,
                 If ʒe wil listen me untill,
                 With hertes and eres understandes;

A large brown discoloration obscures the following words: 104 And sone Si; 105 And said ful; 106 Madame; 107 We sold; 108 Now le; 109 þarfore; 110 þat ʒ; 111 And te   113 M *of* Mi *partly obscured*   135 me: *added above the line in another hand*

And I sal tel ȝow swilk tithandes,   140
þat ȝe herd never none slike
Reherced in no kynges ryke.
Bot word fares als dose þe wind,
Bot if men it in hert bynd;
And, wordes wo so trewly tase,   145
By þe eres into þe hert it gase,
And in þe hert þare es þe horde
And knawing of ilk mans worde.

Ch. 172   'Herkens, hende, unto my spell,
Trofels sal I ȝow nane tell,   150
Ne lesinges forto ger ȝow lagh,
Bot I sal say right als I sagh.
Now als þis time sex ȝere
I rade allane, als ȝe sal here,
Obout forto seke aventurs,   155
Wele armid in gude armurs.
In a frith I fand a strete
Ful thik and hard, I ȝow bihete,
With thornes, breres and moni a quyn.
Nerehand al day I rade þareyn,   160
'And thurgh I past with mekyl payn.
þan come I sone into a playn,
Whare I gan se a bretise brade,
And þederward ful fast I rade.
I saw þe walles and þe dyke,   165
And hertly wele it gan me lyke;
And on þe drawbrig saw I stand
A knight with fawkon on his hand.
þis ilk knight, þat be ȝe balde,
Was lord and keper of þat halde.   170
I hailsed him kindly als I kowth;
He answerd me mildeli with mowth.
Mi sterap toke þat hende knight
And kindly cumanded me to lyght;
His cumandment I did onane,   175
And into hall sone war we tane.

141 never: ever *obscured by rip and discoloration*   142 kynges: *obscured by*
rip   143 als: *obscured by rip*   144 i *of it faded*   145 trewly: trew
obscured by rip   149 *A blue initial capital*

He thanked God, þat gude man,
Sevyn sithes or ever he blan,
And þe way þat me þeder broght,
And als þe aventurs þat I soght.   180

'þus went we in, God do him mede,
And in his hand he led my stede.
When we war in þat fayre palays
(It was ful worthly wroght always),
I saw no man of moder born.   185
Bot a burde hang us biforn,
Was nowther of yren ne of tre,

Ne I ne wist whareof it might be,
And by þat bord hang a mall.
þe knyght smate on þar-with-all   190
Thrise, and by þen might men se
Bifore him come a faire menȝe,
Curtayse men in worde and dede;
To stabil sone þai led mi stede.

'A damisel come unto me,   195
þe semeliest þat ever I se,
Lufsumer lifed never in land.
Hendly scho toke me by þe hand,
And sone þat gentyl creature
Al unlaced myne armure.   200
Into a chamber sho me led,
And with a mantil scho me cled:
It was of purpure faire and fine
And þe pane of rich ermyne.
Al þe folk war went us fra,   205
And þare was none þan bot we twa.
Scho served me hendely te hend;
Hir maners might no man amend.
Of tong sho was trew and renable
And of hir semblant soft and stabile.   210
Ful fain I wald, if þat I might,
Have woned with þat swete wight.
And, when we sold go to sopere,
þat lady with a lufsom chere
Led me down into þe hall.   215

180 I *faded*

þare war we served wele at all;
It nedes noght to tel þe mese,
For wonder wele war we at esse.
Byfor me sat þe lady bright
Curtaisly my mete to dyght; 220
Us wanted nowþer baken ne roste.
And efter soper sayd myne oste
þat he cowth noght tel þe day
þat ani knight are with him lay,
Or þat ani aventures soght. 225
þarfore he prayed me, if I moght,
On al wise, when I come ogayne,
þat I sold cum to him sertayne.
I said, "Sir, gladly, yf I may."
It had bene shame have said him nay. 230

Ch. 269   'þat night had I ful gude rest
And mi stede esed of þe best.
Alsone als it was dayes lyght,
Forth to fare sone was I dyght.
Mi leve of mine ost toke I þare 235
And went mi way withowten mare,
Aventures forto layt in land.
A faire forest sone I fand.
Me thoght mi hap þare fel ful hard,
For þare was mani a wilde lebard, 240
Lions, beres, bath bul and bare,
þat rewfully gan rope and rare.
Oway I drogh me, and with þat
I saw sone whare a man sat
On a lawnd, þe fowlest wight 245
þat euer ȝit man saw in syght.
He was a lathly creature,
For fowl he was out of mesure;
A wonder mace in hand he hade,
And sone mi way to him I made. 250
His hevyd, me thoght, was als grete

---

225 ani: ni *partially obliterated*   240 lebard: bard *partially obliterated*
246 ght *of* syght *partially obliterated*   248 mesure: re *faded*   249–50 *Schl.*
transposes these lines; see note   249 de *of* hade *partially obliterated*   251 te
of grete *obliterated*

Als of a rowncy or a nete;
Unto his belt hang his hare,
And efter þat byheld I mare.
To his forhede byheld I þan,   255
Was bradder þan twa large span;
He had eres als ane olyfant
And was wele more þan geant.
His face was ful brade and flat;
His nese was cutted als a cat;   260
His browes war like litel buskes;
And his tethe like bare-tuskes.
A ful grete bulge opon his bak
(þare was noght made withowten lac);
His chin was fast until his brest;   265
On his mace he gan him rest.
Also it was a wonder-wede,
þat þe cherle yn ȝede;
Nowther of wol ne of line
Was þe wede þat he went yn.   270

Ch. 315   'When he me sagh, he stode upright.
I frayned him if he wolde fight,
For þarto was I in gude will,
Bot als a beste þan stode he still.
I hopid þat he no wittes kowth,   275
No reson forto speke with mowth.
To him I spak ful hardily
And said, "What ertow, belamy?"
He said ogain, "I am a man."
f. 5ᵛ   I said, "Swilk saw I never nane."   280
"What ertow?" alsone said he.
I said, "Swilk als þou here may se."
I said, "What dose þou here allane?"
He said, "I kepe þir bestes ilkane."
I said, "þat es mervaile, think me;   285
For I herd never of man bot þe
In wildernes ne in forestes,
þat kepeing had of wilde bestes,
Bot þai war bunden fast in halde."

252 of *added above the line by same hand*   253–4 *Schl. transposes these lines;*
see note   262 tethe *added above the line by the same hand*

He sayd, "Of þire es none so balde   290
Nowþer by day ne bi night
Anes to pas out of mi sight."
I sayd, "How so? Tel me þi scill."
"Parfay", he said, "gladly I will."

Ch. 344　　　'He said, "In al þis faire foreste   295
Es þare none so wilde beste,
þat remu dar, bot stil stand,
When I am to him cumand.
And ay, when þat I wil him fang
With mi fingers þat er strang   300
I ger him cri on swilk manere,
þat al þe bestes when þai him here,
Obout me þan cum þai all,
And to mi fete fast þai fall,
On þaire manere merci to cry.   305
Bot understand now redyli,
Olyve es þare lifand no ma
Bot I þat durst omang þam ga,
þat he ne sold sone be al torent.
Bot þai er at my comandment;   310
To me þai cum when I þam call,
And I am maister of þam all."
þan he asked onone right,
What man I was. I said, a knight
þat soght aventurs in þat land,   315
My body to asai and fande.
"And I þe pray of þi kownsayle,
þou teche me to sum mervayle."

Ch. 367　　　'He sayd, "I can no wonders tell,
Bot here-bisyde es a well.   320
Wend þeder and do als I say;
þou passes noght al quite oway.
Folow forth þis ilk strete,
And sone sum mervayles sal þou mete.
þe well es under þe fairest tre,   325
þat ever was in þis cuntre;
By þat well hinges a bacyne

295 said *added above the line by the same hand*; sai *very pale*　　　310 o *of*
comandment *changed from* u

þat es of gold gude and fyne,
With a cheyne, trewly to tell,
þat wil reche into þe well.　　　　　　　　330
þare es a chapel nere þarby,
þat nobil es and ful lufely;
By þe well standes a stane.
Tak þe bacyn sone onane
And cast on water with þi hand,　　　　335
And sone þou sal se new tithand.
A storme sal rise and a tempest
Al obout, by est and west;
þou sal here mani thonor-blast
Al obout þe blawand fast.　　　　　　　340
And þare sal cum slik slete and rayne
þat unnese sal þou stand ogayne;
Of lightnes sal þou se a lowe,
Unnethes þou sal þi selven knowe.
And, if þou pas withowten grevance,　　345
þan has þou þe fairest chance,
þat ever ȝit had any knyght,
þat þeder come to kyth his myght."

Ch. 408　　'þan toke I leve and went my way
And rade unto þe midday.　　　　　　350
By þan I come whare I sold be,
I saw þe chapel and þe tre.
þare I fand þe fayrest t[h]orne
þat ever groued sen God was born.
So thik it was with leves grene,　　　355
Might no rayn cum þarbytwene;
And þat grenes lastes ay,
For no winter dere yt may.
I fand þe bacyn als he talde,
And þe wel with water kalde.　　　　　360
An amerawd was þe stane,
Richer saw I never nane,
On fowre rubyes on heght standand;
þaire light lasted over al þe land.
And when I saw þat semely syght,　　365
It made me bath joyful and lyght.

353 tlorne *MS.*; *R's emendation; see l. 641*

I toke þe bacyn sone onane
And helt water opon þe stane.
þe weder wex þan wonder-blak,
And þe thoner fast gan crak.   370
þare come slike stormes of hayl and rayn,
Unnethes I might stand þare ogayn;
þe store windes blew ful lowd,
So kene come never are of clowd.
I was drevyn with snaw and slete,   375

f. 6   Unnethes I might stand on my fete;
In my face þe levening smate,
I wend have brent, so was it hate,
þat weder made me so will of rede,
I hopid sone to have my dede;   380
And sertes, if it lang had last,
I hope I had never þeþin past.
Bot thorgh his might þat tholed wownd,
þe storme sesed within a stownde.
þan wex þe weder fayre ogayne,   385
And þareof was I wonder-fayne;
For best comforth of al thing
Es solace efter myslikeing.

Ch. 460   'þan saw I sone a mery syght:
Of al þe fowles þat er in flyght,   390
Lighted so thik opon þat tre,
þat bogh ne lefe none might I se.
So merily þan gon þai sing,
þat al þe wode bigan to ring;
Ful mery was þe melody   395
Of þaire sang and of þaire cry.
þare herd never man none swilk,
Bot if ani had herd þat ilk.
And when þat mery dyn was done,
Anoþer noyse þan herd I sone,   400
Als it war of horsmen
Mo þan owþer nyen or ten.

Ch. 483   'Sone þan saw I cum a knyght,
In riche armurs was he dight;
And sone, when I gan on him loke,   405

403 *A red initial capital*

Mi shelde and spere to me I toke.
þat knight to me hied ful fast,
And kene wordes out gan he cast.
He bad þat I sold tel him tite,
Whi I did him swilk despite,   410
With weders wakend him of rest
And [did] him wrang in his forest.
'þarfore', he said, 'þou sal aby.'
And with þat come he egerly
And said I had ogayn resowne   415
Done him grete destrucciowne
And might it never more amend,
þarfore he bad I sold me fend.
And sone I smate him on þe shelde,
Mi schaft brac out in þe felde,   420
And þan he bare me sone bi strenkith
Out of my sadel my speres lenkith.
I wate þat he was largely
By þe shuldres mare þan I;
And bi þe ded þat I sal thole,   425
Mi stede by his was bot a fole.
For mate I lay down on þe grownde,
So was I stonayd in þat stownde.
A worde to me wald he noght say,
Bot toke my stede and went his way.   430
Ful sarily þan þare I sat,
For wa I wist noght what was what.
With my stede he went in hy
þe same way þat he come by.
And I durst folow him no ferr   435
For dout me solde bit[id]e werr;
And also ȝit, by Goddes dome,
I ne wist whare he bycome.

Ch. 554   'þan I thoght how I had hight
Unto myne ost, þe hende knyght,   440
And also til his lady bryght,
To com ogayn if þat I myght.

412 done MS.; Schl. emends to did   426 his w: smudged and partially
obliterated   427 down: dow smudged   436 bite MS.; see note
439 A blue initial capital

Mine armurs left I þare ilkane,
For els myght I noght have gane.
Unto myne in I come by day.   445
þe hende knight and þe fayre may
Of my come war þai ful glade,
And nobil semblant þai me made.
In al thinges þai have þam born
Als þai did þe night biforn.   450
Sone þai wist whare I had bene,
And said þat þai had never sene
Knyght þat ever þeder come,
Take þe way ogayn home.
On þis wise þat tyme I wroght;   455
I fand þe folies þat I soght.'

Ch. 581   'Now sekerly,' said Sir Ywayne,
'þou ert my cosyn jermayne;
Trew luf suld be us bytwene,
Als sold bytwyx breþer bene.   460
þou ert a fole at þou ne had are
Tald me of þis ferly fare,
For sertes I sold onone ryght
Have venged þe of þat ilk knyght.
So sal I ȝit, if þat I may.'   465
And þan als smertly sayd Syr Kay
(He karpet to þam wordes grete):
'It es sene now es efter mete!
Mare boste es in a pot of wyne
f. 6ᵛ   þan in a karcas of Saynt Martyne.   470
Arme þe smertly, Syr Ywayne,
And sone, þat þou war cumen ogayne;
Luke þou fil wele þi panele,
And in þi sadel set þe wele;
And, when þou wendes, I þe pray,   475
þi baner wele þat þou desplay;
And, rede I, or þou wende,
þou tak þi leve at ilka frende;
And if it so bytide þis nyght,
þat þe in slepe dreche ani wight   480

457 *A red initial capital*   458 iermayne *MS.*   472 r *of* war *and* en *of*
cumen *partially obliterated by a smudge*

Or any dremis mak þe rad,
Turn ogayn and say I bad.'

Ch. 612   þe quene answerd with milde mode
And said, 'Sir Kay, ertow wode?
What þe devyl es þe withyn,   485
At þi tong may never blyn
þi felows so fowly to shende?
Sertes, Sir Kay, þou ert unhende.
By him þat for us sufferd pine,
Syr, and þe tong war myne,   490
I sold bical it tyte of treson,
And so might þou do, by gude reson.
þi tong dose þe grete dishonowre,
And þarefore es it þi traytowre.'
And þan alsone Syr Ywayne   495
Ful hendly answerd ogayne,
Al if men sayd hym velany,
He karped ay ful curtaysly:
'Madame,' he said unto þe quene,
'þare sold na stryf be us bytwene.   500
Unkowth men wele may he shende
þat to his felows es so unhende.
And als, madame, men says sertayne
þat, wo so flites or turnes ogayne,
He bygins al þe melle: 505
So wil I noght it far by me.
Lates him say halely his thoght;
His wordes greves me right noght.'

Ch. 649   Als þai war in þis spekeing
Out of þe chamber come þe kyng.   510
þe barons þat war þare, sertayn,
Smertly rase þai him ogayne.
He bad þam sit down al bydene,
And down he set him by þe quene.
þe quene talde him fayre and wele,   515
Als sho kowth, everilka dele
Ful apertly al þe chance
Als it bifel Syr Colgrevance.

483 *A blue initial capital*   488 Sertes: es *faded*   509 *A red initial capital*
518 Colgrevance: grey *unclear because of discoloration and shrinkage*

When sho had talde him how it ferd,
And þe king hyr tale had herd, 520
He sware by his owyn crowne
And his fader sowl Uterpendragowne,
þat he sold se þat ilk syght
By þat day þeþin a fowretenight,
On Saint Johns evyn, þe Baptist, 525
þat best barn was under Crist.
'Swith,' he sayd, 'wendes with me,
Who so wil þat wonder se.'

Ch. 673   þe kynges word might noght be hid,
Over al þe cowrt sone was it kyd; 530
And þare was none so litel page
þat he ne was fayn of þat vayage;
And knyghtes and swiers war ful fayne;
Mysliked none bot Syr Ywayne.
To himself he made grete mane, 535
For he wald have went allane;
In hert he had grete myslykyng
For þe wending of þe kyng,
Al for he hopid, withowten fayle,
þat Sir Kay sold ask þe batayle, 540
Or els Sir Gawayn, knyght vailant;
And owþer wald þe king grant.
Who so it wald first crave
Of þam two, sone might it have.

Ch. 691   þe kynges wil wald he noght bide, 545
Worth of him, what may bityde;
Bi him allane he thoght to wend
And tak þe grace þat God wald send.
He thoght to be wele on hys way,
Or it war passed þe thryd day, 550
And to asay if he myght mete
With þat ilk narow strete
With thornes and with breres set,
þat mens way might lightli let,
And also forto fynd þe halde, 555

---

525 Johns: *down stroke of* h *struck through with a short line, without significance*
545 wil *added above line by same hand*   551 *The whole line written over*
erasure   555 also forto *over erasure* y *of* fynd *is changed from* a *by the same hand*

þat Sir Colgrevance of talde,
þe knyght and þe mayden meke.
þe forest fast þan wald he seke
And als þe karl of Kaymes kyn
And þe wilde bestes with him,   560
þe tre with briddes þareopon,
þe chapel, þe bacyn and þe stone.
His thoght wald he tel to no frende,

f. 7   Until he wyst how it wald ende.
Ch. 675   þan went Ywaine to his yn;   565
His men he fand redy þareyn.
Unto a swier gan he say,
'Go swith and sadel my palfray,
And so þou do my strang stede,
And tak with þe my best wede.   570
At ȝone ȝate I wil out ryde,
Withowten town I sal þe bide;
And hy þe smertly unto me,
For I most make a jorne,
Ogain sal þou bring my palfra,   575
And forbede þe oght to say.
If þou wil any more me se,
Lat none wit of my prevete;
And if ani man þe oght frayn,
Luke now lely þat þou layn.'   580
'Sir,' he said, 'with ful gude will,
Als ȝe byd, I sal fulfyll;
At ȝowre awyn wil may ȝe ride,
For me ȝe sal noght be ascryed.'

Ch. 747   Forth þan went Sir Ywayne;   585
He thinkes, or he cum ogayne,
To wreke his cosyn at his myght.
þe squier has his hernays dyght;
He did right als his mayster red;
His stede, his armurs he him led.   590
When Ywayn was withowten town,

---

558 wald *over an erasure?*   565 to *unclear*   566 redy *unclear*
575 brring *MS.*   585 *A blue initial capital*   589 *After* red *a letter*
is erased, probably an e

Of his palfray lighted he down
And dight him right wele in his wede
And lepe up on his gude stede.
Furth he rade onone right,   595
Until it neghed nere þe nyght.
He passed many high mowntayne
In wildernes and mony a playne,
Til he come to þat leþir sty,
þat him byhoved pass by.   600
þan was he seker forto se
þe wel and þe fayre tre.
þe chapel saw he at þe last,
And þeder hyed he ful fast.
More curtaysi and more honowre   605
Fand he with þam in þat toure,
And mare conforth by monyfalde,
þan Colgrevance had him of talde.
þat night was he herberd þare:
So wele was he never are.   610

Ch. 792   At morn he went forth by þe strete,
And with þe cherel sone gan he mete
þat sold tel to him þe way.
He sayned him, þe soth to say,
Twenty sith or ever he blan;   615
Swilk mervayle had he of þat man;
For he had wonder þat nature
Myght mak so fowl a creature.
þan to þe well he rade gude pase,
And doun he lighted in þat place;   620
And sone þe bacyn has he tane
And kest water opon þe stane;
And sone þare wex withowten fayle,
Wind and thonor, rayn and haile.
When it was sesed, þan saw he   625
þe fowles light opon þe tre;
þai sang ful fayre opon þat thorn,
Right als þai had done byforn.

611 *A red initial capital*   615 *Initial* t *of* twenty *faded*   624 *After*
thonor, and hayl *is cancelled by a single line*

And sone he saw cumand a knight
Als fast so þe fowl in flyght   630
With rude sembland and sterne chere,
And hastily he neghed nere.
To speke of lufe na time was þare,
For aiþer hated uþer ful sare.
Togeder smertly gan þai drive,   635
þaire sheldes sone bigan to ryve,
þaire shaftes cheverd to þaire hand,
Bot þai war bath ful wele syttand.
Out þai drogh þaire swerdes kene
And delt strakes þam bytwene;   640
Al to peces þai hewed þaire s[h]eldes,
þe culpons flegh out in þe feldes.
On helmes strake þay so with yre,
At ilka strake outbrast þe fyre.
Aiþer of þam gude buffettes bede,   645
And nowþer wald styr of þe stede;
Ful kenely þai kyd þaire myght
And feyned þam noght forto fight.
[At] þaire hauberkes, þat men myght ken,
þe blode out of þaire bodyes ren;   650
Aiþer on oþer laid so fast,
þe batayl might noght lang last.
Hauberkes er broken and helmes reven,
Stif strakes war þare gyfen;
þai faght on hors stifly always;   655
þe batel was wele more to prays.
Bot at þe last Syr Ywayne

f. 7ᵛ
On his felow kyd his mayne;
So egerly he smate him þan,
He clefe þe helme and þe hernpan.   660

Ch. 873
þe knyght wist he was nere ded;
To fle þan was his best rede,
And fast he fled with al hys mayne,
And fast folow[d] Syr Ywayne.

641 sleldes *MS.*; *R.'s emendation; see l. 353*   649 þaire hauberkes þat
men myght ken *MS.*; *Schl. emends to* At þaire hauberkes þat men might ken
on the basis of ll. 3543 f.; see note   652 ht lang *over an erasure*
653 hauberkes: *Schl. reads* hauberkis   664 folow *MS.*; *Schl.'s emendation*

Bot he ne might him overtake,   665
þarfore grete murning gan he make;
He folowd him ful stowtlyk
And wald have tane him ded or quik;
He folowd him to þe cete,
Na man lyfand met he.   670
When þai come to þe kastel-ȝate,
In he folowd fast þareate.
At aiþer entre was, iwys,
Straytly wroght a portculis
Shod wele with yren and stele   675
And also grunden wonder wele.
Under þat þan was a swyke,
þat made Syr Ywain to myslike.
His hors fote toched þareon,
þan fel þe portculis onone   680
Bytwyx him and his hinder arsown,
Thorgh sadel and stede it smate al down;
His spores of his heles it schare;
þan had Ywaine murnyng mare.
Bot so he wend have passed quite,   685
þa[n] fel þe toþer bifore als tyte.
A faire grace ȝit fel him swa,
Al if it smate his hors in twa
And his spors of aiþer hele,
þat himself passed so wele.   690

Ch. 960   Bytwene þa ȝates now es he tane;
þarfore he mase ful mykel mane,
And mikel murnyng gan he ma,
For þe knyght was went him fra.
Als he was stoken in þat stall,   695
He herd byhind him in a wall
A dore opend faire and wele,
And þareout come a damysel.
Efter hir þe dore sho stak,
Ful hinde wordes to him sho spak.   700
'Syr,' sho said, 'by Saint Myghell,
Here þou has a febil ostell.

685 h of he is corrected   686 þat MS.; Schl. emends to þan

þou mon be ded (es noght at laine)
For my lord þat þou has slayne.
Seker it es þat þou him slogh;   705
My lady makes sorow ynogh
And al his menȝe everilkane.
[He]re has þou famen many ane;
To be þi bane er þai ful balde,
þou brekes noght out of þis halde.   710
And, for þai wate, þai may noght fayl,
þ[ai] wil þe sla in playn batayl.'

Ch. 994   He sayd, 'þai ne sal, so God me rede.
For al þaire might do me to dede,
Ne no handes opon me lay.'   715
Sho said, 'Na, sertes, if þat I may!
Al if þou be here straytly stad,
Me think þou ert noght ful adrad.
And sir,' sho said, 'on al wise
I aw þe honore and servyse;   720
I was in message at þe king
Bifore þis time, whils I was ȝing.
I was noght þan savese,
Als a damysel aght to be;
Fro þe tyme þat I was lyght   725
In cowrt was none so hend knyght,
þat unto me þan walde take hede,
Bot þou allane, God do þe mede.
Grete honore þou did to me,
And þat sal I now quite þe.   730
I wate, if þou be seldom sene,
þou ert þe Kyng son Uriene,
And þi name es Sir Ywayne.
Of me may þou be sertayne.
If þou wil my kownsail leve,   735
þou sal find na man þe to greve;
I sal lene þe here mi ring,
Bot ȝelde it me at myne askyng;
When þou ert broght of al þi payn,

---

707 An *of* And *is obscure*   708 Here: *except for a faint* re *this word is obliterated by a water stain.* R. *suggests* Her; Schl. Þare. *See note*   712 Þe MS.; R. *reads* Ye *and emends to* Thai; Schl. *retains* Þe

ʒelde it þan to me ogayne. 740
Als þe bark hilles þe tre,
Right so sal my ring do þe;
When þou in hand has þe stane,
Dere sal þai do þe nane;
For þe stane es of swilk myght, 745
Of þe sal men have na syght.'

Ch. 1038   Wit ʒe wele þat Sir Ywayne
Of þir wordes was ful fayne.
In at þe dore sho him led
And did him sit opon hir bed. 750
A quylt ful nobil lay þareon,
f. 8   Richer saw he never none.
Sho said if he wald any thing,
He sold be served at his liking.
He said þat ete wald he fayn. 755
Sho went and come ful sone ogain;
A capon rosted broght sho sone,
A clene klath and brede þarone
And a pot with riche wine
And a pece to fil it yne. 760
He ete and drank with ful gude chere,
For þarof had he grete mystere.

Ch. 1055   When he had eten and dronken wele,
Grete noyse he herd in þe kastele.
Þai soght over al him to have slayn; 765
To venge þaire lorde war þai ful bayn,
Or þat þe cors in erth was layd.
Þe damysel sone to him sayd,
'Now seke þai þe fast forto sla,
Bot whosoever com or ga, 770
Be þou never þe more adred,
Ne styr þou noght out of þis stede;
In þis here seke þai wyll,
Bot on þis bed, luke þou be styll,
Of þam al mak þou na force. 775
Bot when þat þai sal bere þe cors
Unto þe kyrk forto bery,

767 O *of* Or *unclear; seems to be written over another letter*   771 n *of*
never *added above the line by the same hand*

þan sal þou here a sary cry;
So sal þai mak a doleful dyn.
þan will þai seke þe eft herein;   780
Bot loke þou be of hert lyght,
For of þe sal þai have no syght.
Here sal þou be mawgre þaire berd,
And þarefore be þou noght aferd,
þi famen sal be als þe blynd;   785
Both byfor þe and byhind,
On ilka side sal þou be soght.
Now most I ga, bot drede þe noght,
For I sal do þat þe es lefe,
If al it turn me to mischefe.'   790

Ch. 1086   When sho come unto þe ȝate,
Ful many men fand sho þarate
Wele armed, and wald ful fayn
Have taken and slane Sir Ywaine.
Half his stede þare fand þai   795
þat within þe ȝates lay;
Bot þe knight þare fand þai n[o]ght:
þan was þare mekil sorow unsoght.
Dore ne window was þare nane,
Whare he myght oway gane.   800
þai said he sold þare be laft,
Or els he cowth of wechecraft;
Or he cowth of nygromancy;
Or he had wenges forto fly.

Ch. 1132   Hastily þan went þai all   805
And soght him in þe maydens hall,
In chambers high (es noght at hide)
And in solers on ilka side.
Sir [Ywaine] saw ful wele al þat,
And still opon þe bed he sat.   810
þare was nane þat anes mynt
Unto þe bed at smyte a dynt;

---

788 I *inserted between* most *and* ga *by the same hand*   noght: o *imperfectly made, a small hook on the bottom making it look like an oversized* e   797 o *in* noght *added above the line by another hand*   803 nygromancy: g *faint* 809 Sir saw *MS.*; *between these two words and above an inverted caret is written* Yw, *the ink of which has faded. In the margin, after a caret,* Ywaine *is written. Both additions are in the same hand, but not in the hand of the MS.*

Al obout þai smate so fast,
þat mani of þaire wapins brast.
Mekyl sorow þai made ilkane,   815
For þai ne myght wreke þaire lord bane.

Ch. 1144   þai went oway with dreri chere,
And sone þareefter come þe bere.
A lady folowd white so mylk,
In al þat land was none swilk;   820
Sho wrang hir fingers, outbrast þe blode;
For mekyl wa sho was nere wode.
Hir fayre hare scho al todrogh,
And ful oft fel sho down in swogh;
Sho wepe with a ful dreri voice.   825
þe hali water and þe croyce
Was born bifore þe procession;
þare folowd mani a moder son;
Bifore þe cors rade a knyght
On his stede þat was ful wight,   830
In his armurs wele arayd,
With spere and target gudely grayd.
þan Sir Ywayn herd þe cry
And þe dole of þat fayre lady;
For more sorow myght nane have,   835
þan sho had when he went to grave.
Prestes and monkes on þaire wyse
Ful solempnly did þe servyse.

Ch. 1258   Als Lunet þare stode in þe thrang,
Until Sir Ywaine thoght hir lang;   840
Out of þe thrang þe wai sho tase,
Unto Sir Ywaine fast sho gase.
Sho [said], 'Sir, how ertow stad?
I hope ful wele þou has bene rad.'
'Sertes,' he said, 'þou sais wele þare;   845
f. 8ᵛ   So abayst was I never are.'
Ch. 1302   He said, 'Leman, I pray þe,
If it any wise may be,
þat I might luke a litel throw

---

835 y *of* myght *written over another letter*   839 Lunet þare *over an*
erasure   841 out of *over an erasure*   843 said *added above the line by*
another hand

Out at sum hole or sum window,   850
For wonder fayn,' he sayd, 'wald I
Have a sight of þe lady.'
þe maiden þan ful sone unshet
In a place a preve weket.
þare of þe lady he had a syght.   855
Lowd sho cried to God almyght,
'Of his sins do hym pardowne,
For sertanly in no regyowne
Was never knight of his bewte,
Ne efter him sal never nane be;   860
In al þe werld fro end to ende
Es none so curtayse ne so hende.
God grante þe grace þou mai won
In hevyn with his owyn son;
For so large lifes none in lede   865
Ne none so doghty of gude dede.'
When sho had þus made hir spell,
In swowny[n]g ful oft sithes sho fell.

Ch. 1302   Now lat we þe lady be,
And of Sir Ywaine speke we.   870
Luf, þat es so mekil of mayne,
Sare had wownded Sir Ywayne,
þat whare so he sal ride or ga,
His hert sho has þat es his fa.
His hert he has set al bydene,   875
Whare himself dar noght be sene.
Bot þus in langing bides he
And hopes þat it sal better be.
Al þat war at þe enterement,
Toke þaire leve at þe lady gent,   880
And hame now er þai halely [g]ane;
And þe lady left allane
Dweland with hir chamberere
And oþer mo þat war hir dere.
Þan bigan hir noyes al new,   885
For sorow failed hir hide and hew.

---

868 swownyg *MS.*; *Schl. and R. have* swowyng   869 *A blue initial capital*
880 ke *of* toke *over erasure*   881 yane *MS. is added over an erasure by a*
later hand. Over y *a dot. R.'s emendation*   886 hew *over an erasure*

Unto his sawl was sho ful hulde;
Opon a sawter al of gulde
To say þe salmes fast sho bigan
And toke no tent unto no man.   890

Ch. 1339   þan had Sir Ywain mekyl drede,
For he hoped noght to spede;
He said, 'I am mekil to blame,
þat I luf þam þat wald me shame.
Bot ʒit I wite hir al with wogh,   895
Sen þat I hir lord slogh.
I can noght se by nakyn gyn,
How þat I hir luf sold wyn.
þat lady es ful gent and small,
Hir yghen clere als es cristall;   900
Sertes þare es no man olive,
þat kowth hir bewtese wele descrive.'
þus was Syr Ywayne sted þat sesowne;
He wroght fu[l] mekyl ogayns resowne
To set his luf in swilk a stede,   905
Whare þai hated him to þe dede.
He sayd he sold have hir to wive,
Or els he sold lose his lyve.

Ch. 1541   þus als he in stody sat,
þe mayden come to him with þat.   910
Sho sayd, "How hasto farn þis day,
Sen þat I went fro þe oway?'
Sone sho saw him pale and wan,
Sho wist wele what him ayled þan.
Sho [said], 'I wote þi hert es set,   915
And sertes I ne sal noght it let;
Bot I sal help þe fra presowne
And bring þe to þi warisowne.'
He said, 'Sertes, damysele,
Out of þis place wil I noght stele;   920
Bot I wil wende by dayes lyght,
þat men may of me have sight
Opinly on ilka syde.
Worth of me what so bityde,

904 fu *MS.*; *Schl. emends to* ful   909 *A red initial capital*   915 said
added above the line by another hand

Manly wil I heþin wende.'   925
þan answerd þe mayden hende,
'Sir, þow sal wend with honowre,
For þou sal have ful gude socowre.
Bot, sir, þou sal be here sertayne
A while unto I cum ogayne.'   930

Ch. 1588   Sho [kend] al trewly his entent,
And þarfore es sho wightly went
Unto þe lady faire and bright.
For unto hir right wele sho myght
Say whatsom hyr willes es;   935
For sho was al hir maystres,
Her keper and hir cownsaylere.
To hir sho said, als ȝe sal here,
Bytwix þam twa in gude cownsayl,
f. 9   'Madame,' sho sayd, 'I have mervayl   940
þat ȝe sorow þus ever onane.
For Goddes luf, lat be ȝowre mane.
ȝe sold think over alkyn thyng
Of þe Kinges Arthurgh cumyng.
Menes ȝow noght of þe message   945
Of þe Damysel Savage,
þat in hir lettre to ȝow send?
Allas, who sal ȝow now defend
ȝowre land and al þat es þareyn,
Sen ȝe wil never of wepeing blyn?   950
A, madame, takes tent to me.
ȝe ne have na knyght in þis cuntre,
þat durst right now his body bede
Forto do a doghty dede,
Ne forto bide þe mekil boste   955
Of King Arthurgh and of his oste;
And if he find none hym ogayn,
ȝowre landes er lorn, þis es sertayn.'

Ch. 1638   þe lady understode ful wele,
How sho hyr cownsaild ilka dele;   960
Sho bad hyr go hir way smertly,

931 MS. sho al trewly his entent. kend *suggested by R.*   949 ȝ *of* ȝowre
unclear. The MS. is badly shrunken here   951 A *is obscure. MS. is disco-
loured and shrunken*   959 A *blue initial capital*

And þat sho war na more hardy
Swilk wordes to hyr at speke;
For wa hir hert wold al tobreke.
Sho bad, 'Go wightly heþin oway.'   965
þan þe maiden þus gan say,
'Madame, it es oft wemens will
þam forto blame þat sais þam scill.'
Sho went oway, als sho noght roght,
And þan þe lady hyr bythoght,   970
þat þe maiden said no wrang,
And so sho sat in stody lang.

Ch. 1664   In stody þus allane sho sat,
þe mayden come ogayn with þat.
'Madame,' she said, 'ȝe er a barn;   975
þus may ȝe sone ȝowre self forfarn.'
Sho sayd, 'Chastise þi hert, madame;
To swilk a lady it es grete shame
þus to wepe and make slike cry;
Think opon þi grete gentri.   980
Trowes þou þe flowre of chevalry
Sold al with þi lord dy
And with him be put in molde?
God forbede þat it so solde!
Als gude als he and better bene.'   985
'þou lyes,' sho sayd, 'by hevyn-quene!
Lat se if þoue me tel kan,
Whare es any so doghty man,
Als he was þat wedded me.'
'ȝis, and ȝe kun me [na] mawgre,   990
And þat ȝe mak me sekernes,
þat ȝe sal luf me never þe les.'
Sho said, 'þou may be ful sertayn,
þat for na thing þat þou mai sayn,
Wil I me wreth on nane manere.'   995
'Madame,' sho said, 'þan sal ȝe here;
I sal ȝow tel a prevete,

---

989 *Between* þat *and* wedded *a caret pointing to two letters above the line,*
now illegible and not necessary to the sense   990 na *added above the line*
over a caret. The n *is faintly discernible; the other letter is illegible. R. emends*
to on

And na ma sal it wit bo[t] we.
Yf twa knyghtes be in þe felde
On twa stedes with spere and shelde   1000
And þe tane þe toþer may sla,
Wheþer es þe better of þa?'
Sho said, 'He þat has þe bataile.'
'3a,' said þe mayden, 'sawnfayle,
þe knyght þat lifes es mare of maine   1005
þan 3owre lord þat was slayne.
3owre lord fled out þe place,
And þe toþer gan hym chace
Heder into his awyn halde;
þare may 3e wit, he was ful balde.'   1010
þe lady said, 'þis es grete scorne,
þat þou nevyns him me biforne;
þou sais nowþer soth ne right.
Swith, out of myne eghen syght!'
þe mayden said, 'So mot I the,   1015
þus ne hight 3e noght me,
þat 3e sold so me myssay.'
With þat sho turned hir oway,
And hastily sho went ogayn
Unto þe chameber to Sir Ywayne.   1020

Ch. 1734   þe lady thoght þan al þe nyght,
How þat sho had na knyght
Forto seke hir land thorghout
To kepe Arthurgh and hys rowt.
þan bigan hir forto shame   1025
And hirself fast forto blame.
Unto hirself fast gan sho flyte
And said, 'With wrang now I hir wite.
Now hopes sho I wil never mare
Luf hir als I have done are.   1030
I wil hir luf with main and mode;
For þat sho said was for my gode.'

Ch. 1785   On þe morn þe mayden rase,
f. 9ᵛ   And unto chamber sone sho gase.
þare sho fyndes þe faire lady   1035
Hingand hir hevyd ful drerily

998 bo *MS.*; *R. emends to* bot

In þe place whare sho hir left;
And ilka dele sho talde hir eft,
Als sho had said to hir bifore.
þan said þe lady, 'Me rewes sore, 1040
þat I missayd þe ȝisterday.
I wil amend, if þat I may.
Of þat knyght now wald I here,
What he war and wheþen he were.
I wate þat I have sayd omys; 1045
Now wil I do als þou me wys.
Tel me baldely, or þou blin,
If he be cumen of gentil kyn.'
'Madame,' sho said, 'I dar warand,
A genteler lord es none lifand; 1050
þe hendest man ȝe sal him fynde,
þat ever come of Adams kynde.'
'How hat he? Sai me for sertayne.'
'Madame,' sho said, 'Sir Ywayne;
So gentil knight have ȝe noght sene, 1055
He es þe Kin[g]s son Uryene.'
Sho held hir paid of þat tiþ[y]ng,
For þat his fader was a kyng;
'Do me have [him] here in my sight
Bitwene þis and þe thrid night 1060
And are, if þat it are myght be.
Me langes sare him forto se;
Bring him, if þou mai, þis night.'
'Madame,' sho sayd, 'þat I ne might,
For his wonyng es heþin oway 1065
More þan þe jorne of a day.
Bot I have a wele rinand page,
Wil stirt þider right in a stage
And bring him by to-morn at nyght.'
þe lady saide, 'Loke yf he myght 1070
To-morn by evyn be here ogayn.'
Sho said, 'Madame, with al his mayn.'

1056 kins *MS.*; *Schl. reads* king. *R. reads* kins *and emends to* kings. *See ll. 944,*
2149, 2175 1057 tiþng *MS.*; *R.'s emendation* 1059 him *added above*
the line by another hand 1070 he *added above the line by the same hand*
1072 Sho *in left margin before* said

'Bid him hy on alkyn wyse.
He sal be quit wele his servyse;
Avancement sal be hys bone,   1075
If he wil do þis erand sone.'
'Madame,' sho said, 'I dar ȝow hight
To have him here or þe thrid nyght.
Towhils efter ȝowre kownsayl send
And ask þam wha sal ȝow defend   1080
Ȝowre well, ȝowre land, kastel and towre
Ogayns þe nobil King Arthure.
For þare es nane of þam ilkane,
þat dar þe batel undertane.
þan sal ȝe say, "Nedes bus me take   1085
A lorde to do þat ȝe forsake." '
Nedes bus ȝow have sum nobil knyght,
þat wil and may defend ȝowre right;
And sais also, to suffer ded
Ȝe wil noght do out of þaire rede.   1090
Of þat worde sal þai be blyth
And thank ȝow ful many siþe.'
þe lady said, 'By God of myght,
I sal areson þam þis night.
Me think þou dwelles ful lang here;   1095
Send forth swith þi messangere.'
    þan was þe lady blith and glad.
Sho did al als hir mayden bad.
Efter hir cownsail sho sent onane.
And bad þai sold cum sone ilkane.   1100
þe maiden redies hyr ful rath;
Bilive sho gert Syr Ywaine bath
And cled him seþin in gude scarlet
Forord wele and with gold fret,
A girdel ful riche for þe nanes   1105
Of perry and of preciows stanes.
Sho talde him al how he sold do,
When þat he come þe lady to.
And þus when he was al redy,
Sho went and talde to hyr lady,   1110
þat cumen was hir messagere.

Sho said smertly, 'Do lat me here,
Cumes he sone als have þou wyn?'
'Medame,' sho said, 'I sal noght blin,
Or þat he be byfor ȝow here.'   1115
þan said þe lady with light chere,
'Go bring him heder prevely,
þat none wit bot þou and I,'

Ch. 1904   þan þe maiden went ogayn
Hastily to Sir Ywayn.   1120
'Sir,' sho sayd, 'als have I wyn,
My lady wate þou ert hereyn.
To cum bifore hir, luke þou be balde,
And tak gode tent what I have talde.'
By þe hand sho toke þe knyght   1125
And led him unto chamber right
Byfor hir lady (es noght at layne),

f. 10   And of þat come was sho ful fayne.
Bot ȝit Sir Ywayne had grete drede,
When he unto chamber ȝede.   1130
þe chamber-flore and als þe bed
With klothes of gold was al overspred
Hir thoght [he] was withowten lac;
Bot no word to him sho spak,
And he for dred oway he drogh.   1135
þan þe mayden stode and logh.
Sho sayd, 'Mawgre have þat knyght
þat haves of swilk a lady syght
And can noght shew to hir his nede.
Cum furth, sir; þe thar noght drede,   1140
þat mi lady wil þe smyte;
Sho loves þe wele withouten lite.
Pray to hir of hir mercy,
And for þi sake right so sal I,
þat sho forgif þe in þis stede   1145
Of Salados þe Rouse ded,
þat was hir lord, þat þou has slayne.'

Ch. 1972   On knese him set þan Syr Ywaine;
'Madame, I ȝelde me ȝow untill

1114 Medame: *Schl. emends to* Madame   1133 he *over an erasure, an-*
other hand

Ever to be at ȝowre wyll;   1150
Yf þat I might, I ne wald noght fle.'
Sho [said], 'Na[y], whi sold so be?
To ded yf I gert do þe now,
To me it war ful litel prow.
Bot for I find þe so bowsum,   1155
þat þou wald þus to me cum,
And for þou dose þe in my grace,
I forgif þe þi trispase.
Syt down,' sho said, 'and lat me here,
Why þou ert þus debonere.'   1160
'Madame,' he said, 'anis with a luke
Al my hert with þe þou toke;
Sen I first of þe had syght,
Have I þe lufed with al my might.
To mo þan þe, mi lady hende,   1165
Sal never more my luf wende;
For þi luf ever I am redy
Lely forto lif or dy.'
Sho said, 'Dar þou wele undertake
In my land pese forto make   1170
And forto maintene al mi rightes
Ogayns King Arthure and his knyghtes?'
He said, 'þat dar I undertane
Ogaynes ilka lyfand man.'
Swilk kownsail byfore had sho tane;   1175
Sho said, 'Sir, þan er we at ane.'
Hir barons hir ful rathly red
To tak a lord hir forto wed.

Ch. 1937   þan hastily sho went to hall;
þare abade hir barons all   1180
Forto hald þaire parlement
And mari hir by þaire asent.
Sho sayd, 'Sirs, with an acorde,
Sen me bus nedely have a lord
My landes forto lede and ȝeme,   1185
Sais me sone howe ȝe wil deme.'
'Madame,' þai said, 'how so ȝe will,

1152 said *added above the line by another hand.* y *of* nay *written in another hand over an illegible letter*

Al we sal assent þartyll.'

    þan þe lady went ogayne
Unto chameber to Sir Ywaine.   1190
'Sir,' sho said, 'so God me save,
Oþer lorde wil I nane have;
If I þe left, I did noght right,
A king son and a noble knyght.'

Ch. 2049   Now has þe maiden done hir thoght: 1195
Sir Ywayne out of anger broght.
þe lady led him unto hall;
Ogains him rase þe barons all,
And al þai said ful sekerly:
'þis knight sal wed þe lady.'   1200
And ilkane said þamself bitwene,
So faire a man had þai noght sene:
'For his bewte in hal and bowre
Him semes to be an emperowre.
We wald þat þai war trowth-plight   1205
And weded sone þis ilk night.'
þe lady set hir on þe dese
And cumand al to hald þaire pese,
And bad hir steward sumwhat say,
Or men went fra cowrt oway.   1210
þe steward said, 'Sirs, understandes,
Were es waxen in þir landes:
þe king Arthure es redy dight
To be here byn þis fowretenyght.
He and his menȝe ha thoght   1215
To win þis land if þai moght.
þai wate ful wele þat he es ded,
þat was lord here in þis stede.
None es so wight wapins to welde
Ne þat so boldly mai us belde,   1220
And wemen may maintene no stowre,

f. 10ᵛ   þai most nedes have a governowre.
þarefor mi lady most nede
Be weded hastily for drede;
And to na lord wil sho tak tent,   1225
Bot if it be by ȝowre assent.'

1189 *A red initial capital*   1222 v *of* governowre *is blotted*

Ch. 2105   þan þe lordes al on raw
Held þam wele payd of þis saw;
Al assented hyr untill
To tak a lord at hyr owyn wyll.   1230
þan said þe lady onone right,
'How hald ȝe ȝow paid of þis knight?
He profers hym on al wyse
To myne honore and my servyse;
And sertes, sirs, þe soth to say,   1235
I saw him never or þis day;
Bot talde unto me has it bene,
He es þe kyng son Uriene.
He es cumen of hegh parage
And wonder doghty of vasselage.   1240
War and wise and ful curtayse,
He ȝernes me to wife alwayse,
And nere þe lese, I wate, he might
Have wele better, and so war right.'
With a voice halely þai sayd,   1245
'Madame, ful wele we hald us payd.
Bot hastes fast, al þat ȝe may,
þat ȝe war wedded þis ilk day.'
And grete prayer gan þai make
On al wise, þat sho suld hym take.   1250

Ch. 2150   Sone unto þe kirk þai went
And war wedded in þaire present.
þare wedded Ywaine in plevyne
þe riche lady Alundyne,
þe dukes doghter of Landuit;   1255
Els had hyr lande bene destruyt.
þus þai made þe maryage
Omang al þe riche barnage;
þai made ful mekyl mirth þat day,
Ful grete festes on gude aray.   1260
Grete mirthes made þai in þat stede,
And al forgetyn es now þe ded
Of him þat was þaire lord fre.
þai say þat þis es worth swilk thre,
And þat þai lufed him mekil more   1265

1264 a *of* say *added above the line by the same hand*

þan him þat lord was þare byfore.
þe bridal sat, for soth to tell,
Til Kyng Arthure come to þe well
With al his knyghtes everilkane;
Byhind leved þare noght ane.   1270
þan sayd Sir Kay, 'Now, whare es he,
þat made slike bost here forto be
Forto venge his cosyn germayne?
I wist his wordes war al in vayne;
He made grete boste bifor þe quene,   1275
And here now dar he noght be sene.
His prowd wordes er now al purst,
For, in fayth, ful ill he durst
Anes luke opon þat knyght
þat he made bost with to fyght.'   1280
þan sayd Gawayn hastily:
'Syr, for Goddes luf, mercy!
For I dar hete þe for sertayne,
þat we sal here of Sir Ywayne
þis ilk day, þat be þou balde,   1285
Bot he be ded or done in halde;
And never in no cumpany
Herd I him speke þe velany.'
þan sayd Sir Kay, 'Lo, at þi will
Fra þis time forth I sal be still.'   1290

þe king kest water on þe stane;
þe storme rase ful sone onane
With wikked weders, kene and calde,
Als it was byforehand talde.
þe king and his men ilkane   1295
Wend þarwith to have bene slane,
So blew it store with slete and rayn;
And hastily þan Syr Ywayne
Dight him graythly in his gere
With nobil shelde and strong spere.   1300
When he was dight in seker wede,
þan he umstrade a nobil stede;
Him thoght þat he was als lyght,

1270 byhind: hin *faded*   1291 *A blue initial capital*

Als a fowl es to þe flyght.
Unto þe well fast wendes he,   1305
And sone when þai myght him se,
Syr Kay (for he wald noght fayle)
Smertly askes þe batayl;
And alsone þan said þe kyng,
'Sir Kay, I grante þe þine askyng.'   1310
þan Sir Ywayn neghed þam nere
þaire cowntenance to se and here.
Sir Kay þan on his stede gan spring;
'Bere þe wele now,' sayd þe kyng.
Ful glad and blith was Syr Ywayne,   1315

f. 11
When Sir Kay come him ogayn.
Bot Kay wist noght wha it was;
He findes his fere now or he pas.
Syr Ywaine thinkes now to be wroken
On þe grete wordes þat Kay has spoken.   1320

Ch. 2248
    þai rade togeder with speres kene;
þare was no reverence þam bitwene.
Sir Ywayn gan Sir Kay bere
Out of his sadel lenkith of his spere;
His helm unto þe erth smate,   1325
A fote depe þarein yt bate.
He wald do him na more despite,
Bot down he lighted als tyte;
Syr Kay stede he toke in hy
And presand þe king ful curtaysly.   1330
Wonder glad þan war þai all
þat Kay so fowl a shame gan fall;
And ilkone sayd til oþer þen,
'þis es he þat scornes al men';
Of his wa war þai wele paid.   1335
Syr Ywain þan to þe kyng said,
'Sir Kyng, I gif to þe þis stede,
For he may help þe in þi nede;
And to me war it grete trispas
Forto withhald þat ȝowres was.'   1340
'What man ertow?' quod þe kyng;

1319 Ywaine *added above the line by the same hand*   1321 *A red initial*
capital

'Of þe have I na knawyng,
Bot if þou unarmed were
Or els þi name þat I might here.'
'Lord,' he sayd, 'I am Ywayne.'   1345
þan was þe king ferly fayne;
A sari man þan was Sir Kay,
þat said þat he was stollen oway;
Al descumfite he lay on grownde,
To him þat was a sary stownde.   1350
þe king and his men war ful glad,
þat þai so Syr Ywayne had;
And ful glad was Sir Gawayne
Of þe welefare of Sir Ywayne;
For nane was to him half so dere   1355
Of al þat in þe court were.
þe king Sir Ywayn sone bisoght
To tel him al how he had wroght;
And sone Sir Ywaine gan him tell
Of al his fare how it byfell: 1360
With þe knight how þat he sped,
And how he had þe lady wed,
And how þe mayden hym helped wele;
þus tald he to him ilka dele.

Ch. 2302   'Sir King,' he sayd, 'I ȝow byseke   1365
And al ȝowre menȝe milde and meke,
þat ȝe wald grante to me þat grace
At wend with me to my purchace,
And se my kastel and my towre;
þan myght ȝe do me grete honowre.'   1370
þe kyng granted him ful right
To dwel with him a fowretenyght.
Sir Ywayne thanked him oft sith;
þe knyghtes war al glad and blyth
With Sir Ywaine forto wend;   1375
And sone a squier has he send.
Unto þe kastel þe way he nome
And warned þe lady of þaire come,
And þat his lord come with þe kyng;

1363 m *of* hym, ped *of* helped, *and* w *of* wele *faded and unclear*   1364 lk
of ilka *blotched and unclear*   1365 *A blue initial capital*

And when þe lady herd þis thing,   1380
It es no lifand man with mowth,
þat half hir cumforth tel kowth.

Ch. 2324   Hastily þat lady hende
Cumand al hir men to wende
And dight þam in þaire best aray   1385
To kepe þe king þat ilk day.
þai keped him in riche wede
Rydeand on many a nobil stede;
þai hailsed him ful curtaysly
And also al his cumpany.   1390
þai said he was worthy to dowt,
þat so fele folk led obowt.
þare was grete joy, I ȝow bihete,
With clothes spred in ilka strete
And damysels danceand ful wele   1395
With trompes, pipes and with fristele.
þe castel and þe cete rang
With mynstralsi and nobil sang.
þai ordand þam ilkane infere
To kepe þe king on faire manere.   1400
þe lady went withowten towne
And with hir many. bald barowne
Cled in purpure and ermyne
With girdels al of gold ful fyne;
þe lady made ful meri chere,   1405
Sho was al dight with drewries dere.
Abowt hir was ful mekyl thrang;
þe puple cried and sayd omang,
'Welkum ertou, Kyng Arthoure;
f. 11�v   Of al þis werld þou beres þe flowre, 1410
Lord Kyng of al kynges,
And blissed be he þat þe brynges.'
Ch. 2372   When þe lady þe kyng saw,
Unto him fast gan sho draw
To hald his sterap whils he lyght.   1415

1388 Rydeand: y *seems to be changed from* a   1394 spered *MS.*, *the* d,
very faint, is just discernible above the final e. *Above and below the first* e *dots are*
placed to indicate that the letter is to be omitted   1409 ou *of* ertou *over an*
erasure

Bot sone, when he of hir had syght,
With mekyl myrth þai samen met.
With hende wordes sho him gret,
'A thowsand sithes welkum,' sho says,
'And so es Sir Gawayne þe curtayse.' 1420
þe king said, 'Lady white so flowre,
God gif þe joy and mekil honowre,
For þou ert fayre with body gent.'
With þat he hir in armes hent,
And ful faire gan hir falde; 1425
þare was many to bihalde.
It es no man with tong may tell
þe mirth þat was þam omell.
Of maidens was þare so gude wane,
þat ilka knight myght tak ane. 1430
Ful mekil joy Syr Ywayn made
þat he þe king til his hows hade;
þe lady omang þam al samen
Made ful mekyl joy and gamen.

Ch. 2466   In þe kastel þus þai dwell, 1435
Ful mekyl myrth wase þam omell;
þe king was þare with his knyghtes
Aght dayes and aght nyghtes;
And Ywayn þam ful mery made
With alkyn gamyn þam for [to] glade. 1440
He prayed þe kyng to thank þe may,
þat hym had helpid in his jornay;
And ilk day had þai solace sere
Of huntyng and als of revere;
For þare was a ful fayre cuntre 1445
With wodes and parkes grete plente,
And castels wroght with lyme and stane,
þat Ywayne with his wife had tane.

Ch. 2476   Now wil þe king no langer lende,
Bot til his cuntre wil he wende. 1450
Aywhils þai war þare, for sertayne,
Syr Gawayn did al his mayne
To pray Sir Ywaine on al manere

1436 wase *altered from* ware?   1440 to *added above the line by another hand*   1449 *A red initial capital*

Forto wende with þam infere.
He said, 'Sir, if þou ly at hame,　　　　　1455
Wonderly men wil þe blame.
þat knyght es nothing to set by,
þat leves al his chevalry
And ligges bekeand in his bed,
When he haves a lady wed.　　　　　1460
For when þat he has grete endose,
þan war tyme to win his lose;
For when a knyght es chevalrouse,
His lady es þe more jelows,
Also sho lufes him wele þe bet.　　　　　1465
þarfore, sir, þou sal noght let
To haunt armes in ilk cuntre;
þan wil men wele more prayse þe.
þou has inogh to þi despens;
Now may þow wele hante turnamentes.　　　　　1470
þou and I sal wende infere,
And I will be at þi banere.
I dar noght say, so God me glad,
If I so fayre a leman had,
þat I ne most leve al chevalry　　　　　1475
At hame ydel with hir to ly.
Bot ȝit a fole þat litel kan,
May wele cownsail anoþer man.'

Ch. 2539　　So lang Sir Gawayn prayed so,
Syr Ywayne grantes him forto go　　　　　1480
Unto þe lady and tak his leve;
Loth him was hir forto greve.
Til hyr onane þe way he nome,
Bot sho ne wist noght whi he come.
In his arms he gan hir mete,　　　　　1485
And þus he said, 'My leman swete,
My life, my hele and al my hert,
My joy, my comforth and my quert,
A thing prai I þe unto
For þine honore and myne also.'　　　　　1490
þe lady said, 'Sir, verrayment,
I wil do al ȝowre cumandment.'

　　　　　1474 leman: a *changed from* o

'Dame,' he said, 'I wil þe pray,
þat I might þe king cumvay
And also with my feres founde   1495
Armes forto haunte a stownde.
For in bourding men wald me blame,
If I sold now dwel at hame.'

Ch. 2554   þe lady was loth him to greve;
'Sir,' sho said, 'I gif ȝow leve   1500
Until a terme þat I sal sayn,
Bot þat ȝe cum þan ogayn!
Al þis ȝere hale I ȝow grante
f. 12   Dedes of armes forto hante;
Bot, syr, als ȝe luf me dere,   1505
On al wise þat ȝe be here
þis day twelmoth how som it be,
For þe luf ȝe aw to me.
And if ȝe com noght by þat day,
My luf sal ȝe lose for ay.   1510
Advise ȝow wele now or ȝe gone.
þis day es þe evyn of Saint Jon;
þat warn I ȝow now or ȝe wende,
Luke ȝe cum by þe twelmoth ende.'

Ch. 2581   'Dame,' he sayd, 'I sal noght let   1515
To hald þe day þat þou has set;
And if I might be at my wyll,
Ful oft are sold I cum þe till.
Bot, madame, þis understandes,
A man þat passes divers landes,   1520
May sum tyme cum in grete destres,
In preson or els in sekenes;
þarefore I pray ȝow, or I ga,
þat ȝe wil out-tak þir twa.'
þe lady sayd, 'þis grant I wele,   1525
Als ȝe ask, everilka dele;
And I sal lene to ȝow my ring,
þat es to me a ful dere thing:
In nane anger sal ȝe be,
Whils ȝe it have and thinkes on me.   1530
I sal tel to ȝow onane

1493 i *of* said *added above the line, same hand*

þe vertu þat es in þe stane:
It es na preson 3ow sal halde,
Al if 3owre fase be manyfalde;
With sekenes sal 3e noght be tane,   1535
Ne of 3owre blode 3e sal lese nane;
In batel tane sal 3e noght be,
Whils 3e it have and thinkes on me;
And ay, whils 3e er trew of love,
Over al sal 3e be obove.   1540
I wald never for nakyn wight
Lene it are unto na knyght.
For grete luf I it 3ow take;
3emes it wele now for my sake.'

Ch. 2615   Sir Ywayne said, 'Dame, gramercy!'   1545
þan he gert ordain in hy
Armurs and al oþer gere,
Stalworth stedes, both sheld and spere,
And also squyere, knave and swayne.
Ful glad and blith was Sir Gawayne.   1550
No lenger wald Syr Ywayne byde,
On his stede sone gan he stride,
And þus he has his leve tane;
For him murned many ane.
þe lady toke leve of þe kyng   1555
And of his men3e ald and 3ing;
Hir lord, Sir Ywayne, sho bisekes
With teris trikland on hir chekes,
On al wise þat he noght let
To halde þe day þat he had set.   1560

Ch. 2639   þe knightes þus þaire ways er went
To justing and to turnament.
Ful dughtily did Sir Ywayne,
And also did Sir Gawayne;
þai war ful doghty both infere,   1565
þai wan þe prise both fer and nere.
þe kyng þat time at Cester lay;
þe knightes went þam forto play.

1539 o of love *changed from* u, *same hand*   1551 *A blue initial capital*
1563 Vwayne *MS.*

Ful really þai rade obout
Al þat twelmoth out and out 1570
To justing and to turnament;
þan wan grete wirships, als þai went;
Sir Ywayne oft had al þe lose,
Of him þe word ful wide gose;
Of þaire dedes was grete renown 1575
To and fra in towre and towne.
On þis wise in þis life þai last,
Unto Saint Johns day was past;
þan hastily þai hied home,
And sone unto þe kyng þai come; 1580
And þare þai held grete mangeri,
þe kyng with al his cumpany.

Ch. 2695 Sir Ywaine umbithoght him þan,
He had forgeten his leman.
'Broken I have hir cumandment. 1585
Sertes,' he said, 'now be I shent;
þe terme es past þat sho me set.
How ever sal þis bale be bet?'
Unnethes he might him hald fra wepe;
And right in þis þan toke he kepe, 1590
Into court come a damysele
On a palfray ambland wele;
And egerly down gan sho lyght
Withouten help of knave or knyght;
And sone sho lete hyr mantel fall 1595
And hasted hir fast into hall.
'Syr Kyng,' sho sayd, 'God mot þe se,

f. 12ᵛ My lady gretes þe wele by me,
And also Sir gude Gawayne
And al þi knyghtes bot Sir Ywayne. 1600
He es ateyned for trayture,
A fals and lither losenjoure;
He has bytrayed my lady,
Bot sho es war with his gilry.
Sho hopid noght, þe soth to say, 1605
þat he wald so have stollen oway;
He made to hir ful mekyl boste
And said of al he lufed hir moste.

Al was treson and trechery,
And þat he sal ful dere haby.   1610
It es ful mekyl ogains þe right
To cal so fals a man a knight.
My lady wend he had hir hert
Ay forto kepe and hald in quert,
Bot now with grefe he has hir gret   1615
And broken þe term þat sho him set,
Þat was þe evyn of Saynt John;
Now es þat tyme for ever gone.
So lang gaf sho him respite,
And þus he haves hir led with lite.   1620
Sertainly, so fals a fode
Was never cumen of kynges blode,
Þat so sone forgat his wyfe,
Þat lofed him better þan hyr life.'

Ch. 2768   Til Ywayne sais sho þus, 'þou es   1625
Traytur untrew and trowthles
And also an unkind cumlyng.
Deliver me my lady ring!'
Sho stirt to him with sterne loke,
Þe ring fro his finger sho toke;   1630
And alsone als sho had þe ring,
Hir leve toke sho of þe king
And stirted up on hir palfray.
Withowten more sho went hir way;
With hir was nowþer knave ne grome,   1635
Ne no man wist where sho bycome.

Ch. 2780   Sir Ywayn, when he þis gan here,
Murned and made simpil chere;
In sorow þan so was he stad,
Þat nere for murni[n]g wex he mad.   1640
It was no mirth þat him myght mend;
At worth to noght ful wele he wend,
For wa he es ful wil of wane.
'Allas, I am myne owin bane;
Allas,' he sayd, 'þat I was born,   1645
Have I my leman þus forlorn,

1637 *A red initial capital*   1640 murnig *MS.*

And al es for myne owen foly.
Allas, þis dole wil mak me dy.'
An evyl toke him als he stode;
For wa he wex al wilde and wode.   1650
Unto þe wod þe way he nome;
No man wist whore he bycome.
Obout he welk in þe forest,
Als it wore a wilde beste;
His men on ilka syde has soght   1655
Fer and nere and findes him noght.

Ch. 2814   On a day als Ywayne ran
In þe wod, he met a man;
Arowes brade and bow had he,
And when Sir Ywaine gan him se,   1660
To him he stirt with bir ful grim,
His bow and arwes reft he him.
Ilka day þan at þe leste
Shot he him a wilde beste;
Fless he wan him ful gude wane,   1665
And of his arows lost he nane.
þare he lifed a grete sesowne
With rotes and raw venysowne;
He drank of þe warm blode,
And þat did him mekil gode.   1670

Ch. 2827   Als he went in þat boskage,
He fand a litil ermytage.
þe ermyte saw and sone was war,
A naked man a bow bare.
He hoped he was wode þat tide;   1675
þarefore no lenger durst he bide.
He sperd his ȝate and in he ran
Forfered of þat wode man;
And for him thoght it charite,
Out at his window set he   1680
Brede and water for þe wode man;
And þarto ful sone he ran.
Swilk als he had, swilk he him gaf,
Barly-brede with al þe chaf;
þarof ete he ful gude wane,   1685

1675 *Following* hoped *the word* hepid *is cancelled by a single line*

And are swilk ete he never nane.
Of þe water he dra[n]k þarwith;
þan ran he forth into þe frith,
For if a man be never so wode,
He wil kum whare man dose him gode,   1690
And, sertanly, so did Ywayne.

f. 13   Everilka day he come ogayne,
And with him broght he redy boun
Ilka day new venisowne;
He laid it at þe ermite ȝate   1695
And ete and drank and went his gate.
Ever alsone als he was gane,
þe ermyt toke þe flesh onane;
He flogh it and seth it fayre and wele;
þan had Ywayne at ilke mele   1700
Brede and sothen venysowne.
þan went þe ermyte to þe towne
And salde þe skinnes þat he broght,
And better brede þarwith he boght;
þan fand Sir Ywayne in þat stede   1705
Venyson and better brede.
þis life led he ful fele ȝere,
And sethen he wroght als ȝe sal here.

Ch. 2888   Als Ywaine sleped under a tre,
By him come þare rideand thre: 1710
A lady, twa bourewemen alswa.
þan spak ane of þe maidens twa,
'A naked [man] me think I se;
Wit I wil what it may be.'
Sho lighted doun and to him ȝede,   1715
And unto him sho toke gude hede;
Hir thoght wele sho had him sene
In many stedes whare sho had bene.
Sho was astonyd in þat stownde,
For in hys face sho saw a wonde,   1720
Bot it was heled and hale of hew;

1687 drak MS.; R.'s emendation   1702 Schl. suggests that the t of went
was added by a later hand   1709 A blue initial capital   1712 p of spak
changed from t, same hand   1713 man R.'s suggestion; see note   1719 asto-
nayd MS. A dot under the second a indicates that this letter is to be omitted

þarby, hir thoght, þat sho him knew.
Sho sayd, 'By God þat me has made,
Swilk a wound Sir Ywayne hade.
Sertaynly þis ilk es he.   1725
Allas,' sho sayd, 'how may þis be?
Allas, þat him es þus bityd,
So nobil a knyght als he was kyd.
It es grete sorow þat he sold be
So ugly now opon to se.'   1730
So tenderly for him sho gret,
þat hir teres al hir chekes wet.
'Madame,' sho said, 'for sertayn,
Here have we funden Sir Ywayne,
þe best knyght þat on grund mai ga.   1735
Allas, him es bytid so wa;
In sum sorow was he stad,
And þarefore es he waxen mad.
Sorow wil meng a mans blode
And make him forto wax wode.   1740
Madame, and he war now in quert
And al hale of will and hert,
Ogayns ȝowre fa he wald ȝow were,
þat has ȝow done so mekyl dere.
And he ware hale, so God we mend,   1745
Ȝowre sorow war sone broght to end.'
þe lady said, 'And þis ilk be he
And [þat] he wil noght heþin fle,
Thorgh Goddes help þan, hope I, ȝit
We sal him win ynto his wyt.   1750
Swith at hame I wald we were,
For þare I have an unement dere;
Morgan þe Wise gaf it to me
And said als I sal tel to þe.
He sayd, "þis unement es so gode,   1755
þat if a man be braynwode
And he war anes anoynt with yt,
Smertly sold he have his wit." '
Fro hame þai wer bot half a myle;
þeder come þai in a whyle.   1760

Ch. 2956

1748 þan *MS.*; *R. suggests* þat

þe lady sone þe boyst has soght,
And þe unement has sho broght.
'Have,' sho said, 'þis unement here,
Unto me it es ful dere;
And smertly þat þou wend ogayne.   1765
Bot luke þou spend it noght in vaine;
And fra þe knight anoynted be,
þat þou leves, bring it to me.'
Hastily þat maiden meke
Tok hose and shose and serk and breke.   1770
A riche robe als gan sho ta
And a saint of silk alswa
And also a gude palfray;
And smertly come sho whare he lay;
On slepe fast ȝit sho him fande.   1775
Hir hors until a tre sho band,
And hastily to him sho ȝede,
And þat was a ful hardy dede.
Sho enoynt hys heved wele
And his body ilka dele;   1780
Sho despended al þe unement
Over hir ladies cumandment;
For hir lady wald sho noght let;
Hir thoght þat it was ful wele set.
Al his atyre sho left hym by   1785

f. 13ᵛ   At his rising to be redy,
                   þat he might him cleth and dyght,
                   Or he sold of hyr have syght.
Ch. 3016   þan he wakend of his slepe;
                   þe maiden to him toke gude kepe;   1790
                   He luked up ful sarily
                   And said, 'Lady Saynt Mary,
                   What hard grace to me es maked,
                   þat I am here now þus naked?
                   Allas, where any have here bene?   1795
                   I trow, sum has my sorow sene.'
                   Lang he sat so in a thoght,
                   How þat gere was þeder broght.
                   þan had he noght so mekyl myght

                   1789 *A red initial capital*

On his fete to stand upright; 1800
Him failed might of fete and hand,
þat he myght nowþer ga ne stand.
Bot ȝit his clathes on he wan;
þarfore ful wery was he þan.
þan had he mister forto mete 1805
Sum man þat myght his bales bete.
þan lepe þe maiden on hir palfray
And nere byside him made hir way.
Sho lete als sho him noght had sene
Ne wetyn þat he þare had bene. 1810
Sone when he had of hir had syght,
He cried unto hyr on hight;
þan wald sho ne ferrer ride,
Bot fast sho luked on ilka syde
And waited obout fer and nere. 1815
He cried and sayd, 'I am here.'
þan sone sho rade him till
And sayd, 'Sir, what es þi will?'
'Lady, þi help war me ful lefe,
For I am here in grete meschefe, 1820
I ne wate never by what chance
þat I have al þis grevance.
P[ar] charite I walde þe pray
Forto lene me þat palfray,
þat in þi hand es redy bowne, 1825
And wis me sone unto some towne.
I wate noght how I had þis wa,
Ne how þat I sal heþin ga.'
Sho answerd him with wordes hende,
'Syr, if þou wil with me wende, 1830
Ful gladly wil I ese þe,
Until þat þou amended be.'
Ch. 3086   Sho helped him up on his hors ryg,
And sone þai come until a bryg;
Into þe water þe boist sho cast, 1835
And seþin hame sho hied fast.
When þai come to þe castel-ȝate,

1823 p charite MS. (*abbreviation mark for -ar om.*)

þai lighted and went in þarate.
þe maiden to þe chameber went;
þe lady asked þe unement.   1840
'Madame,' sho said, 'þe boyst es lorn,
And so was I nerehand þarforn.'
'How so,' sho said, 'for Goddes tre?'
'Madame,' sho said, 'I sal tel þe
Al þe soth how þat it was.   1845
Als I over þe brig sold pas,
Evyn inmyddes, þe soth to say,
þare stombild my palfray;
On þe brig he fell al flat,
And þe boyst right with þat   1850
Fel fra me in þe water down;
And had I noght bene titter boun
To tak my palfray bi þe mane,
þe water sone had bene my bane.'
þe lady said, 'Now am I shent,   1855
þat I have lorn my gude unement;
It was to me, so God me glade,
þe best tresure þat ever I hade.
To me it es ful mekil skath,
Bot better es lose it þan ʒow bath.   1860
Wend, sho said, unto þe knight
And luke þou ese him at þi myght.'
'Lady,' sho said, 'els war me lathe.'
þan sho gert him washe and bathe
And gaf him mete and drink of main,   1865
Til he had geten his might ogayn.
þai ordand armurs ful wele dight,
And so þai did stedes ful wight.

Ch. 3086   So it fell sone on a day,
Whils he in þe castel lay,   1870
þe ryche eryl, Syr Alers,
With knightes, serjantes and swiers,
And with swith grete vetale
Come þat kastel to asayle.
Sir Ywain þan his armurs tase   1875

          1869 *A blue initial capital*

With oþer socure þat he hase.
þe erel he kepes in þe felde,
And sone he hit ane on þe shelde,
þat þe knyght and als þe stede

f. 14 Stark ded to þe erth þai ȝede. 1880
Sone anoþer, þe thrid, þe ferth
Feld he doun ded on þe erth;
He stird him so omang þam þan,
At ilka dint he slogh a man.
Sum he losed of hys men, 1885
Bot þe eril lost swilk ten;
Al þai fled fast fra þat syde,
Whare þai saw Sir Ywayn ride.
He herted so his cumpany,
þe moste coward was ful hardy 1890
To fel al þat þai fand in felde.

Ch. 3199 þe lady lay ever and bihelde;
Sho sais, 'Yon es a nobil knyght,
Ful eger and of ful grete myght;
He es wele worthy forto prayse, 1895
þat es so doghty and curtayse.'
þe mayden said, 'Withowten let,
Ȝowre oynement mai ȝe think wele set;
Sese, madame, how [h]e prikes,
And sese also, how fele he stikes. 1900
Lo, how he fars omang his fase;
Al þat he hittes sone he slase.
War þare swilk oþer twa als he,
þan, hope I, sone þaire fase sold fle.
Sertes, þan sold we se ful tyte, 1905
þe eril sold be descumfite.
Madame, God gif, his wil were
To wed ȝow and be loverd here.'

Ch. 3270 þe erils folk went fast to ded;
To fle þan was his best rede. 1910
þe eril sone bigan to fle,
And þan might men bourd se,
How Sir Ywayne and his feres
Folowd þam on fel maners;

1899 he: þe *MS.*; *R.'s emendation*   1900 stikes *MS.*; *R. emends to* strikes

And fast þai slogh þe erils men,   1915
Olive þai left noght over ten.
þe eril fled ful fast for drede,
And þan Sir Ywaine strake his stede
And overtoke him þat tide
At a kastel þarbysyde.   1920
Sir Ywayne sone withset þe ȝate,
þat þe eril myght noght in þarate.
þe eril saw al might noght gain;
He ȝalde him sone to Sir Ywayn,
And sone he has his trowth plyght   1925
To wend with him þat ilk night
Unto þe lady of grete renowne
And profer him to hir presowne,
And to do him in hir grace
And also to mend his trispase.   1930

Ch. 3290   þe eril þan unarmed his hevid,
And none armure on him he levid.
Helm, shelde and als his brand,
þat he bare naked in his hand,
Al he gaf to Sir Ywayne,   1935
And hame with him he went ogaine.
In þe kastel made þai joy ilkane,
When þai wist þe eril was tane;
And when þai saw þam cumand nere,
Ogayns him went þai al infere;   1940
And when þe lady gan þam mete,
Sir Ywaine gudely gan hir grete.
He said, 'Madame, have þi presoun
And hald him here in þi baundoun.'
Bot he gert hir grante him grace   1945
To mak amendes yn þat space.
On a buke þe erl sware
Forto restore bath les and mare,
And big ogayn bath toure and toune,
þat by him war casten doune,   1950
And evermare to be hir frende.

1923 Before noght *there seems to be an erasure*   1931 i *of* hevid *added*
above the line, same hand   1934 hand *changed from* ham   1949 y *of*
ogayn *over an erasure*

Umage made he to þat hende;
To þis forward he borows fand,
þe best lordes of al þat land.

Ch. 3315   Sir Ywaine wald no lenger lend,   1955
Bot redies him fast forto wend.
At þe lady his leve he takes,
Grete murnyng þarfore sho makes.
Sho said, 'Sir, if it be ȝowre will,
I pray ȝow forto dwel here still;   1960
And I wil ȝelde into ȝowre handes
Myne awyn body and al my landes.'
Hereof fast sho hym bysoght,
Bot al hir speche avayles noght.
He said, 'I wil no thing to mede   1965
Bot myne armurs and my stede.'
Sho said, 'Bath stede and oþer thing
Es ȝowres at ȝowre owyn likyng;
And if ȝe walde herewith us dwell,
Mekyl mirth war us omell.'   1970
It was na bote to bid him bide,
He toke his stede and on gan stride;
þe lady and hyr maydens gent
f. 14ᵛ   Wepid sare when þat he went.

Ch. 3341   Now rides Ywayn als ȝe sal here,   1975
With hevy herte and dreri chere
Thurgh a forest by a sty;
And þare he herd a hydose cry.
þe gaynest way ful sone he tase,
Til he come whare þe noys was.   1980
þan was he war of a dragoun,
Had asayled a wilde lyown;
With his tayl he drogh him fast,
And fire ever on him cast;
þe lyoun had over litel myght   1985
Ogaynes þe dragon forto fyght.
þan Sir Ywayn made him bown
Forto sucore þe lyown;

1967 stedes *MS.*; *R. and Schl. emend to* stede   1975 *A red initial capital*
1976 herte and: rte and *obscured by a dark spot*

His shelde bifore his face he fest
For þe fyre þat þe dragon kest;   1990
He strake þe dragon in at þe chavyl,
þat it come out at þe navyl;
Sunder strake he þe throte-boll,
þat fra þe body went þe choll.
By þe lioun tail þe hevid hang ȝit,   1995
For þarby had he tane his bit;
þe tail Sir Ywayne strake in twa,
þe dragon hevid þan fel þarfra.
He thoght, 'If þe lyoun me asayle,
Redy sal he have batayle.'   2000
Bot þe lyoun wald noght fyght,
Grete fawnyng made he to þe knyght.
Down on þe grund he set him oft,
His forþerfete he held oloft,
And thanked þe knyght als he kowth,   2005
Al if he myght noght speke with mowth;
So wele þe lyon of him lete,
Ful law he lay and likked his fete.
When Syr Ywayne þat sight gan se,
Of þe beste him thoght pete,   2010
And on his way forth gan he ride;
þe lyown folowd by hys syde.
In þe forest al þat day
þe lyoun mekely foloud ay,
And never for wele ne for wa   2015
Wald he part Sir Ywayn fra.

Ch. 3416
    þus in þe forest als þai ware,
þe lyoun hungerd swith sare.
Of a beste savore he hade;
Until hys lord sembland he made,   2020
þat he wald go to get his pray;
His kind it wald, þe soth to say.
For his lorde sold him noght greve,
He wald noght go withowten leve.
Fra his lord þe way he laght   2025
þe mountance of ane arow-draght;
Sone he met a barayn da,

      1997 k *of* strake *over an erasure*

And ful sone he gan hir sla;
Hir throte in twa ful sone he bate
And drank þe blode whils it was hate. 2030
þat da he kest þan in his nek,
Als it war a mele-sek.
Unto his lorde þan he it bare;
And Sir Ywayn parsayved þare,
þat it was so nere þe nyght, 2035
þat no ferrer ride he might.

Ch. 3456 A loge of bowes sone he made,
And flynt and fire-yren bath he hade,
And fire ful sone þare he slogh
Of dry mos and many a bogh. 2040
þe lion has þe da undone;
Sir Ywayne made a spit ful sone,
And rosted sum to þaire sopere.
þe lyon lay als ȝe sal here:
Unto na mete he him drogh 2045
Until his maister had eten ynogh.
Him failed þare bath salt and brede,
And so him did whyte wine and rede;
Bot of swilk thing als þai had,
He and his lyon made þam glad. 2050
þe lyon hungerd for þe nanes,
Ful fast he ete raw fless and banes.
Sir Ywayn in þat ilk telde
Laid his hevid opon his shelde;
Al nyght þe lyon about ȝede 2055
To kepe his mayster and his stede.
þus þe lyon and þe knyght
Lended þare a fouretenyght.

Ch. 3485 On a day so it byfell,
Syr Ywayne come unto þe well. 2060
He saw þe chapel and þe thorne
And said allas þat he was born;
And when he loked on þe stane,
He fel in swowing sone onane.
Als he fele his swerde outshoke; 2065

2040 boght *MS.*; *R.'s emendation; see ll. 2347, 3931*   2059 *A blue initial capital*

þe pomel into þe erth toke,
þe poynt toke until his throte.
(Wel nere he made a sari note.)
Thorgh his armurs sone it smate,
A litel intil hys hals it bate;   2070
And wen þe lyon saw his blude,
He brayded als he had bene wode.
þan kest he up so lathly rerde,
Ful mani fok myght he have ferde;
He wend wele, so God me rede,   2075
þat his mayster had bene ded.
It was ful grete pete to here
What sorow he made on his manere.
He stirt ful hertly, I ȝow hete,
And toke þe swerde bytwix his fete;   2080
Up he set it by a stane,
And þare he wald himself have slane;
And so he had sone, for sertayne,
Bot right in þat rase Syr Ywayne;
And alsone als he saw hym stand,   2085
For fayn he liked fote and hand.
Sir Ywayn said oft sithes, 'Allas,
Of alkins men hard es my grace.
Mi leman set me sertayn day,
And I it brak, so wayloway.   2090
Allas, for dole how may I dwell
To se þis chapel and þis well,
Hir faire thorn, hir riche stane?
My gude dayes er now al gane,
My joy es done now al bidene,   2095
I am noght worthi to be sene.
I saw þis wild beste was ful bayn
For my luf himself have slayne.
þan sold I, sertes, by more right
Sla my self for swilk a wyght   2100
þat I have for my foly lorn.
Allas þe while þat I was born!'

Ch. 3563
    Als Sir Ywayn made his mane
In þe chapel ay was ane

2078 manere: a *changed from* e

And herd his murnyng haly all   2105
Thorgh a crevice of þe wall,
And sone it said with simepel chere,
'What ertou, þat murnes here?'
'A man,' he sayd, 'sum tyme I was.
What ertow? Tel me or I pas.'   2110
'I am,' it sayd, 'þe sariest wight,
þat ever lifed by day or nyght.'
'Nay,' he said, 'by Saynt Martyne,
þare es na sorow mete to myne,
Ne no wight so wil of wane.   2115
I was a man, now am I nane;
Whilom I was a nobil knyght
And a man of mekyl myght;
I had knyghtes of my menȝe
And of reches grete plente;   2120
I had a ful fayre seignory,
And al I lost for my foly.
Mi maste sorow als sal þou here:
I lost a lady þat was me dere.'

Ch. 3586   þe toþer sayd, 'Allas, allas,   2125
Myne es a wele sarier case:
To-morn I mun bere my jewyse,
Als my famen wil devise.'
'Allas,' he said, 'what es þe skill?'
'þat sal þou here, sir, if þou will.   2130
I was a mayden mekil of pride
With a lady here-nere-biside;
Men me bikalles of tresown
And has me put here in presown;
I have no man to defend me,   2135
þarfore to-morn brent mun I be.'
He sayd, 'What if þou get a knyght,
þat for þe with þi fase wil fight?'
'Syr,' sho sayd, 'als mot I ga,
In þis land er bot knyghtes twa,   2140
þat me wald help to cover of care:
þe tane es went, I wate noght whare;

2115 of *over erasure*   2119 had *added over the line, same hand*

þe toþer es dweland with þe king
And wate noght of my myslykyng.
þe tane of þam hat Syr Gawayn,   2145
And þe toþer hat Syr Ywayn.
For hym sal I be done to dede
To-morn right in þis same stede;
He es þe Kinges son Uriene.'
'Parfay,' he sayd, 'I have hym sene;   2150
I am he, and for my gilt
Sal þou never more be spilt.
þou ert Lunet, if I can rede,
þat helpyd me yn mekyl drede;
I had bene ded had þou noght bene.   2155
þarfore tel me us bytwene,
How bical þai þe of treson
þus forto sla and for what reson?'

Ch. 3648   'Sir, þai say þat my lady
Lufed me moste specially,   2160
And wroght al efter my rede;
f. 15ᵛ   þarefore þai hate me to þe ded.
þe steward says þat done have I
Grete tresone unto my lady.
His twa breþer sayd it als,   2165
And I wist þat þai said fals;
And sone I answerd als a sot —
For fole bolt es sone shot —
I said þat I sold find a knyght,
þat sold me mayntene in my right   2170
And feght with þam al thre;
þus þe batayl wajed we.
þan þai granted me als tyte
Fourty dayes unto respite;
And at þe kynges court I was;   2175
I fand na cumfort ne na solase
Nowþer of knyght, knave ne swayn.'
þan said he, 'Whare was Syr Gawayn?
He has bene ever trew and lele,
He fayled never no damysele.'   2180

2155 *After* ded, ben ded *is repeated and cancelled by a single line. As a result
the verse is so extended that final* bene *is added below the line*

Ch. 3703   Scho said, 'In court [he] was noght sene,
                For a knyght led oway þe quene.
                þe king þarfore es swith grym;
                Syr Gawayn folowd efter him,
                He coms noght hame, for sertayne,   2185
                Until he bryng þe quene ogayne.
                Now has þou herd, so God me rede,
                Why I sal be done to ded.'
                He said, 'Als I am trew knyght,
                I sal be redy forto fyght   2190
                To-morn with þam al thre,
                Leman, for þe luf of þe.
                At my might I sal noght fayl,
                Bot how so bese of þe batayle,
                If ani man my name þe frayne,   2195
                On al manere luke þou yt layne;
                Unto na man my name þou say.'
                'Syr,' sho sayd, 'for soth, nay.
                I prai to grete God alweldand,
                þat þai have noght þe hegher hand;   2200
                Sen þat ȝe wil my murnyng mend,
                I tak þe grace þat God wil send.'
                Syr Ywayn sayd, 'I sal þe hyght
                To mend þi murnyng at my myght;
                Thorgh grace of God in trenyte   2205
                I sal þe wreke of þam al thre.'

Ch. 3770   þan rade he forth into frith,
                And hys lyoun went hym with.
                Had he redyn bot a stownde,
                A ful fayre castell he fownde;   2210
                And Syr Ywaine, þe soth to say,
                Unto þe castel toke þe way.
                When he come at þe castel-ȝate,
                Foure porters he fand þarate.
                þe drawbryg sone lete þai doun,   2215
                Bot al þai fled for þe lyown.
                þai said, 'Syr, withowten dowt,

2181 MS. lacks he; R.'s suggestion   2217 said added above the line,
same hand

þat beste byhoves þe leve þarout.'
He sayd, 'Sirs, [so] have I wyn,
Mi lyoun and I sal noght twyn;   2220
I luf him als wele, I ȝow hete,
Als my self at ane mete;
Owþer sal we samyn lende,
Or els wil we heþin wende.'
Bot right with þat þe lord he met —   2225
And ful gladly he him gret—
With knyghtes and swiers grete plente
And faire ladies and maydens fre;
Ful mekyl joy of him þai made,
Bot sorow in þaire hertes þai hade.   2230
Unto a chameber was he led
And unarmed and seþin cled
In cloþes þat war gay and dere.
Bot ofttymes changed þaire chere;
Sum tyme, he saw, þai weped all   2235
Als þai wald to water fall;
þai made slike murny[n]g and slik mane
þat gretter saw he never nane;
þai feynyd þam oft for hys sake
Fayre semblant forto make.   2240
Ful grete wonder Sir Ywayn hade
For þai swilk joy and sorow made;
'Sir,' he said, 'if ȝowre wil ware,
I wald wyt why ȝe make slike kare.'

Ch. 3851   'þis joy,' he said, 'þat we mak now,   2245
Sir, es al for we have ȝow;
And, sir, also we mak þis sorow
For dedys þat sal be done to-morow.
A geant wons here-nere-bysyde,
þat es a devil of mekil pryde;   2250
His name hat Harpyns of Mowntain.
For him we lyf in mekil payn;
My landes haves he robbed and reft,

2219 so *added above the line, another hand*   2232 unarmed: *MS. has*
unharmed *with a dot over the* h. *Schl. retains* unharmed *on the grounds that the
dot is a spatter of ink*   2237 murnyg *MS.*

Noght bot þis kastel es me left;
And, by God þat in hevyn wons,   2255
Syr, I had sex knyghtis to sons;
I saw my self þe twa slogh he,
To-morn þe foure als slane mun be—
He has al in hys presowne—
And, sir, for nane oþer enchesowne,   2260
Bot for I warned hym to wyve
My doghter, fayrest fode olyve.
þarfore es he wonder-wrath,
[And] depely has he sworn hys ath,
With maystry þat he sal hir wyn,   2265
And þat þe laddes of his kychyn
And also þat his werst fote-knave
His wil of þat woman sal have,
Bot I to-morn might find a knight,
þat durst with hym selven fyght;   2270
And I have none to him at ga.
What wonder es if me be wa?'

Ch. 3899   Syr Ywayn lystend hym ful wele,
And when he had talde ilka dele,
'Syr,' he sayd, 'me think mervayl   2275
þat 3e soght never no kounsayl
At þe kynges hous here-bysyde;
For, sertes, in al þis werld so wyde
Es no man of so mekil myght,
Geant, champioun ne knight,   2280
þat he ne has knyghtes of his men3e
þat ful glad and blyth wald be
Forto mete with swilk a man
þat þai myght kyth þaire myghtes on.'
He said, 'Syr, so God me mend,   2285
Unto þe kynges kourt I send
To seke my mayster Syr Gawayn;
For he wald socore me ful fain.
He wald noght leve for luf ne drede,

f. 16 *(left margin, opposite line 2256)*

2255 *In the tail-margin of f. 15ᵛ are written the catchwords* Syr I had, *same hand*
2264 And: *MS. has* In; *Schl.'s emendation*   2282 *Between* blyth *and* wald
a blank space, perhaps an erasure   2284 t *of* kyth *changed from another letter*
myghtes: *Schl. extends the abbreviation as* myghtis

Had he wist now of my nede;   2290
For his sister es my wyfe,
And he lufes hyr als his lyfe.
Bot a knyght þis oþer day,
þai talde, has led þe quene oway;
Forto seke hyr went Sir Gawayn,   2295
And ȝit ne come he noght ogayn.'

Ch. 3940
    þan Syr Ywayne sighed sare
And said unto þe knyght right þare;
'Syr,' he sayd, 'for Gawayn sake
þis batayl wil I undertake   2300
Forto fyght with þe geant;
And þat opon swilk a covenant,
Yif he cum at swilk a time,
So þat we may fight by prime.
No langer may I tent þarto,   2305
For oþer thing I have to do;
I have a dede þat most be done
To-morn nedes byfor þe none.'
þe knyght sare sighand sayd him till,
'Sir, God ȝelde þe þi gode wyll.'   2310
And al þat ware þare in þe hall,
On knese byfor hym gan þai fall.
Forth þare come a byrd ful bryght,
þe fairest man might se in sight;
Hir moder come with hir infere,   2315
And both þai morned and made yll chere.
þe knight said, 'Lo, verraiment,
God has us gude socure sent,
þis knight þat of his grace wil grant
Forto fyght with þe geant.'   2320
On knese þai fel doun to his fete
And thanked him with wordes swete.
'A, God forbede', said Sir Ywain,
'þat þe sister of Sir Gawayn
Or any oþer of his blode born   2325
Sold on þis wise knel me byforn.'
He toke þam up tyte both infere
And prayd þam to amend þaire chere:
'And praies fast to God alswa,

þat I may venge ȝow on ȝowre fa,   2330
And þat he cum swilk tyme of day,
þat I by tyme may wend my way
Forto do anoþer dede;
For, sertes, þeder most I nede.
Sertes, I wald noght þam byswike   2335
Forto win þis kinges rike.'
His thoght was on þat damysel,
þat he left in þe chapel.
þai said, 'He es of grete renowne,
For with hym dwels þe lyoun.'   2340
Ful wele confort war þai all
Bath in boure and als in hall;
Ful glad war þai of þaire gest;
And when tyme was at go to rest,
þe lady broght him to his bed;   2345
And for þe lyoun sho was adred.
Na man durst negh his chamber nere,
Fro· þai war broght þareyn infere.

Ch. 4030
f. 16^v

    Sone at morn, when it was day,
þe lady and þe fayre may   2350
Til Ywayn chamber went þai sone,
And þe dore þai have undone.
Sir Ywayn to þe kyrk ȝede
Or he did any oþer dede;
He herd þe servise of þe day   2355
And seþin to þe knyght gan say,
'Sir,' he said, 'now most I wend,
Lenger here dar I noght lende;
Til oþer place byhoves me fare.'
þan had þe knyght ful mekel care;   2360
He said, 'Syr, dwells a litel thraw
For luf of Gawayn þat ȝe knaw;
Socore us now or ȝe wende.
I sal ȝow gif withowten ende
Half my land with toun and toure,   2365
And ȝe wil help us in þis stoure.'

2335 I: *Schl. emends to he; see note on this line*   2343 of: *Schl. reads on erroneously*   2347 neght *MS.; R. (iii. 442) suggests this reading; see ll. 2040, 3931*   2353 *A red initial capital*

Sir Ywayn said, 'Nai, God forbede
þat I sold tak any mede.'
þan was grete dole, so God me glade,
To se þe sorow þat þai made.　　　　　　　　　2370
Of þam Sir Ywayn had grete pete;
Him thoght his hert myght breke in thre;
For in grete drede ay gan he dwell
For þe mayden in þe chapell;
For, sertes, if sho war done to ded,　　　　　　2375
Of him war þan none oþer rede
Bot oiþer he sold hymselven sla
Or wode ogain to þe wod ga.

Ch. 4088　　Ryght with þat þare come a grome
And said þam þat geant come:　　　　　　　2380
'ȝowre sons bringes he him byforn,
Wel nere naked als þai war born.'
With wreched ragges war þai kled
And fast bunden; þus er þai led.
þe geant was bath large and lang　　　　　　2385
And bare a levore of yren ful strang;
þarwith he bet þam bitterly;
Grete rewth it was to here þam cry;
þai had nothing þam forto hyde.
A dwergh ȝode on þe toþer syde;　　　　　　2390
He bare a scowrge with cordes ten;
þarewith he bet þa gentil men
Ever onane als he war wode.
Efter ilka band brast out þe blode;
And when þai at þe walles were,　　　　　　2395
He cried loud þat men myght here,
'If þou wil have þi sons in hele,
Deliver me þat damysele.
I sal hir gif to warisowne
Ane of þe foulest quisteroun,　　　　　　　2400
þat ever ȝit ete any brede;
He sal have hir maydenhede.
þar sal none oþer lig hir by
Bot naked herlotes and lowsy.'
When þe lord þir wordes herd,　　　　　　2405
Als he war wode for wa he ferd.

Sir Ywayn þan þat was curtays,
Unto þe knyght ful sone he sais:
'þis geant es ful fers and fell
And of his wordes ful kruell;   2410
I sal deliver hir of his aw
Or els be ded within a thraw.
For, sertes, it war a misaventure
þat so gentil a creature
Sold ever so foul hap byfall   2415
To be defouled with a thrall.'

Ch. 4158 Sone was he armed, Sir Ywayn;
þarfore þe ladies war ful fayn.
þai helpid to lace him in his wede,
And sone he lepe up on his stede.   2420
þai prai to God þat grace him grant
Forto sla þat foul geant.
þe drawbrigges war laten doun,
And forth he rides with his lioun.
Ful mani sari murnand man   2425
Left he in þe kastel þan,
þat on þaire knese to God of might
Praied ful hertly for þe knyght.

Ch. 4182 Syr Ywayn rade into þe playne,
And þe geant come hym ogayne.   2430
His levore was ful grete and lang
And himself ful mekyl and strang;
He said, 'What devil made þe so balde
Forto cum heder out of þi halde?
Whosoever þe heder send,   2435
Lufed þe litel, so God me mend;
Of þe he wald be wroken fayn.'
'Do forth þi best,' said Sir Ywayn.
Al þe armure he was yn,
Was noght bot of a bul-skyn.   2440
Sir Ywayn was to him ful prest,
He strake to him inmiddes þe brest;
f. 17 þe spere was both stif and gode;
Whare it toke bit, outbrast þe blode;

2428 *Between* 2428 *and* 2429 *appears the following rubric in red, same hand:*
here es þe myddes of þis boke. 2429 *A blue initial capital*

So fast Sir Ywayn on yt soght,   2445
þe bul-scyn availed noght.
þe geant stombild with þe dynt,
And unto Sir Ywayn he mynt,
And on þe shelde he hit ful fast,
It was mervayl þat it myght last.   2450
þe levore bended þarwithall,
With grete force he lete it fall,
þe geant was so strong and wight,
þat never for no dint of knyght
Ne for batayl þat he sold make,   2455
Wald he none oþer wapyn take.
Sir Ywain left his spere of hand
And strake obout him with his brand,
And þe geant mekil of mayn
Strake ful fast to him ogayn,   2460
Til at þe last within a throw
He rest him on his sadelbow;
And þat parcayved his lioun,
þat his hevid so hanged doun,
He hopid þat hys lord was hyrt,   2465
And to þe geant sone he styrt.
þe scyn and fless bath rafe he down
Fro his hals to hys cropoun;
His ribbes myght men se onane,
For al was bare unto bane.   2470
At þe lyown oft he mynt,
Bot ever he lepis fro his dynt,
So þat no strake on him lyght.
By þan was Ywain cumen to myght,
þan wil he wreke him if he may.   2475
þe geant gaf he ful gude pay;
He smate oway al his left cheke,
His sholder als of gan he kleke,
þat both his levore and his hand
Fel doun law op[o]n þe land.   2480
Seþin with a stoke to him he stert
And smate þe geant unto þe hert:
þan was nane oþer tale to tell,

2447 geant: a *written over another letter*   2480 open *MS.*; *Schl's emendation*

Bot fast unto þe erth he fell,
Als it had bene a hevy tre.   2485
Ch. 4248   Þan myght men in þe kastel se
Ful mekil mirth on ilka side.
Þe ȝates kest þai opyn wyde;
Þe lord unto Syr Ywaine ran,
Him foloud many a joyful man;   2490
Also þe lady ran ful fast,
And hir doghter was noght þe last.
I may noght tel þe joy þai had;
And þe foure brether war ful glad,
For þai war out of bales broght.   2495
Þe lord wist it helpid noght
At pray Sir Ywayn forto dwell,
For tales þat he byfore gan tell;
Bot hertly with his myght and mayn
He praied him forto cum ogayn   2500
And dwel with him a litel stage,
When he had done hys vassage.
He said, 'Sir, þat may I noght do;
Bileves wele, for me bus go.'
Þam was ful wo he wald noght dwell,   2505
Bot fain þai war þat it so fell.
Ch. 4313   Þe neghest way þan gan he wele,
Until he come to þe chapele.
Þare he fand a mekil fire;
And þe mayden with lely lire   2510
In hyr smok was bunden fast
Into þe fire forto be kast.
Unto himself he sayd in hy
And prayed to God almyghty,
Þat he sold for his mekil myght   2515
Save fro shame þat swete wight.
'Yf þai be many and mekil of pryse,
I sal let for no kouwardise;
For with me es bath God and right,
And þai sal help me forto fight,   2520
And my lyon sal help me;
Þan er we foure ogayns þam thre.'

Ch. 4337

Sir Ywayn rides and cries þen,
'Habides, I bid 3ow, fals men!
It semes wele þat 3e er wode,   2525
þat wil spill þis sakles blode.
3e sal noght so, yf þat I may.'
His lyown made hym redy way.
Naked he saw þe mayden stand
Bihind hir bunden aiþer hand: 2530
þan sighed Ywain wonder-oft,
Unnethes might he syt oloft.
þare was no sembland þam bitwene,
þat ever owþer had oþer sene.
Al obout hyr myght men se   2535
Ful mykel sorow and grete pete

f. 17ᵛ

Of oþer ladies þat þare were,
Wepeand with ful sory chere.
'Lord,' þai sayd, 'what es oure gylt?
Oure joy, oure confort sal be spilt.   2540
Who sal now oure erandes say?
Allas, who sal now for us pray?'

Ch. 4385

Whils þai þus karped, was Lunet
On knese byfore þe prest set,
Of hir syns hir forto schrive.   2545
And unto hir he went bylive,
Hir hand he toke, and up sho rase;
'Leman,' he sayd, 'whore er þi fase?'
'Sir, lo þam 3onder in 3one stede
Bideand until I be ded;   2550
þai have demed me with wrang.
Wel nere had 3e dwelt over lang.
I pray to God he do 3ow mede
þat 3e wald help me in þis nede.'
þir wordes herd þan þe steward;   2555
He hies him unto hir ful hard.
He said, 'þou lies, fals woman!
For þi treson ertow tane.
Sho has bitraied hir lady,
And, sir, so wil sho þe in hy.   2560

2523 *A red initial capital*   2533 sembland: la *seem written over other*
letters   2553 God: G *seems to be changed from* d

And þarefore, syr, by Goddes dome,
I rede þou wend right als þou com;
þou takes a ful febil rede,
If þou for hir will suffer ded.'

Ch. 4424   Unto þe steward þan said he,   2565
'Who so es ferd, I rede he fle;
And, sertes, I have bene þis day,
Whare I had ful large pay;
And ʒit,' he sayd, 'I sal noght fail.'
To þam he waged þe batayl.   2570
'Do oway þi lioun,' said þe steward;
'For þat es noght oure forward.
Allane sal þou fight with us thre.'
And unto him þus answerd he,
'Of my lioun no help I crave;   2575
I ne have none oþer fote-knave;
If he wil do ʒow any dere,
I rede wele þat ʒe ʒow were.'
þe steward said, 'On alkins wise
þi lyoun, sir, þou most chastise,   2580
þat he do here no harm þis day,
Or els wend forth on þi way;
For hir warand mai þou noght be,
Bot þou allane fight with us thre.
Al þir men wote, and so wote I,   2585
þa[t] sho bitrayed hir lady.
Als traytures sal sho have hyre,
Sho be brent here in þis fire.'
Sir Ywayn sad, 'Nai, God forbede!'
(He wist wele how þe soth ʒede)   2590
'I trow to wreke hir with þe best.'
He bad his lyoun go to rest;
And he laid him sone onane
Doun byfore þam everilkane;
Bitwene his legges he layd his tail   2595
And so biheld to þe batayl.
Ch. 4478   Al thre þai ride to Sir Ywayn,
And smertly rides he þam ogayn;
In þat time nothing tint he,

2586 þai *MS.*; *R.'s emendation*

For his an strake was worth þaires thre.   2600
He strake þe steward on þe shelde,
þat he fel doun flat in þe felde;
Bot up he rase ȝit at þe last
And to Sir Ywayn strake ful fast.
þarat þe lyoun greved sare,   2605
No lenger wald he þan lig þare;
To help his mayster he went onane;
And þe ladies everilkane,
þat war þare forto se þat sight,
Praied ful fast ay for þe knight.   2610

Ch. 4521   þe lyoun hasted him ful hard,
And sone he come to þe steward.
A ful fel mynt to him he made:
He bigan at þe shulder-blade,
And with his pawm al rafe he downe   2615
Bath hauberk and his actoune
And al þe fless doun til his kne,
So þat men myght his guttes se;
To ground he fell so al torent
Was þare no man þat him ment.   2620
þus þe lioun gan hym sla.
þan war þai bot twa and twa,
And, sertanly, þare Sir Ywayn
Als with wordes did his main
Forto chastis hys lyowne;   2625
Bot he ne wald na more lig doun.
þe liown thoght, how so he sayd,
þat with his help he was wele payd.
þai smate þe lyoun on ilka syde
And gaf him many woundes wide.   2630

f. 18   When þat he saw hys lyoun blede,
He ferd for wa als he wald wede,
And fast he strake þan in þat stoure,
Might þare none his dintes doure.
So grevosly þan he bygan   2635
þat doun he bare bath hors and man.
þai ȝald þam sone to Sir Ywayn,
And þarof war þe folk ful fayne;

2611 *A blue initial capital*

And sone quit to þam þaire hire,
For both he kest þam in þe fire   2640
And said, 'Wha juges men with wrang,
þe same jugement sal þai fang.'
þus he helpid þe maiden ȝing,
And seþin he made þe saghtelyng
Bitwene hyr and þe riche lady.   2645

Ch. 4580   þan al þe folk ful hastily
Proferd þam to his servise
To wirship him ever on al wise.
Nane of þam al wist bot Lunet,
þat þai with þaire lord war met.   2650
þe lady prayed him als þe hend
þat he hame with þam wald wende
Forto sojorn þare a stownd,
Til he wer warist of his wound.
By his sare set he noght a stra,   2655
Bot for his lioun was him wa.
'Madame,' he said, 'sertes, nay,
I mai noght dwel, þe soth to say.'
Sho said, 'Sir, sen þou wyl wend,
Sai us þi name, so God þe mend.'   2660
'Madame,' he said, 'bi Saint Symoun,
I hat þe knight with þe lyoun.'
Sho said, 'We saw ȝow never or now,
Ne never herd we speke of ȝow.'
'þarby,' he sayd, 'ȝe understand,   2665
I am noght knawen wide in land.'
Sho said, 'I prai þe forto dwell,
If þat þou may, here us omell.'
If sho had wist wele wha it was,
She wald wele lever have laten him pas;   2670
And þarefore wald he noght be knawen
Both for hir ese and for his awyn.
He said, 'No lenger dwel I ne may;
Beleves wele and haves goday.
I prai to Crist, hevyn kyng,   2675

2659 wyl: y *changed from* e, *same hand*   2670 wele: *first* e *seems adapted from an* i, *same hand*   2671 be: e *is very small and may be made from another letter, same hand*

Lady, len ȝow gude lifing,
And len grace, þat al ȝowre anoy
May turn ȝow unto mykel joy.'
Sho said, 'God grant þat it so be.'
Unto himself þan þus said he, 2680
'þou ert þe lok and kay also
Of al my wele and al my wo.'

Ch. 4635 Now wendes he forth and morning mase,
And nane of þam wist what he was,
Bot Lunet þat he bad sold layn; 2685
And so sho did with al hir mayne,
Sho cunvayd him forth on his way.
He said, 'Gude leman, I þe pray,
þat þou tel to no moder son,
Who has bene þi champion; 2690
And als I pray þe, swete wight,
Late and arly þou do þi might
With speche unto my lady fre
Forto make hir frende with me.
Sen ȝe er now togeder glade, 2695
Help þou þat we war frendes made.'
'Sertes, sir,' sho sayd, 'ful fayn
þareobout wil I be bayn;
And þat ȝe have done me þis day,
God do ȝow mede, als he wele may.' 2700

Ch. 4644 Of Lunet þus his leve he tase,
Bot in hert grete sorow he hase;
His lioun feled so mekill wa,
þat he ne myght no ferrer ga.
Sir Ywayn puld gres in þe felde 2705
And made a kouche opon his shelde;
þareon his lyoun laid he þare,
And forth he rides and sighes sare;
On his shelde so he him led,
þan was he ful evyl sted. 2710
Forth he rides by frith and fell,
Til he come to a fayre castell.
þare he cald and swith sone

2683 *A red initial capital*

þe porter has þe ȝates undone,
And to him made he ful gude chere. 2715
He said, 'Sir, ȝe er welcum here.'
Syr Ywain said, 'God do þe mede,
For þarof have I mekil nede.'
Yn he rade right at þe ȝate;
Faire folk kepid hym þarate. 2720
þai toke his shelde and his lyoun,
And ful softly þai laid it doun;
Sum to stabil led his stede,
And sum also unlaced his wede.

f. 18ᵛ   þai talde þe lord þan of þat knyght; 2725
And sone he and his lady bryght
And þaire sons and doghters all
Come ful faire him forto kall;
þai war ful fayn he þore was sted.
To chaumber sone þai have him led; 2730
His bed was ordand richely,
And his lioun þai laid him by;
Him was no mister forto crave,
Redy he had what he wald have.
Twa maydens with him þai laft 2735
þat wele war lered of lechecraft;
þe lordes doghters both þai wore
þat war left to kepe hym þore.
þai heled hym everilka wound,
And hys lyoun sone made þai sownd. 2740
I can noght tel how lang he lay;
When he was helyd he went his way.

Ch. 4703   Bot whils he sojorned in þat place,
In þat land byfel þis case.
A litil þeþin in a stede 2745
A grete lord of þe land was ded.
Lifand he had none oþer ayre
Bot two doghters þat war ful fayre.
Als sone als he was laid in molde,
þe elder sister sayd sho wolde 2750
Wend to court sone als sho myght,

2743 *A blue initial capital*   2748 two: *added above the line, same hand*

Forto get hir som doghty knyght
Forto win hir al þe land
And hald it halely in hir hand.
Þe ȝonger sister saw sho ne myght   2755
Have þat fell until hir right,
Bot if þat it war by batail;
To court sho wil at ask cownsayl.
Þe elder sister sone was ȝare,
Unto þe court fast gan sho fare.   2760
To Sir Gawayn sho made hir mane,
And he has granted hyr onane,
'Bot yt bus be so prevely,
Þat nane wit bot þou and I.
If þou of me makes any ȝelp,   2765
Lorn has þou al my help.'

Ch. 4737   Þan efter on þe toþer day
Unto kourt come þe toþer may,
And to Sir Gawayn sone sho went
And talde unto him hir entent;   2770
Of his help sho him bysoght.
'Sertes,' he sayd, 'þat may I noght.'
Þan sho wepe and wrang hir handes;
And right with þat come new tithandes,
How a knyght with a lyoun   2775
Had slane a geant ful feloun.
Þe same knight þare talde þis tale
Þat Syr Ywayn broght fra bale
Þat had wedded Gawayn sister dere.
Sho and hir sons war þare infere;   2780
Þai broght þe dwergh, þat be ȝe balde,
And to Sir Gawayn have þai talde
How þe knyght with þe lyowne
Delivred þam out of presowne,
And how he for Syr Gawayn sake   2785
Gan þat batayl undertake,
And als how nobilly þat he wroght.
Sir Gawayn said, 'I knaw him n[o]ght.'
Þe ȝonger mayden þan alsone

2784 Delivred: r *added above the line, same hand*   2788 nght *MS.*; *R.'s*
emendation

Of þe king askes þis bone   2790
To have respite of fourti dais,
Als it fel to landes lays.
Sho wist þare was no man of main
þat wald fyght wi[t]h Sir Gawayn;
Sho thoght to seke by frith and fell   2795
þe knyght þat sho herd þam of tell.
Respite was granted of þis thing;
þe mayden toke leve at [þe] king
And seþen at al þe baronage,
And forth sho went on hir vayage.   2800

Ch. 4821   Day ne nyght wald sho noght spare;
Thurgh al þe land fast gan sho fare,
Thurgh castel and thurgh ilka toun
To seke þe knight with þe lyown:
He helpes al in word and dede,   2805
þat unto him has any nede.
Sho soght hym thurgh al þat land,
Bot of hym herd sho na tythand;
Na man kouth tel hir whare he was;
Ful grete sorow in hert sho has.   2810
So mikel murning gan sho make
þat a grete sekenes gan sho take.
Bot in hir way right wele sho sped;
At þat kastell was sho sted,
Whare Sir Ywayn are had bene   2815
Helid of his sekenes clene.
þare sho was ful wele knawen
And als welcum als til hyr awyn;
f. 19   With alkyn gamyn þai gan hir glade,
And mikel joy of hir þai made.   2820
Unto þe lord sho tald hyr case,
And helping hastily sho hase.

Ch. 4832   Stil in lecheing þare sho lay;
A maiden for hir toke þe way
Forto seke yf þat sho myght   2825
In any land here of þat knyght;
And þat same kastel come sho by,

2794 with: t *by another hand over an erasure*   2798 *MS. lacks the second*
þe, *which R. suggests*

Whare Ywayn wedded þe lavedy;
And fast sho spird in ylk sesown
Efter þe knight with þe lioun.　　　　2830
þai tald hir how he went þam fra,
And also how þay saw him sla
Thre nobil knyghtes for þe nanes
þat faght with him al at anes.
Sho said, 'Par charite, I ȝow pray,　　　　2835
If þat ȝe wate wil ȝe me say,
Whederward þat he es went?'
þai said, for soth, þai toke na tent;
'Ne here es nane þat þe can tell,
Bot if it be a damysell,　　　　2840
For whas sake he heder come,
And for hir þe batayl he name.
We trow wele þat sho can þe wis;
ȝonder in ȝone kyrk sho ys;
þarfore we rede to hyr þou ga';　　　　2845
And hastily þan did sho swa.
Aiþer oþer ful gudeli gret,
And sone sho frayned at Lunet
If sho kouth ani sertain sayne;
And hendly answerd sho ogayne,　　　　2850
'I sal sadel my palfray
And wend with þe forth on þi way
And wis þe als wele als I can.'
Ful oft siþes thanked sho hir þan.

Ch. 4970　　　Lunet was ful smertly ȝare,　　　　2855
And with þe mayden forth gan sho fare.
Als þai went, al sho hyr talde,
How sho was taken and done in halde,
How wikkedly þat sho was wreghed,
And how þat trayturs on hir leghed,　　　　2860
And how þat sho sold have bene brent,
Had noght God hir socore sent
Of þat knight with þe lyoun—
'He lesed me out of presoun.'
Sho broght hir sone into a playn,　　　　2865
Whare sho parted fra Sir Ywayn;
Sho said, 'Na mare can I tel þe,

Bot here parted he fra me.
How þat he went wate I no mare;
Bot wounded was he wonder-sarc.   2870
God þat for us sufferd wounde,
Len us to se him hale and sownde.
No lenger with þe may I dwell;
Bot cumly Crist þat heried hell,
Len þe grace þat þou may spede   2875
Of þine erand als þou has nede.'
Lune[t] hastily hies hir home,
And þe mayden sone to þe kastel come
Whare he was helid byforehand.
þe lord sone at þe ȝate sho fond   2880
With knyghtes and ladies grete cumpani;
Sho haylsed þam al ful hendely,
And ful fayre praied sho to þam þen
If þai couth þai sold hyr ken
Whare sho myght fynd in toure or toun   2885
A kumly knyght with a lyoun.
þan said þe lord, 'By swete Jhesus,
Right now parted he fra us;
Lo here þe steppes of his stede,
Evyn unto him þai wil þe lede.'   2890

Ch. 5032 þan toke sho leve and went hir way,
With sporrs sho sparid noght hir palfray;
Fast sho hyed with al hyr myght,
Until sho of him had a syght
And of hys lyoun þat by him ran.   2895
Wonder-joyful was sho þan,
And with hir force sho hasted so fast
þat sho overtoke him at þe last.
Sho hailsed him with hert ful fayn,
And he hir hailsed fayre ogayn.   2900
Sho said, 'Sir, wide have I ȝow soght;
And for my self ne es it noght,
Bot for a damysel of pryse
þat halden es both war and wise.
Men dose to hir ful grete outrage,   2905

2877 Luned *MS.*; *R.'s emendation*   2887 Jhesus: *the usual abbreviation*
jhs *with a curved line over the* hs

þai wald hir reve hyr heritage;
And in þis land now lifes none
þat sho traystes hyr opone
Bot anly opon God and þe,
For þou ert of so grete bounte;   2910
Thorgh help of þe sho hopes wele
To win hyr right everilka dele.

f. 19ᵛ   Scho sais no knyght þat lifes now
Mai help hir half so wele als þou;
Gret word sal gang of þi vassage,   2915
If þat þou win hir heritage.
For thoght sho toke slike sekenes sare,
So þat sho might travail no mare,
I have ȝow soght on sydes sere;
þarfore ȝowre answer wald I here,   2920
Wheþer ȝe wil with me wend,
Or elswhare ȝow likes to lend.'
He said, 'þat knyght þat idil lies
Oft siþes winnes ful litel pries.
Forþi mi rede sal sone be tane: 2925
Gladly with þe wil I gane,
Wheder so þou wil me lede,
And hertly help þe in þi nede.
Sen þou haves me so wide soght,
Sertes, fail þe sal I noght.'   2930

Ch. 5107   þus þaire wai forth gan þai hald
Until a kastel þat was cald
þe Castel of þe Hevy Sorow.
þare wald he bide until þe morow;
þare to habide him thoght it best,   2935
For þe son drogh fast to rest.
Bot al þe men þat þai met,
Grete wonder sone on þam þai set
And [said], 'þou wreche, unsely man,
Whi wil þou here þi herber tane?   2940
þou passes noght without despite.'

2911 þe *added above the line, same hand*   2931 *A red initial capital*
2939 *MS. lacks* said; *R. suggests* seyde

Sir Ywain answerd þam als tyte
And said, 'For soth, ӡe er unhende
An unkouth man so forto shende;
Ӡe sold noght say hym velany,   2945
Bot if ӡe wist encheson why.'
þai answerd þan and said ful sone,
'þou sal wit or to-morn at none.'
Syr Ywaine said, 'For al ӡowre saw
Unto ӡon castel wil I draw.'   2950
He and his lyoun and þe may
Unto þe castel toke þe way.
When þe porter of þam had sight,
Sone he said unto þe knight,
'Cumes forth,' he said, 'ӡe al togeder!   2955
Ful ille hail er ӡe cumen heder.'
Ch. 5185   þus war þai welkumd at þe ӡate,
And ӡit þai went al in þarate;
Unto þe porter no word þai said.
A haƚ þai fand ful gudeli graid,   2960
And als Sir Ywaine made entre,
Fast bisyde him þan saw he
A proper place and faire, iwis
Enclosed obout with a palis.
He loked in bitwix þe trese,   2965
And many maidens þare he sese
Wirkand silk and gold-wire;
Bot þai war al in pover atire.
þaire cloþes war reven on evil arai;
Ful tenderly al weped þai.   2970
þaire face war lene and als unclene,
And blak smokkes had þai on bidene;
þai had mischef[s] ful manifalde
Of hunger, of threst and of calde;
And ever onane þai weped all,   2975
Als þai wald to water fall.
Ch. 5212   When Ywaine al þis understode,
Ogayn unto þe ӡates he ӡode;
Bot þai war sperred ferli fast
With lokkes þat ful wele wald last.   2980

2973 mischefs: s *added by another hand*

þe porter kepid þam with his main
And said, 'Sir, þou most wend ogain;
I wate þou wald out at þe ȝate,
Bot þou mai noght by na gate.
þi herber es tane til to-morow, 2985
And þarfore getes þou mekill sorow.
Omang þi fase here sted ertow.'
He said, 'So have I bene or now
And past ful wele; so sal I here.
Bot, leve frend, wiltou me lere 2990
Of þise maidens what þai are,
þat wirkes al þis riche ware?'
He said, 'If þou wil wit trewly,
Forþermare þou most aspy.'
'þarfore,' he said, 'I sal n[o]ght lett.' 2995
He soght and fand a dern weket,
He opind it and in he ȝede.
'Maidens,' he said, 'God mot ȝow spede,
And als he sufferd woundes sare,
He send ȝow covering of ȝowre care, 3000
So þat ȝe might mak merier chere.'
'Sir,' þai said, 'God gif so were.'
'ȝowre sorow,' he said, 'unto me say,
And I sal mend it, yf I may.'

Ch. 5250 Ane of þam answerd ogayne 3005
And said, 'þe soth we sal noght layne;

f. 20 We sal ȝow tel or ȝe ga ferr,
Why we er here and what we err.
Sir, ȝe sal understand
þat we er al of Maydenland. 3010
Oure kyng opon his jolite
Passed thurgh many cuntre
Aventures to spir and spy
Forto asay his owen body.
His herber here anes gan he ta; 3015
þat was biginyng of oure wa.
For heryn er twa champions;
Men sais þai er þe devil sons,
Geten of a woman with a ram;

2995 nght *MS.*; *R.'s emendation*

Ful many man have þai done gram. 3020
What knight so herbers here a nyght,
With both at ones bihoves him fight.
So bus þe do, by bel and boke;
Allas, þat þou þine yns here toke.
Oure king was wight himself to welde 3025
And of fourtene ʒeres of elde,
When he was tane with þam to fyght;
Bot unto þam had he no myght,
And when he saw him bud be ded,
þan he kouth no better rede, 3030
Bot did him haly in þaire grace
And made þam surete in þat place,
Forto ʒeld þam ilka ʒere,
So þat he sold be hale and fere,
Threty maidens to trowage, 3035
And al sold be of hegh parage
And þe fairest of his land;
Herto held he up his hand.
þis ilk rent byhoves hym gyf,
Als lang als þe fendes lyf, 3040
Or til þai be in batayl tane,
Or els unto þai be al slane.
þan sal we pas al heþin quite,
þat here suffers al þis despite.
Bot herof es noght for speke; 3045
Es none in werld þat us mai wreke.
We wirk here silver, silk and golde,
Es none richer on þis molde,
And never þe better er we kled,
And in grete hunger er we sted; 3050
For al þat we wirk in þis stede,
We have noght half oure fil of brede;
For þe best þat sewes here any styk,
Takes bot foure penys in a wik,
And þat es litel wha som tase hede, 3055
Any of us to kleth and fede.
Ilkone of us withouten lesyng

3036 And *faded*   3037 And þ *faded*   3039 *After* rent *an erasure or*
an imperfection in the parchment

Might win ilk wike fourty shilling;
And ȝit, bot if we travail mare,
Oft þai bete us wonder-sare.   3060
It helpes noght to tel þis tale,
For þare bese never bote of oure bale.
Oure maste sorow, sen we bigan,
þat es þat we se mani a man,
Doghty dukes, yrels and barouns,   3065
Oft sithes slane with þir champiowns;
With þam to-morn bihoves þe fight.'
Sir Ywayn said, 'God, maste of myght,
Sal strenkith me in ilka dede
Ogains þa devils and al þaire drede;   3070
þat lord deliver ȝow of ȝowre fase.'
þus takes he leve and forth he gase.

Ch. 5347   He passed forth into þe hall,
þare fand he no man him to call;
No bewtese wald þai to him bede,   3075
Bot hastily þai toke his stede
And also þe maydens palfray,
War served wele with corn and hay,
For wele þai hoped þat Sir Ywayn
Sold never have had his stede ogayn.   3080
Thurgh þe hal Sir Ywain gase
Intil ane orcherd playn pase;
His maiden with him ledes he.
He fand a knyght under a tre,
Opon a clath of gold he lay;   3085
Byfor him sat a ful fayre may;
A lady sat with þam infere.
þe mayden red at þai myght here,
A real romance in þat place;
Bot I ne wote of wham it was.   3090
Sho was bot fiftene ȝeres alde;
þe knyght was lord of al þat halde,
And þat mayden was his ayre;
Sho was both gracious, gode and fare.

Ch. 5400   Sone, when þai saw Sir Ywaine,   3095
Smertly rase þai hym ogayne,
And by þe hand þe lord him tase,

And unto him grete myrth he mase.
He said, 'Sir, by swete Jhesus,
þou ert ful welcum until us.'   3100
f. 20ᵛ   þe mayden was bowsom and bayne
Forto unarme Syr Ywayne;
Serk and breke bath sho hym broght,
þat ful craftily war wroght
Of riche cloth soft als þe sylk   3105
And þarto white als any mylk.
Sho broght hym ful riche wedes to were,
Hose and shose and alkins gere.
Sho payned hir with al hir myght
To serve him and his mayden bright.   3110
Sone þai went unto sopere,
Ful really served þai were
With metes and drinkes of þe best,
And seþin war þai broght to rest.
In his chaumber by hym lay   3115
His owin lyoun and his may.

Ch. 5448   At morn, when it was dayes lyght,
Up þai rase and sone þam dyght.
Sir Ywayn and hys damysele
Went ful sone til a chapele,   3120
And þare þai herd a mes in haste
þat was sayd of þe haly gaste.
Efter mes ordand he has
Forth on his way fast forto pas;
At þe lord hys leve he tase,   3125
And grete thanking to him he mase.
þe lord said, 'Tak it to na greve,
To gang heþin ȝit getes þou na leve.
Herein es ane unsely law,
þat has bene used of ald daw   3130
And bus be done for frend or fa.
I sal do com byfor þe twa
Grete serjantes of mekil myght;
And, wheþer it be wrang or right,
þou most tak þe shelde and spere   3135

3127 þe: þ partly obliterated   3131 Between or and fa a letter is cancelled

Ogaynes þam þe forto were.
If þou overcum þam in þis stoure,
þan sal þou have al þis honoure
And my doghter in mariage
And also al myne heritage.'   3140
þan said Sir Ywayn, 'Als mot I the,
þi doghter sal þou have for me;
For a king or ane emparoure
May hir wed with grete honoure.'
þe lord said, 'Here sal cum na knyght,   3145
þat he ne sal with twa champions fight;
So sal þou do on al wise,
For it es knawen custum assise.'
Sir Ywaine said, 'Sen I sal so,
þan es þe best þat I may do   3150
To put me baldly in þaire hend
And tak þe grace þat God wil send.'

Ch. 5512   þe champions sone war forth broght.
Sir Ywain sais, 'By him me boght,
Ʒe seme wele þe devils sons,   3155
For I saw never swilk champions.'
Aiþer broght unto þe place
A mikel rownd talvace
And a klub ful grete and lang,
Thik fret with mani a thwang;   3160
On bodies armyd wele þai ware,
Bot þare hedes bath war bare.
þe lioun bremly on þam blist;
When he þam saw ful wele he wist
þat þai sold with his mayster fight;   3165
He thoght to help him at his myght;
With his tayl þe erth he dang,
For to fyght him thoght ful lang.
Of him a party had þai drede;
þai said, 'Syr knight, þou most nede   3170
Do þi lioun out of þis place
For to us makes he grete manace,
Or Ʒelde þe til us als creant.'

3148 kn of knawen *not clear*   3160 thawang *MS.; R.'s emendation*
3161 bodies: o *changed from* i

He said, 'þat war noght mine avenant.'
þai said, 'þan do þi beste oway, 3175
And als sone sal we samyn play.'
He said, 'Sirs, if ȝe be agast,
Takes þe beste and bindes him fast.'
þai said, 'He sal be bun or slane,
For help of him sal þou have nane; 3180
þi self allane sal with us fight,
For þat es custume and þe right.'
þan said Sir Ywain to þam sone:
'Whare wil ȝe þat þe best be done?'
'In a chamber he sal be loken 3185
With gude lokkcs ful stifly stoken.'
Sir Ywain led þan his lioun
Intil a chamber to presoun;
þan war bath þa devils ful balde,
When þe lioun was in halde. 3190

Ch. 5570
    Sir Ywayn toke his nobil wede
And dight him yn, for he had nede;
And on his nobil stede he strade,
And baldely to þam bath he rade.

f. 21
His mayden was ful sare adred, 3195
þat he was so straitly sted,
And unto God fast gan sho pray
Forto wyn him wele oway.
þan strake þai on him wonder-sare
With þaire clubbes þat ful strang ware; 3200
Opon his shelde so fast þai feld
þat never a pece with oþer held;
Wonder it es þat any man
Might bere þe strakes þat he toke þan.
Mister haved he of socoure, 3205
For he come never in swilk a stoure;
Bot manly evyr with al his mayn
And graithly hit he þam ogayn;
And als it telles in þe boke,
He gaf þe dubbil of þat he toke. 3210

Ch. 5594
    Ful grete sorow þe lioun has
In þe chameber whare he was;
And ever he thoght opon þat dede,

How he was helpid in his nede,
And he might now do na socowre   3215
To him þat helpid him in þat stoure;
Might he out of þe chamber breke,
Sone he walde his maister wreke.
He herd þaire strakes þat war ful sterin,
And ȝern he waytes in ilka heryn,   3220
And al was made ful fast to hald.
At þe last he come to þe thriswald;
þe erth þare kest he up ful sone,
Als fast als foure men sold have done
If þai had broght bath bill and spade;   3225
A mekil hole ful sone he made.
Yn al þis was Sir Ywayn
Ful straitly parred with mekil payn,
And drede he had, als him wele aght,
For nowþ[e]r of þam na woundes laght.   3230
Kepe þam cowth þai wonder-wele
þat dintes derid þam never a dele;
It was na wapen þat man might welde,
Might get a shever out of þaire shelde.
þarof cowth Ywayn no rede,   3235
Sare he douted to be ded;
And also his damysel
Ful mekil murny[n]g made omell,
And wele sho wend he sold be slane,
And, sertes, þan war hir socore gane.   3240
Bot fast he stighteld in þat stowre,
And hastily him come socowre.

Ch. 5627   Now es þe lioun outbroken,
His maister sal ful sone be wroken.
He rynnes fast with ful fell rese,   3245
þan helpid it noght to prai for pese;
He stirt unto þat a glotowne,
And to þe erth he brayd him downe.
þan was þare nane obout þat place,
þat þai ne war fayn of þat faire chace   3250
(þe maiden had grete joy in hert);

3230 nowþr MS.; R.'s emendation   3238 murnyg MS.   3243 A blue
initial capital

þai said, 'He sal never rise in quert.'
His felow fraisted with al his mayn
To raise him smertly up ogayn;
And right so als he stowped doun,   3255
Sir Ywain with his brand was boun,
And strake his nek-bane right insonder,
þareof þe folk had mekil wonder.
His hevid trindeld on þe sand;
þus had Ywain þe hegher hand.   3260

When he had feld þat fowl feloun,

Ch. 5659

Of his stede he lighted down.
His lioun on þat oþer lay;
Now wil he help him, if he may.
þe lioun saw his maister cum,   3265
And to hys part he wald have som.
þe right sholder oway he rase,
Both arm and klob with him he tase,
And so his maister gan he wreke;
And, als he might, ʒit gan he speke   3270
And said, 'Sir knight, for þi gentry,
I pray þe have of me mercy;
And by scill sal he mercy have,
What man so mekely wil it crave,
And þarfore grantes mercy to me.'   3275
Sir Ywain said, 'I grant it þe,
If þat þou wil þi selven say,
þat þou ert overcumen þis day.'
He said, 'I grant, withowten fail,
I am overcumen in þis batail   3280
For pure ataynt and recreant.'
Sir Ywayn said, 'Now I þe grant
Forto do þe na mare dere,
And fro my liown I sal þe were;
I grant þe pese at my powere.'   3285

Ch. 5694

þan come þe folk ful faire infere;
þe lord and þe lady als
þai toke him faire obout þe hals;

3260 had *added above the line, same hand*   3265 s *of* his *written over*
another letter

þai [saide], 'Sir, now saltou be
Lord and syre in þis cuntre,   3290
And wed oure doghter, for sertayn.'
Sir Ywain answerd þan ogayn;
He said, 'Sen ȝe gif me hir now,
I gif hir evyn ogayn to ȝow;
Of me forever I grant hir quite.   3295
Bot, sir, takes it til no despite;
For, sertes, whif may I none wed,
Until my nedes be better sped.
Bot þis thing, sir, I ask of þe,
þat al þir prisons may pas fre.   3300
God has granted me þis chance,
I have made þaire delyverance.'
þe lord answerd þan ful tyte
And said, 'I grant þe þam al quite.
My doghter als, I rede, þou take;   3305
Sho es noght worthi to forsake.'
Unto þe knyght Sir Ywain sais,
'Sir, I sal noght hir mysprays;
For sho es so curtays and hende,
þat fra hethin to þe werldes ende   3310
Es no king ne emparoure
Ne no man of so grete honowre,
þat he ne might wed þat bird bright;
And so wald I, if þat I myght.
I wald hir wed with ful gude chere,   3315
Bot, lo, I have a mayden here;
To folow hir now most I nede,
Wheder so sho wil me lede.
þarfore at þis time haves goday.'
He said, 'þou passes noght so oway.   3320
Sen þou wil noght do als I tell,
In my prison sal þou dwell.'
He said, 'If I lay þare al my live,
I sal hir never wed to wive;
For with þis maiden most I wend   3325
Until we cum whare sho wil lend.'
þe lord saw it was na bote

3289 saide *added above the line, another hand*

Obout þat mater more to mote.
He gaf him leve oway to fare,
Bot he had lever he had bene þare.   3330

Ch. 5771   Sir Ywayn takes þan forth infere
Al þe prisons þat þare were;
Bifore hym sone þai come ilkane,
Nerehand naked and wo-bigane;
Stil he hoved at þe ȝate,   3335
Til þai war went al forth þareate.
Twa and twa ay went þai samyn
And made omang þam mikel gamyn;
If God had cumen fra hevyn on hight
And on þis mold omang þam light,   3340
þai had noght made mare joy, sertain,
þan þai made to Syr Ywayne.
Folk of þe toun com him biforn
And blissed þe time þat he was born;
Of his prowes war þai wele payd: 3345
'In þis werld es none slike,' þai said.
þai cunvayd him out of þe toun
With ful faire processiowne.
þe maidens þan þaire leve has tane,
Ful mekil myrth þai made ilkane;   3350
At þaire departing prayed þai þus:
'Oure lord God, mighty Jhesus,
He help ȝow, sir, to have ȝowre will
And shilde ȝow ever fra alkyns ill.'
'Maidens,' he said, 'God mot ȝow se   3355
And bring ȝow wele whare ȝe wald be.'
þus þaire way forther þai went:
Na more unto þam wil we tent.

Ch. 5812   Sir Ywayn and his faire may
Al þe sevenight traveld þai.   3360
þe maiden knew þe way ful wele
Hame until þat ilk castele
Whare sho left þe seke may;
And þeder hastily come þai.
When þai come to þe castel-ȝate,   3365
Sho led Sir Ywain yn þareate.
      3331 _A red initial capital_

þe mayden was ȝit seke lyand;
Bot, when þai talde hir þis tithand,
þat cumen was hir messagere
And þe knyght with hyr infere,   3370
Swilk joy þareof sho had in hert,
Hir thoght þat sho was al in quert.
Sho said, 'I wate my sister will
Gif me now þat falles me till.'
In hir hert sho was ful light;   3375
Ful hendly hailsed sho þe knight:
'A, sir,' sho said, 'God do þe mede,
þat þou wald cum in swilk a nede';
And al þat in þat kastel were
Welkumd him with meri chere.   3380
I can noght say, so God me glade,
Half þe myrth þat þai him made.

f. 22   þat night he had ful nobil rest
With alkins esement of þe best.
Als sone als þe day was sent,   3385
þai ordaind þam and forth þai went.

Ch. 5842   Until þat town fast gan þai ride
Whare þe kyng sojorned þat tide;
And þare þe elder sister lay,
Redy forto kepe hyr day.   3390
Sho traisted wele on Sir Gawayn,
þat no knyght sold cum him ogayn;
Sho hopid þare was no knyght lifand,
In batail þat might with him stand.
Al a sevenight dayes bidene   3395
Wald noght Sir Gawayn be sene,
Bot in ane oþer toun he lay;
For he wald cum at þe day
Als aventerous into þe place,
So þat no man sold se his face;   3400
þe armes he bare war noght his awyn,
For he wald noght in court be knawyn.

Ch. 5862   Syr Y[w]ayn and his damysell
In þe town toke þaire hostell;

3389 þe: þ *written over an e*   3390 forto: r *obscure*   3403 Ywayn:
w *added above the line by another hand*

And þare he held him prevely,   3405
So þat none sold him ascry.
Had þai dwelt langer by a day,
þan had sho lorn hir land for ay.
Sir Ywain rested þare þat nyght,
And on þe morn he gan hym dyght;   3410
On slepe left þai his lyowne
And wan þam wightly out of toun.
It was hir wil and als hys awyn
At cum to court als knyght unknawyn.

Ch. 5872   Sone obout þe prime of day   3415
Sir Gawayn fra þeþin þare he lay,
Hies him fast into þe felde
Wele armyd with spere and shelde;
No man knew him, les ne more,
Bot sho þat he sold fight fore.   3420
þe elder sister to court come
Unto þe king at ask hir dome;
Sho said, 'I am cumen with my knyght
Al redy to defend my right.
þis day was us set sesowne,   3425
And I am here al redy bowne;
And sen þis es þe last day,
Gifes dome and lates us wend oure way.
My sister has al sydes soght,
Bot, wele I wate, here cums sho noght;   3430
For, sertainly, sho findes nane,
þat dar þe batail undertane
þis day for hir forto fyght
Forto reve fra me my right.
Now have I wele wonnen my land   3435
Withowten dint of knightes hand;
What so my sister ever has mynt,
Al hir part now tel I tynt;
Al es myne to sell and gyf,
Als a wreche ay sal sho lyf.   3440
þarfore, Sir King, sen it es swa,
Gifes ȝowre dome and lat us ga.'

Ch. 5909   þe king said, 'Maiden, think noght lang.'
                3443 *A blue initial capital*

(Wele he wist sho had þe wrang.)
'Damysel, it es þe assyse,   3445
Whils sityng es of þe justise,
þe dome nedes þou most habide;
For par aventure it may bityde,
þi sister sal cum al bi tyme,
For it es litil passed prime.'   3450
When þe king had tald þis scill,
þai saw cum rideand over a hyll
þe ȝonger sister and hir knyght;
þe way to town þai toke ful right.
On Ywains bed his liown lay,   3455
And þai had stollen fra him oway.
þe elder maiden made il chere,
When þai to court cumen were.
þe king withdrogh his jugement,
For wele he trowed in his entent   3460
þat þe ȝonger sister had þe right,
And þat sho sold cum with sum knyght;
Himself knew hyr wele inogh.
When he hir saw, ful fast he logh;
Him liked it wele in his hert,   3465
þat he saw hir so in quert.

Ch. 5942

   Into þe court sho toke þe way,
And to þe king þus gan sho say,
'God þat governs alkin thing,
þe save and se, Syr Arthure þe Kyng,   3470
And al þe knyghtes þat langes to þe,
And also al þi mery menȝe.
Unto ȝowre court, sir, have I broght
An unkouth knyght þat ȝe knaw noght;
He sais þat sothly for my sake   3475
þis batayl wil he undertake;

f. 22ᵛ

And he haves ȝit in oþer land
Ful felle dedes under hand;
Bot al he leves, God do him mede,
Forto help me in my nede.'   3480
Hir [elder] sister stode hyr by,

3481 elder: *MS. has* ȝonger *written by a later hand on an erasure. R.'s emendation. Schl. sees the vestige of an* l *of an original* elder

And tyl hyr sayd sho hastily,
'For hys luf þat lens us life,
Gif me my right withouten strife,
And lat no men þarfore be slayn.'   3485
þe elder sister sayd ogayn:
'þi right es noght, for al es myne,
And I wil have yt mawgre þine.
þarfore, if þou preche al day,
Here sal þou nothing bere oway.'   3490
þe ȝonger mayden to hir says,
'Sister, þou ert ful curtays,
And gret dole es it forto se,
Slike two knightes al[s] þai be,
For us sal put þamself to spill.   3495
þarefore now, if it be þi will,
Of þi gude wil me þou gif
Sumthing þat I may on lif.'

Ch. 5976   þe elder said, 'So mot I the,
Who so es ferd, I rede þai fle.   3500
þou getes right noght, withowten fail,
Bot if þou win yt thurgh batail.'
þe ȝonger said, 'Sen þou wil swa,
To þe grace of God here I me ta;
And lord als he es maste of myght,   3505
He send his socore to þat knyght
þat þus in dede of charite
þis day antres hys lif for me.'

Ch. 5991   þe twa knightes come bifor þe king
And þare was sone ful grete gedering;   3510
For ilka man þat walk might,
Hasted sone to se þat syght.
Of þam þis was a selly case,
þat nowþer wist what oþer wase;
Ful grete luf was bitwix þam twa,   3515
And now er aiþer oþer fa;
Ne þe king kowth þam noght knaw,
For þai wald noght þaire faces shew.
If owþer of þam had oþer sene,

3490 nothing: *Schl. has* no thing   3494 als: al *MS.*; *R.'s emendation*
3498 lif *is obscured by a spot*

Grete luf had bene þam bitwene;   3520
Now was þis a grete selly
þat trew luf and so grete envy,
Als bitwix þam twa was þan,
Might bath at anes be in a man.
þe knightes for þase maidens love   3525
Aiþer til oþer kast a glove,
And wele armed with spere and shelde
þai riden both forth to þe felde;
þai stroke þaire stedes þat war kene;
Litel luf was þam bitwene.   3530
Ful grevosly bigan þat gamyn,
With stalworth speres strake þai samen;
And þai had anes togeder spoken,
Had þare bene no speres broken;
Bot in þat time bitid it swa,   3535
þat aiþer of þam wald oþer sla.
þai drow swerdes and swang obout,
To dele dyntes had þai no dout.
þaire sheldes war shiferd and helms rifen,
Ful stalworth strakes war þare gifen.   3540
Bath on bak and brestes þare
War bath wounded wonder-sare;
In many stedes might men ken
þe blode out of þaire bodies ren.
On helmes þai gaf slike strakes kene   3545
þat þe riche stanes al bidene
And oþer gere þat was ful gude,
Was overcoverd al in blode.
þaire helmes war evel brusten bath,
And þai also war wonder-wrath.   3550
þaire hauberkes als war al totorn
Both bihind and als byforn;
þaire sheldes lay sheverd on þe ground.
þai rest þan a litil stound
Forto tak þaire ande þam till,   3555
And þat was with þaire boþer will.
Bot ful lang rested þai noght,
Til aiþer of þam on oþer soght;

3525 maidens: *Schl. reads* maydens   3551 *Schl. extends to* hauberkis

A stronge stowre was þam bitwene,
Harder had men never sene.   3560
þe king and oþer þat þare ware,
Said þat þai saw never are
So nobil knightes in no place
So lang fight bot by Goddes grace.
Barons, knightes, squiers and knaves   3565
Said, 'It es no man þat haves
So mekil tresore ne nobillay,
þat might þam quite þaire dede þis day.'
þir wordes herd þe knyghtes twa,
It made þam forto be more thra.   3570

Knightes went obout gude wane
To mak þe two sisters at ane:
Bot þe elder was so unkinde,
In hir þai might no mercy finde;
And þe right þat þe ȝonger hase,   3575
Puttes sho in þe kinges grace.
þe king himself and als þe quene
And oþer knightes al bidene
And al þat saw þat dede þat day,
Held al with þe ȝonger may;   3580
And to þe king al þai bisoght,
Wheþer þe elder wald or noght,
þat he sold evin þe landes dele
And gif þe ȝonger damysele
þe half or els sum porciowne,   3585
þat sho mai have to warisowne,
And part þe two knightes intwyn.
'For, sertis,' þai said, 'it war grete syn,
þat owþer of þam sold oþer sla,
For in þe werld es noght swilk twa.   3590
When oþer knightes,' said þai, 'sold sese,
þamself wald noght asent to pese.'
Al þat ever saw þat batayl,
Of þaire might had grete mervayl;
þai saw never under þe hevyn   3595
Twa knightes þat war copled so evyn.

3571 *A red initial letter*   3589 þat: a *indistinct*   owþer: w *seems to be written*
over another letter

Of al þe folk was none so wise,
þat wist wheþer sold have þe prise;
For þai saw never so stalworth stoure,
Ful dere boght þai þat honowre.   3600
Grete wonder had Sir Gawayn,
What he was þat faght him ogain;
And Sir Ywain had grete ferly,
Wha stode ogaynes him so stifly.
On þis wise lasted þat fight   3605
Fra midmorn unto mirk night;
And by þat tyme, I trow, þai twa
War ful weri and sare alswa.
þai had bled so mekil blode,
It was grete ferly þat þai stode;   3610
So sare þai bet on bak and brest,
Until þe sun was gone to rest;
For nowþer of þam wald oþer spare.
For mirk might þai þan na mare,
þarfore to rest þai both þam ȝelde.   3615

Ch. 6215   Bot or þai past out of þe felde,
Bitwix þam two might men se
Both mekil joy and grete pete.
By speche might no man Gawain knaw,
So was he hase and spak ful law;   3620
And mekil was he out of maght
For þe strakes þat he had laght;
And Sir Ywain was ful wery,
Bot þus he spekes and sais in hy;
He said, 'Syr, sen us failes light,   3625
I hope it be no lifand wight,
þat wil us blame if þat we twin.
For of al stedes I have bene yn,
With no man ȝit never I met
þat so wele kowth his strakes set;   3630
So nobil strakes has þou gifen
þat my sheld es al toreven.'
      Sir Gawayn said, 'Sir, sertanly,
þou ert noght so weri als I;

3616 Bot: B *unclear*   3633 Gawayn: w *written over another letter, same hand*
3634 noght: g *written over another letter, same hand*

For if we langer fightand were, 3635
I trow I might do þe no dere.
þou ert nothing in my det
Of strakes þat I on þe set.'
Sir Ywain said, 'In Cristes name,
Sai me what þou hat at hame.' 3640
He said, 'Sen þou my name wil here
And covaites to wit what it were,
My name in þis land mani wote;
I hat Gawayn, þe King son Lote.'
þan was Sir Ywayn sore agast; 3645
His swerde fra him he kast.
He ferd right als he wald wede,
And sone he stirt down of his stede.
He said, 'Here es a fowl mischance
For defaut of conisance. 3650
A, sir,' he said, 'had I þe sene,
þan had here no batel bene;
I had me ȝolden to þe als tite,
Als worthi war for descumfite.'
'What man ertou?' said Sir Gawain. 3655
'Syr,' he sayd, 'I hat Ywayne,
þat lufes þe more by se and sand
þan any man þat es lifand,
For mani dedes þat þou me did,
And curtaysi ȝe have me kyd. 3660
þarfore, sir, now in þis stoure
I sal do þe þis honowre:
I grant þat þou has me overcumen
And by strenkyth in batayl nomen.'
Sir Gawayn answerd als curtays: 3665
'þou sal noght do, sir, als þou sais;
þis honowre sal noght be myne,
Bot, sertes, it aw wele at be þine;
I gif it þe here withowten hone
And grantes þat I am undone.' 3670
Sone þai light, so sais þe boke,
And aiþer oþer in armes toke

f. 23ᵛ

3640 hat over an erasure   3642 what: except for the very end of the cross-
stroke, the t is obliterated   3670 grantes: nt obliterated by spot on MS.

And kissed so ful fele sithe;
þan war þai both glad and blithe.
In armes so þai stode togeder,   3675
Unto þe king com ridand þeder;
And fast he covait forto here
Of þir knightes what þai were,
And whi þai made so mekil gamyn,
Sen þai had so foghten samyn.   3680
Ful hendli þan asked þe king,
Wha had so sone made saghteling
Bitwix þam þat had bene so wrath
And aiþer haved done oþer scath.
He said, 'I wend ʒe wald ful fain   3685
Aiþer of ʒow have oþer slayn,
And now ʒe er so frendes dere.'
'Sir King,' said Gawain, 'ʒe sal here.
For unknawing and hard grace
þus have we foghten in þis place;   3690
I am Gawayn, ʒowre awin nevow,
And Sir Ywayn faght with me now.
When we war nere weri, iwys,
Mi name he frayned and I his;
When we war knawin, sone gan we sese.   3695
Bot, sertes, sir, þis es no lese,
Had we foghten forth a stownde,
I wote wele I had gone to grounde;
By his prowes and his mayne,
I wate, for soth, I had bene slayne.'   3700
þir wordes menged al þe mode
Of Sir Ywain als he stode;
'Sir,' he said, 'so mot I go,
ʒe kn[a]w ʒowre self it es noght so.
Sir King,' he said, 'withowten fail,   3705
I am overcumen in þis batayl.'
'Nai, sertes,' said Gawain, 'bot am I.'
þus nowþer wald have þe maistri,
Bifore þe king gan aiþer grant,
þat himself was recreant.   3710
þan þe king and hys menʒe

3681 *A blue initial capital*   3704 knaw: knw *MS.; R.'s emendation*

Had bath joy and grete pete;
He was ful fayn þai frendes were,
And þat þai ware so funden infere.

Ch. 6372 þe kyng said, 'Now es wele sene 3715
þat mekil luf was ȝow bitwene.'
He said, 'Sir Ywain, welkum home!'
For it was lang sen he þare come.
He said, 'I rede ȝe both assent
To do ȝow in my jujement; 3720
And I sal mak so gude ane ende
þat ȝe sal both be halden hende.'
þai both assented sone þartill
To do þam in þe kynges will,
If þe maydens wald do so. 3725
þan þe king bad knyghtes two
Wend efter þe maydens bath,
And so þai did ful swith rath.

Ch. 6384 Bifore þe kyng when þai war broght,
He tald unto þam als him thoght, 3730
'Lystens me now, maydens hende,
ȝowre grete debate es broght til ende;
So fer forth now es it dreven
þat þe dome most nedes be gifen,
And I sal deme ȝow als I can.' 3735
þe elder sister answerd þan:
'Sen ȝe er king þat us sold were,
I pray ȝow do to me na dere.'
He said, 'I wil let for na saw
Forto do þe landes law. 3740
þi ȝong sister sal have hir right,
For I se wele þat þi knyght
Es overcumen in þis were.'
þus said he anely hir to fere,
And for he wist hir wil ful wele, 3745
þat sho wald part with never a dele.
'Sir,' sho said, 'sen þus es gane,
Now most I wheþer I wil or nane,
Al ȝowre cumandment fufill,
And þarfore dose right als ȝe will.' 3750
þe king said, 'þus sal it fall,

Al ȝowre landes depart I sall.
Þi wil es wrang, þat have I knawin;
Now sal þou have noght bot þin awin,
Þat es þe half of al bydene.'   3755
Þan answerd sho ful tite in tene
And said, 'Me think ful grete outrage
To gif hir half myne heritage.'

f. 24   Þe king said, 'For ȝowre bother esse
In hir land I sal hir sese,   3760
And sho sal hald hir land of þe
And to þe þarfore mak fewte;
Sho sal þe luf als hir lady,
And þou sal kith þi curtaysi,
Luf hir efter þine avenant,   3765
And sho sal be to þe tenant.'
Þis land was first, I understand,
Þat ever was parted in Ingland.
Þan said þe king, withow[t]en fail,
For þe luf of þat batayl   3770
Al sisters þat sold efter bene
Sold part þe landes þam bitwene.

Ch. 6447   Þan said þe king to Sir Gawain,
And als he prayed Sir Ywain
Forto unlace þaire riche wede;   3775
And þarto had þai bath grete nede.
Als þai þusgate stod and spak,
Þe lyown out of þe chamber brak.
Als þai þaire armurs sold unlace,
Come he rinand to þat place.   3780
Bot he had, or he come þare,
Soght his mayster whideware;
And ful mekil joy he made
When he his mayster funden hade.
On ilka side þan might men se,   3785
Þe folk fast to toun gan fle;
So war þai ferd for þe liowne
Whan þai saw him þeder bown.
Syr Ywain bad þam cum ogayn

3769 withowten: *second t added above the line, another hand*
initial capital   3789 Syr: y *changed from* a, *same hand*   3773 *A red*

And said, 'Lordinges, for sertayn,   3790
Fra þis beste I sal ȝow were,
So þat he sal do ȝow no dere;
And, sirs, ȝe sal wele trow mi sawes;
We er frendes and gude felaws.
He es mine and I am his;   3795
For na tresore I wald him mys.'

Ch. 6469   When þai saw þis was sertain,
þan spak þai al of Sir Ywaine,
'þis es þe knight with þe liown,
þat es halden of so grete renown.   3800
þis ilk knight þe geant slogh;
Of dedis he es doghty inogh.'
þan said Sir Gawayn sone in hi,
'Me es bitid grete velani;
I cri þe mercy, Sir Ywayne,   3805
þat I have trispast þe ogayn.
þou helped mi syster in hir nede;
Evil have I quit þe now þi mede.
þou anterd þi life for luf of me;
And als mi sister tald of þe,   3810
þou said þat we ful fele dawes
Had bene frendes and gude fel[a]wes.
Bot wha it was ne wist I noght
Sethen have I had ful mekil thoght,
And ȝit for al þat I do can,   3815
I cowth never here of na man,
þat me cowth tell in toure ne town
Of þe knight with þe liown.'

Ch. 6493   When þai had unlaced þaire wede,
Al þe folk toke ful gode hede,   3820
How þat beste his bales to bete
Likked his maister both hend and fete.
Al þe men grete mervail hade
Of þe mirth þe lyown made.
When þe knightes war broght to rest,   3825
þe king gert cum sone of ɼe best
Surgiens þat [e]ver war sene

3812 felawes: a *changed from* o *by another hand, undoubtedly because of rhyme*
3827 ever: over *MS.*; *Schl. reads* over *and emends to* ever

Forto hele þam both bidene.
    Sone so þai war hale and sownd,
Sir Ywayn hies him fast to found.   3830
Luf was so in his hert fest,
Night ne day haved he no rest;
Bot he get grace of his lady,
He most go wode or for luf dy.
Ful preveli forth gan he wende   3835
Out of þe court fra ilka frende.
He rides right unto þe well,
And þare he thinkes forto dwell.
His gode lyon went with him ay,
He wald noght part fro him oway.   3840
He kest water opon þe stane:
þe storm rase ful sone onane,
þe thoner grisely gan outbrest;
Him thoght als al þe grete forest
And al þat was obout þe well   3845
Sold have sonken into hell.

    þe lady was in mekyl dout,
For al þe kastel walles obout
Quoke so fast þat men might think
þat al into þe erth sold synk;   3850
þai trembled fast, both boure and hall,
Als þai unto þe grund sold fall.

Was never in þis mydlerde
In no kastell folk so ferde.
Bot wha it was wele wist Lunet;   3855
Sho said, 'Now er we hard byset;
Madame, I ne wate what us es best,
For here now may we have no rest.
Ful wele I wate ȝe have no knight,
þat dar wende to ȝowre wel and fight   3860
With him þat cumes ȝow to asaile;
And, if he have here no batayle
Ne findes none ȝow to defend,
ȝowre lose bese lorn withouten end.'
þe lady said sho wald be dede;   3865
'Dere Lunet, what es þi rede?
Wirk I wil by þi kounsail,

For I ne wate noght what mai avail.'
'Madame,' sho said, 'I wald ful fayn
Kownsail ȝow if it might gayn.   3870
Bot in þis case it war mystere
To have a wiser kownsaylere.'
And by desait þan gan sho say,
'Madame, par chance þis ilk day
Sum of ȝowre knightes mai cum hame   3875
And ȝow defend of al þis shame.'
'A,' sho said, 'Lunet, lat be;
Speke na more of my menȝe;
For wele I wate, so God me mend,
I have na knight me mai defend.   3880
þarfore my kownsail bus þe be,
And I wil wirk al efter þe,
And þarfore help at al þi myght.'
'Madame,' sho said, 'had we þat knyght,
þat es so curtais and avenant   3885
And has slane þe grete geant,
And als þat þe thre knightes slogh,
Of him ȝe myght be trist inogh.
Bot forþermar, madame, I wate,
He and his lady er at debate   3890
And has bene so ful many day;
And als I herd hym selvyn say,
He wald bileve with no lady
Bot on þis kownand utterly,
þat þai wald mak sertayn ath   3895
To do þaire might and kunyng bath
Trewly both by day and naght
To mak him and hys lady saght.'
Ch. 6615   þe lady answerd sone hir tyll,
'þat wil I do with ful gode will;   3900
Unto þe here mi trowth I plight
þat I sal þarto do mi might.'
Sho said, 'Mada[m]e, be ȝe noght wrath,
I most nedes have of ȝow an ath,
So þat I mai be sertayn.'   3905
þe lady said, 'þat will I fayn.'

3874 chance: h *changed from* b   3903 Madane *MS.; R.'s emendation*

Lunet þan riche relikes toke,
Þe chalis and þe mes-boke;
On knese þe lady down hir set
(Wit ȝe wele, þan liked Lunet),   3910
Hir hand opon þe boke sho laid,
And Lunet alþus to hir said,
'Madame,' sho said, 'þou salt sw[e]re here
Þat þou sal do þi powere
Both dai and night opon al wise   3915
Withouten a[ni]kyns fayntise
To saghtel þe knyght with þe liown
And his lady of grete renowne,
So þat no faut be funden in þe.'
Sho said, 'I grant, it sal so be.'   ·   3920
Þan was Lunet wele paid of þis;
Þe boke sho gert hir lady kys.

Ch. 6659   Sone a palfray sho bistrade,
And on hir way fast forth sho rade;
Þe next way ful sone sho nome,   3925
Until sho to þe well come.
Sir Ywain sat under þe thorn,
And his lyoun lay him byforn.
Sho knew him wele by his lioun,
And hastily sho lighted downe;   3930
And als sone als he Lunet sagh,
In his hert þan list him lagh.
Mekil mirth was when þai met,
Aiþer oþer ful faire has gret.
Sho said, 'I love grete God in trone   3935
Þat I have ȝow fun so sone,
And tiþandes tel I ȝow biforn;
Oþer sal my lady be manesworn
On relikes and bi bokes brade,
Or els ȝe twa er frendes made.'   3940
Sir Ywain þan was wonder-glad
For þe tiþandes þat he had;

3912 alþus MS.; R. reads alyns and emends to alkyns   3913 swere here
over an erasure; the first e of swere is added above the line by another hand
3916 akyns MS.; R. emends to alkyns   3931 saght MS.; R.'s emendation
3937 Schl. reads now   3941 A blue initial capital

He thanked hir ful fele sith
þat sho wald him slike gudenes kith,
And sho him thanked mekill mare   3945
For þe dedes þat war done are.

So aþer was in oþer det,
þat both þaire travail was wele set.
He sais, 'Talde þou hir oght my name?'
Sho said, 'Nay, þan war I to blame;   3950
þi name sho sal noght wit for me,
Til ȝe have kyssed and saghteld be.'

Þan rade þai forth toward þe town,
And with þam ran þe gude lyoun.
When þai come to þe castel-ȝate,   3955
Al went þai in þareat.
þai spak na word to na man born
Of al þe folk þai fand byforn.
Als sone so þe lady herd sayn,
Hir damisel was cumen ogayn   3960
And als þe liown and þe knight,
þan in hert sho was ful lyght;
Scho covait ever of al thing
Of him to have knawlageing.
Sir Ywain sone on knese him set,   3965
When he with þe lady met.
Lunet said to þe lady sone,
'Take up þe knight, madame, have done!
And, als covenand bituix us was,
Makes his pese fast or he pas.'   3970
þan did þe ladi him up rise;
'Sir,' sho said, 'opon al wise,
I wil me pain in al thing
Forto mak þi saghtelyng
Bitwix þe and þi lady bryght.'   3975
'Medame,' said Lunet, 'þat es right,
For nane bot ȝe has þat powere.
Al þe soth now sal ȝe here.
Madame,' sho said, 'es noght at layn,
þis es my lord Sir Ywaine.   3980

3953 *A red initial capital*   3963 *Schl. reads* sho *erroneously*

Swilk luf God bitwix ȝow send,
þat may last to ȝowre lives end.'

Ch. 6759
   þan went þe lady fer obak,
And lang sho stode or þat sho spak.
Sho said, 'How es þis, damysele?   3985
I wend þou sold be to me lele,
þat makes me, whether I wil or noght,
Luf þam þat me wa has wroght,
So þat me bus be forsworn
Or luf þam þat wald I war lorn.   3990
Bot, wheþer it torn to wele or ill,
þat I have said, I sal fulfill.'
Wit ȝe wele, þan Sir Ywaine
Of þa wordes was ful fayne.
'Madame,' he said, 'I have miswroght,   3995
And þat I have ful dere boght.
Grete foly I did, þe soth to say,
When þat I past my terme-day;
And, sertes, wha so had so bityd,
þai sold have done right als I dyd.   4000
Bot I sal never thorgh Goddes grace
At mi might do more trispase;
And what man so wil mercy crave,
By Goddes law he sal it have.'
þan sho asented saghteling to mak;   4005
And sone in arms he gan hir tak
And kissed hir ful oft sith:
Was he never are so blith.

Ch. 6799
   Now has Sir Ywain ending made
Of al þe sorows þat he hade.   4010
Ful lely lufed he ever hys whyfe
And sho him als hyr owin life;
þat lasted to þaire lives ende.
And trew Lunet, þe maiden hende,
Was honord ever with ald and ȝing   4015
And lifed at hir owin likyng;
Of alkins thing sho has maystri
Next þe lord and þe lady;

3995 misworoght *MS.*; *a dot over the first* o   4009 *A blue initial capital*

Al honord hir in toure and toun.
þus þe knyght with þe liown   4020
Es turned now to Syr Ywayn
And has his lordship al ogayn;
And so Sir Ywain and his wive
In joy and blis þai led þaire live.
So did Lunet and þe liown   4025
Until þat ded haves dreven þam down.
Of þam na mare have I herd tell
Nowþer in rumance ne in spell.
Bot Jhesu Criste for his grete grace
In hevyn-blis grante us a place   4030
To bide in, if his wills be.
Amen, amen, par charite.

4029 jhu *MS.*; *over the* h *a short mark of contraction*   Below 4032 *Added
in red ink and in the same hand are the lines*: Ywain and Gawayn þus makes
endyng, / God grant us al hys dere blyssing. Amen.

COMMENTARY

THE notes which follow call attention to rare or interesting constructions, attempt to illuminate difficult passages, and provide what literary and historical background is necessary for an understanding of the text. The more controversial emendations are justified, and the suggestions of previous editors and commentators are noticed, even when we have chosen to reject them. Divergences from the French source are only sporadically noted since these have been systematically treated in Section III of the Introduction. For the abbreviations used in the references, see ABBREVIATIONS, pp. lviii–lx.

Title. The poem is referred to as *Ywain and Gawain* three times, once in the rubric at the beginning of the poem, once in the rubric at the end, and once in l. 4: . . . *þat herkens Ywayne and Gawayne.* The rubrics are undoubtedly the work of the scribe, but the internal reference indicates that this was also the poet's title. Although Ywain son of King Urien was by no means an obscure knight, his reputation never had the lustre of a Gawain or a Lancelot. It is perhaps for this reason that the poet and scribe sought to help the popularity of the work by attaching to it the name of Sir Gawain, an especial favourite of the northern English romancers.

For the second name of the title Ritson read *Gawin* and Schleich *Ga-w[a]in.* The manuscript reading, however, is *Gawain,* the second *a* being the flat open superior *a* not uncommon in manuscripts of this date. The same superior form of *a* is used in *þat* 3742. *Gawain* or *Gawayn(e)* is the usual spelling in the body of the romance, the first form occurring five times, the second form thirty-five times, and the closing rubric also has *Gawayn.*

Title. Ywain is the historic Owein, son of Urien (Owain ap Uryen), a British king or prince of Rheged, a territory generally considered to be somewhere in northern England or southern Scotland. It was King Urien who led a successful confederation against the sons of Ida, kings of Northumbria, in the latter part of the sixth century. According to the *Historia Brittonum* of Nennius (F. Lot, *Nennius et l'Historia Brittonum* [Paris, 1934], pp. 71–75, 202, 224) Urien later drove the Angles under King Deodric to take refuge in what is now called Lindisfarne. It was on this campaign that he was killed because of the jealousy of Morgan, one of his confederates. When Urien fell, his men carried away his head lest it be dishonoured by his enemies, and this circumstance furnishes the subject for a lament on Urien by his kinsman, the Welsh bard Llywarch Hên. Later in the same poem we learn that Owein son of Urien and his brother Pasgen continued the struggle, and that finally they were killed, leaving the court of Rheged in desolation. On this poem see Ifor Williams, 'The Poems of Llywarch Hên', *Proc. Brit. Acad.* xviii

(1932), 289–93. The reputation of Owein and his equally famous father Urien continued to grow among the Britons, and the glorious details of their exploits became the subject of songs, stories, and legends, the most famous of which are the songs of the great early bard Taliesin.

Ywain, then, like Arthur and Tristram, was an historical personage whose outlines may still be faintly perceived. As Loomis has pointed out (*Arth. Trad.*, p. 269), it is a chronological blunder to connect Owein with the exploits of Arthur, who must have lived almost a hundred years earlier. In retrospect, however, it seems almost inevitable that Owein, son of a famous king and celebrated among the Britons for his valour, should eventually become associated in the popular imagination with the legendary Arthur, symbol of Celtic military glory. At any rate he appears as Eventus in the *Historia* of Geoffrey of Monmouth where he is said to have inherited the kingdom of his uncle Anguselus *rex Albaniae* and to have performed many famous exploits in the wars between the petty principalities of the north of England.

In a Welsh triad Owein is represented as the son of Urien by Modron, daughter of Avallach. This Modron Loomis identifies (*Arth. Trad.*, pp. 93, 269–73) as Morgain la Fée, who is also the daughter of Avaloc or Avallo, and who frequently appears in romances (though not explicitly in *YG*) as the mother of Owein by the mortal King Urien. Since Morgain is also the sister of Arthur, this would make Owein the nephew of the King. He is not, however, identified as such in either Chrétien or *YG*. Owein also appears in the twelfth-century *Life of St. Kentigern* where the anonymous Scots author tells the undoubtedly apocryphal story how Ewen, the son of King Urien, ravished the stepdaughter of Leudonus, King of Leudonia (Lothian), and got upon her a son who became St. Kentigern (*Lives of St. Ninian and St. Kentigern*, ed. A. P. Forbes [Edinburgh, 1874], pp. 245–7).

In addition to 'Yvain li filz au roi Uriien', who frequently appears in French romances with the title *messire*, indicating royal descent, there are, according to Ernst Brugger, at least sixteen other personages who bear the name Yvain—a fact which is probably explained by the popularity of the name in the British languages (Welsh Owein, Breton Ivan(us), Irish Eogan). (See E. Brugger, 'Ywain and his Lion', *MP*. xxxviii [1941], 267–87). Of these sixteen knights one, 'Yvain li Avoutres [the Bastard], qui estoit fiex au roy vrien de la feme son seneschal' (Vulgate *Merlin*, ed. H. O. Sommer, ii. 165), is identified by Loomis (*Arth. Trad.*, p. 270) with the legitimate *filz au roi Uriien*, who is described none the less as born out of wedlock in an ancient account which has come down through a Welsh tale of the sixteenth century. On the occurrences of the name Ywain and variants in the romances, see R. W. Ackerman, 'An Index of the Arthurian Names in Middle English', *Stanford Univ. Publ. in Lang. and Lit.* x (1952).

Between the Welsh name Owein and the English form Ywain, the critical development took place in Armoric Britain, where we find the Breton equivalent Ivan recorded as early as the eleventh century in the latinized forms Ivani and Ivanus (Hyacinthe Morice, *Mémoires pour servir de preuves à l'histoire ecclésiastique et civile de Bretagne* [Paris, 1742–46], i. 457, 469). The Breton Ivan became OF. Ivain, quite possibly, as Loomis has suggested (*Arth. Trad.*, p. 273), by contagion from Gauvain. This in turn became Iwain when turned into English, once again undoubtedly on the model of Gawain. The ending *-wain*, typical of many Celtic names, can be traced to the Primitive Celtic ending *-*ganios*. Thus Welsh Owein is derived from the ancient form Esuganios, which is preserved in a Gallo-Roman inscription Esugen(ius). (See *Sir Gawain and the Green Knight*, ed. J. R. R. Tolkien and E. V. Gordon [Oxford, 1925], p. 83.)

Title. Gawain, the most celebrated of Arthur's knights, was traditionally the son of Loth, king of Lothian, and Arthur's half-sister Anna. He was originally the very model of the medieval ideal of courtesy, but as B. J. Whiting has demonstrated (*Mediaeval Studies*, ix [1947], 189 ff.), the history of Gawain's reputation in the French romances is a study in epic degeneration. In *YG* the role of Gawain is subsidiary to that of his 'cousin' Ywain. It is Ywain who is the hero of the romance, but it is against Gawain, the model of chivalry, that he finally must measure his military prowess. To fight to a draw with Gawain is the highest distinction possible for a knight, and it is clear that both Chrétien and the English author considered Ywain's ability to match Gawain in combat the climactic point of the romance. In all other respects Gawain appears here in his traditional role.

1. *Almyghti God þat made mankyn.* This prayer does not occur in Chrétien and is the addition of E. Such an invocation (frequently *Jhesu, lorde,* &c.) was conventional at the beginning of English minstrel romances and was often echoed at the close. See ll. 4029–32 and *Erle of Toulous* 1–6, 1222–4; *Emaré* 1–6, 1033–5; *Amis and Amiloun* 1–2; *Avowing of Arthur* 1–8, 1145–8; *Sir Gowther* 1–6, 25–27, 754–6; *Morte Arthure* 1–11; *Isumbras* 1–3, 793–4; *Guy of Warwick* 11973–6; *Sir Degrevant* 1–8, 1917–20. For similar invocations, see Carleton Brown and R. H. Robbins, *The Index of Middle English Verse* (New York, 1943), pp. 39–43. In *Emaré* 13–18, 'menstralles' are enjoined that they 'Sholde, at her bygynnyng, / Speke of þat ryghtwes Kyng / That made bothe see and sonde'.

2. Besides *out of, fra* (3354) is used with *schilde.*

16. In the *Roman de Lancelot* it is stated that Arthur held court and wore his crown five times a year, at Easter, Ascension Day, Pentecost, All Saints, and Christmas. Of these festivals Pentecost, coming as it does at the beginning of the summer, was the most joyful. The ceremony of wearing the crown on high feast days seems to have been some sort of minor coronation. According to the *Anglo-Saxon Chronicle* (i. 219–20) William the Conqueror wore his crown three times a year—at Christmas, Easter, and Pentecost—and the decline of England during the reign of Stephen was attributed to his failure to follow this custom. See *Perlesvaus*, ed. W. A. Nitze (Chicago, 1937), ii. 203 f., n. to l. 70.

17. In Chrétien this line reads (Ch. 7): *La corz fu a Carduel an Gales,* which E takes to be incorrect geography and emends to *At Kerdyf þat es in*

Wales. Chrétien is referring, of course, to modern Carlisle in Cumberland—'Cardeol' for Carlisle is found in the *Anglo-Saxon Chronicle* (E) in the annal for 1092 and 'Carduill' is common up to the fifteenth century (the *d* being a dissimilated *l*). In placing Carlisle 'an Gales' Chrétien is drawing upon sources in which Carlisle was recognized as formerly (into the tenth century) a seat of the Strathclyde Welsh. Its location in Cumbria/ Cumberland, 'land of the Cymry', would reinforce the Welsh connexion. On the name Carduel, see E. Ekwall, *Concise Oxf. Dict. of Eng. Place-Names* (Oxford, 1960); on the name and the Arthurian associations of Carlisle and Cumberland, see *The Place-Names of Cumberland* (E.P.N.S.), ed. A. Armstrong and others, pt. i (1950), 40–42, pt. iii (1952), introd., pp. xviii f. Cardiff, though not without Arthurian associations, was not so popular a residence as Camelot, Caerleon, or Carlisle. Nevertheless, it was from Cardiff that Arthur set sail to make war on Lancelot, and it was there that the lady Annowre tried to lure Arthur to the Forest Perilous (see F. J. Snell, *King Arthur's Country* [London, 1926], pp. 137–9, 193–6).

37. *it* is used indefinitely as the object of a verb. Cf. 'I cannot daub *it* further'—*Lear*, IV. i. 54.

40. *trew trowth.* For other examples of words of the same stem in close juxtaposition, see *desspised desspytusely* 96, *armid in gude armurs* 156, *olyve . . . lifand* 307, *saw . . . syght* 246, 365, 389, &c., *dedys . . . done* 2248 (similarly 2307, 2333, &c.), *to tel þe tale* 90 (similarly 123, 2483, &c.), *bled . . . blode* 3609.

55. *Sir Dedyne and Sir Segramore.* Sir Dedyne (in Chrétien, Dodiniaus) appears in this spelling only in *YG*. It is quite possible, however, that he is identical with Dodynas (Dodinell, Dedinet) le Saueage who, according to Malory, was killed by Lancelot in a tournament. Sir Segramore is undoubtedly the son of the King of Hungary. He assisted Arthur at Carmelide and became a knight of the Round Table. He appears in episodes of *Cliges, Erec, Conte del Graal, Arthour and Merlin, Morte Arthure, Morte d'Arthur,* and *Lancelot of the Laik.* His usual sobriquet is 'le Desyrus'. On Segramore see Nitze, *Perlesvaus,* ii. 332 f.

56. Sir Kay is the son of Ector and the foster-brother of Arthur. When Arthur ascended the throne, he was made steward at the request of his father. He appears frequently in Arthurian romances where he is noted for his churlishness. Kay's rudeness, according to the Merlin group of romances, is explained by the fact that Arthur usurped his place at his mother's breast, leaving Kay to the care of an ill-spoken nursemaid. Here, as in other romances, Kay's sharp tongue is contrasted with the courtesy of other knights. Also, as in other romances, Kay's reward for his churlishness is a well-merited defeat.

58. Colgrevance is a minor knight of the Round Table. He appears fleetingly in Malory (*Morte d'Arthur,* ii. 971–3) where he is slain by Lyonel, and in *Arthour and Merlin. YG* is the only romance where he plays a major role. In Chrétien this name appears as Calogrenant, a form which Loomis

(*Arth. Trad.*, p. 275) suggests is actually Cai-lo-grenant, 'Kay the Grumbler'. In this event Calogrenant is really a double of Cai. The identification is bolstered by Calogrenant's humiliation at the storm-making spring, which parallels Kay's humiliation in the same circumstances later.

72. *Ful light of lepes.* Chrétien has (Ch. 72): *Mout vos voi or preu et saillant.*

80 f. The French renders this passage more clearly (Ch. 80–82):

> Ja le leissames por peresce,
> Espoir, que nos ne nos levames,
> Ou por ce, que nos ne deignames!

The sense of the English passage seems to be: 'Surely the Queen will understand that although you rose at her entrance while we sat still, none of us is so boorish as to remain seated out of malice or indifference.'

84. *despise.* Schleich emends to *despised* to suit the tense of *left* (83), but it is better to accept the reading of the manuscript and construe *despise* as the present subjunctive.

86. As Schleich has suggested, it is possible that *þi* is a mistake for *ʒowre.* Kay elsewhere (89, 106, 108, 119, 121 f.) is careful to address the Queen in the 'plural of politeness' which one would expect in someone speaking to a person of royal rank. But this usage tends to be irregular. Although Colgrevance says *ʒe* to the Queen (135 ff.), and both Gawain and the elder sister address Arthur as *ʒe*, the younger sister sometimes says *þe* (3470–2), sometimes *ʒowre* (3473). Lunet also addresses Alundyne familiarly (977, 980–2, 3913–14, 3919), but usually she uses the polite form (941–3, 945, 947, 952, 958, 975–6, &c.). With one exception (1844) the bower-woman addresses her mistress as *ʒe*, and so does Ywain's squire his master (582–4). Parliament addresses Alundyne as *ʒe* (1187, 1247–8), but the crowds hail Arthur as *þou* (1409–10, 1412).

Passing from *ʒe* to *þou* and back may indicate a change in relations between people. At their first meeting Ywain uses *ʒow* in addressing Alundyne (1149), but by l. 1162 he has progressed far enough to use the familiar form. In the same context Alundyne wavers between the two forms. After their marriage, when Ywain indicates to Alundyne that he wishes to leave with Gawain, she consistently uses *ʒow* (1492, 1500, 1502 f.). Prior to this she has normally used the familiar form. Knights of the Round Table use the familiar form among themselves. See the conversations between Kay and Colgrevance (72–73, 77, 93, 96, 99–101), between Kay and Ywain (471–8, 480), between Kay and Gawain (1288 f.), between Ywain and Gawain (1455, 1466, 1468, 1470, &c.). When Ywain and Gawain meet incognito they address one another formally. Persons of higher station (Arthur, the Queen, Ywain, and Alundyne) always address their inferiors familiarly.

88. *takes to no velany.* Cf. *tak to no grevance* 126, *tak it to na greve* 3127, *takes it til no despite* 3296.

98. *A brok omang men forto stynk.* The malodorousness of the badger is proverbial. Besides the quotation from *YG*, *OED.* gives the following from Skelton (1528): *She seyd your brethe stank lyke a broke.* The sense of this passage is that it is in the nature of things for a badger (Kay) to stink, so there is nothing to be done about it.

103. The text appears corrupt here. Colgrevance seems to be contradicting himself, unless by *parto* we are to understand a reference to his altercation with Kay. The sense would then be, 'Since your language is insulting, I should like to end this conversation and continue with the story that I began.' F. Holthausen (*Anglia*, xiv [1891–2], 319) proposes emending *of* to *lef* on the basis of the French, Swedish, Norse, and German analogues. Schleich in his note on this line suggested the possibility that a verb (*blyn?*) is missing after *Bot*. In the French (119) Colgrevance refuses to go on with the story: *Mes je n'an conterai hui mes.*

132. *At* seems rather to be the normal Northern use preceding an infinitive than (as *OED.*) an aberrant form of *ac* conj. 'but'.

149. *Herkens, hende, unto my spell.* Colgrevance begins his account with a minstrel formula of frequent occurrence in ME. verse, both religious and secular. (See Brown and Robbins, *Index of Middle English Verse*, pp. 173–7.)

157. *In a frith.* E purposely omits Chrétien's reference to Broceliande (Ch. 189), the wonderful forest in Brittany which contained the Fountain of Barenton. (See Introduction, III. B. 4.)

169. *þat be ȝe balde* is a favourite expression of E. See also 1285, 2781.

176. Are we to understand 'courtyard' here for *hall*? It seems clear that Colgrevance has dismounted on the *drawbrig* (167) and that the Hospitable Host has taken his horse. As we discover some lines later (182), however, the host has not yet disposed of the mount, nor have they entered the *fayre palays* (183). Some sort of courtyard with attached stables is indicated.

179–80. Like *God* 177 and *þe way* 179, *þe aventurs* is the object of the verb *thanked*.

186. *burde* (*bord*, 189) translates OF. *table*. As W. Lister remarks (*MLR.* xxv. 56–57), *OED.* incorrectly cites this line under *board* (*burde*, *bord*), 'a tablet upon which public notices and intimations are written, or to which they are affixed'. The meaning in this context is 'sheet of metal', one so suspended as to yield a thunderous sound upon being struck by a hammer. E uses *burde* because in its basic meaning ('a rectangular piece of timber having considerable expanse of surface') the word conveys the shape of the percussive apparatus he is describing. Realizing, however, that the word also denotes something wooden, he hastily adds that the *burde* is *nowþer of yren ne of tre* (187) but of some rare metal—the French specifies copper. Chrétien's *table* represents a parallel semantic development.

In Chrétien's source, according to C. B. Lewis (*Classical Mythology*, pp. 19 ff.), the gong was at the spring, hung from the magic tree indeed, and was used in rites of sympathetic magic to conjure up dark skies and thunder, just as the pouring of water upon the stone was intended to make rain. The rite and the bronze gong are traced by Lewis to the sacred spring of Zeus the Rain-maker at Dodona. Clearly Chrétien did not understand the ritual significance of the gong or he would not have separated it from the spring and rationalized it as a household signal.

187. The relative pronoun is missing. See also ll. 256, 1068, 1981, 3076–8, 3154.

196. E's damsel is described as the *semeliest* and *lufsum(er)*; Chrétien's as *bele et jante* (227) and *longue et gresle et droite* (229). Here, as elsewhere, E economizes the French poet's defining details.

235. *leve of mine ost toke.* Cf. 1555 f., 1632, 2701 for other examples of this phrase with *of*; in 478, 880, 1957, 2798–9, 3125, *at* is used.

249–50. Schleich transposes these lines without explanation, apparently on the ground that the detail of the *wonder mace* (249) is logically one of the things that Colgrevance sees after he has come closer to the Herdsman (250). This is not sufficient reason to disrupt the order of the manuscript which follows Chrétien (292–4) closely: *Vi je seoir sor une çoche, / Une grant maçue an sa main. / Je m'aprochai vers le vilain.*

253–4. Again Schleich unnecessarily transposes the lines. They fail to reproduce the original, he argues, and also they perpetrate an awkward repetition (*byheld I mare* followed by *byheld I þan* in the next line). But repetition of this sort is a common minstrel device (cf. 972–3, 2934–5).

260. *cutted* is a strange word in this use and was perhaps suggested by Ch. 302: *Iauz de çuëte* (*choete* in some manuscripts) *et nes de chat.*

297. *remu.* Ritson reads *renin* and glosses as 'run', but Schleich rejects this reading on the ground that the text offers no other infinitive ending in *-in*. The manuscript reading *remu* (OF. *remuer*), 'to move or shift from a place', is a less rare word than Schleich believed; cf. Chaucer, *Boece*, ii, pr. 6, 48–49 (*Works*, ed. Robinson, p. 337); Robert of Gloucester's *Chronicle*, 10835, 11016; *William of Palerne*, 1326.

327–8. *a bacyne . . . of gold gude and fyne.* In all manuscripts of *Yvain* except V, the first mention of the basin has it *de fer* (386); it is *del plus fin or* in all manuscripts on its next appearance (420).

344. *Unnethes þou sal þi selven knowe.* This *non sequitur* is traceable to a misunderstanding by E of the French. Chrétien has (404) *Se tu t'an puez departir*, where *departir* means 'come away'. E, however, uses the alternative meaning 'know' or 'distinguish' (see Ch. 2626) with the result that the sense is difficult. The meaning of Chrétien (404–6) is, 'You will be lucky if you come away', which E takes up at 345–6.

353. The tree in Chrétien (414, 460, 774, 808) is a pine, which is perhaps his way of rationalizing its remaining green throughout the winter. E may have made the tree a thorn because he read *espine* for *pins*, or because the reference to leaves did not suit the pine, or, most probably, because the thorn had stronger magical connotations in England, where it was associated with the Glastonbury thorn, the crown of thorns (see Mandeville,

Travels, ed. P. Hamelius, E.E.T.S., o.s., 153, pp. 8–9), and with May festivals. (On the sacredness of the hawthorn, see I. Teirlinck, *Flora Magica* [Antwerp, 1930], s.v. *Crataegus oxyacantha*.) In Hartmann von Aue's *Iwein* (572) the marvellous tree is a linden (lime); at Dodona it was an oak; the Welsh version describes the tree as 'greener . . . than the greenest fir-trees' (*Mabinogion*, ii. 25). On the supernatural associations of the thorn, see also L. C. Wimberly, *Folklore in the English and Scottish Ballads* (Chicago, 1928), p. 351.

361. E omits the detail that the stone was *perciez aussi come une boz* (Ch. 425).

363. With the pleonastic use of *on heght* here compare *fra hevyn on hight* 3339. E omits Chrétien's ornate figure (Ch. 426–9):

> S'i ot quatre rubiz dessoz
> Plus flanboianz et plus vermauz,
> Que n'est au matin li solauz,
> Quant il apert an oriant.

383. Such periphrastic expressions are common, as elsewhere in ME.; see also *For hys luf þat lens us life* 3483, *by him me boght* 3154, *By him þat for us sufferd pine* 489.

393–4. Schleich points out that after *bigan* the infinitive always has *to* (636, 1911), but after *gan* never (163, 2011, 3843).

403. E omits Chrétien's simile on the coming of the knight (Ch. 487 f.): *Vint plus tost qu'uns alerions, | Fiers par sanblant come lions.* The knight's name, as we discover later (1146), is *Salados þe Rouse*.

409–17. E reduces the knight's elaborate complaint and challenge (Ch. 491–514) to nine lines of predominantly indirect discourse.

426. As Schleich remarks in his note on this line, *fole* has its original meaning of 'young horse'. In this romance *stede* always means a horse suitable for knightly combat. A *palfray*, on the other hand, may mean either a horse that a knight uses for travel (568 ff., 1773, 1824) or a horse used by women. *Hors* is the generic term.

436. *bit[id]e.* Suggested by E. Kölbing in *Engl. Stud.* xxiv (1897), 146. F. Holthausen proposed *abide* (*Anglia*, xiv [1891–2], 319).

441. E evidently considers the woman who entertains Colgrevance and Ywain to be the wife of the Hospitable Host. Chrétien specifically calls her *sa fille* (274, 566).

470. E's free rendering of *Plus a paroles an plain pot | De vin, qu'an un mui de cervoise* (Ch. 592–3) sets a difficult problem in interpretation. Schleich notes that St. Martin of Tours was known for his abstemiousness and mortifications, and suggests that he is being contrasted as a symbol of abstinence with a *pot of wyne*, a glutton, and heavy drinker. The idea, then, is that boasts and brave talk are more readily found in a drunkard than in a person who eats and drinks with moderation. French and Hale

(*Metrical Romances*, p. 499) propose that by *a karcas of Saynt Martyne* a flitch of dried beef is meant, pointing out that Martinmas was the usual time of year for drying meat for the winter. A more exact interpretation, perhaps, is indicated by such proverbs as the Provençal *Cadë por a soun San-Marti*, the French *À chaque porc vient la Saint-Martin*, and the German *Jede Sau hat ihren Martinstag* (see I. von Düringsfeld, *Sprichwörter* [1872], No. 815), which fix St. Martin's Day as a time for butchering. The knights have just risen from a banquet, as Kay reminds them (468). Kay ascribes Ywain's vow to avenge Colgrevance to drunkenness, i.e. 'bottle' courage. The volatile *pot of wyne* represents the drunken boaster; the inert carcass of dressed meat—that it be dried is unnecessary —is a symbol of sobriety. Mention merely of a carcass would have served Kay's purpose, but *a karcas of Saynt Martyne* conjures up an image of Martinmas slaughtering, when dressed carcasses were much in evidence. That the allusion to St. Martin is gratuitous is suggested by the frequency with which his name occurs as a convenient rhyming word in other romances—see references gathered in L. F. Casson's edition of *Sir Degrevant* (E.E.T.S., o.s. 241 (1949), p. 135). Besides the value in rhymes, the saint was so frequently invoked, Casson believes, because the best-known legend about him told of his dividing his cloak with a beggar, 'and gifts of clothes were welcome to minstrels'.

479–82. The lines may be freely rendered 'And if it so happen . . . that a dream frighten you, change your mind and admit that I (Kay) predicted it'. It is barely possible to take *bad* as 1 pr. ind. of *biden*, 'stay, endure, await', distorted to fit the rhyme: '. . . change your mind and say "I shall remain".' The latter interpretation comes nearer the French (610 f.): 'Et se vos anquenuit songiez / Mauvés songe, si remanez.'

522. *fader sowl Uterpendragowne.* For other examples of the genitive without an inflexional ending see Introduction, p. xlv.

Uterpendragowne (Uther Pen Dragon) is traditionally the father of Arthur. The name probably means chief or head of the dragons, with dragons used in the sense of warriors.

525. *Saint Johns evyn.* 23 June, the eve of Midsummer Day and the festival of John the Baptist, because it coincided with the summer solstice, inherited many pagan observances. It was a night when fairies and elves were abroad—the herbal decorations on houses and the bonfires, which until recently marked this day in Europe and Quebec, were originally intended to ward off supernatural visitations—and was thus an advantageous time for the meeting of mortals and fairies.

527–8. The plural feeling of *who so* accounts for the ending of *wendes.* Cf. *Who so es ferd, I rede þai fle* 3500, and *wha had so bityd, / þai sold have done right als I dyd* 3999–4000.

539. *al* intensifies the conjunction here, as elsewhere it frequently intensifies the preposition.

559. *karl of Kaymes kyn.* According to tradition monsters, elves, giants, and spirits of hell were descended from Cain, who was the father of all evil progeny. Both Hebrew tradition and Christian interpretation of Scripture are responsible for this belief, which is the subject of a long discussion by O. F. Emerson, 'Legends of Cain, Especially in Old and Middle English', *PMLA*. xxi (1906), 831–929.

The mention of *Kaymes kyn* is an addition by E and is not found in the French original. The expression had a long history in English. Grendel is described as being descended from Cain, and the *Beowulf*-poet (ll. 106 f.) goes on to explain how all monstrous births, giants, and spirits of hell represent the Lord's revenge for the murder of Abel. Other allusions to *Kaymes kyn* may be found in *Havelok the Dane* (Skeat, ll. 2044–6) and *Kyng Alisaunder* (ed. G. V. Smithers, E.E.T.S. 227, B 1933).

Kaymes is the usual spelling in Middle English. Emerson suggests (op. cit. 885, n. 3) that it may be based on OF. *Cai(y)m*, and has possibly been confused with Cham (Ham), the son of Noah.

587. *at his myght*. This frequent expression seems best rendered by 'as best he can' or 'to the best of his power'. Other instances occur in ll. 1862, 2204, 3166, 3883, 4002.

599. *sty* is used here and in 1977 with the meaning 'path' or 'lane' (Ch. 768 *santier*), and not, as Ritson and Schleich suggest, 'place' or 'building'. Cf. *Havelok the Dane* 2618 (*sti*); *Ipomedon*, Auchl. 3088 (*sty*); *Seven Sages of Rome*, ed. K. Campbell, 3621 (*sty*).

601–4. These lines translate the following passage in Chrétien (770–8):

> Et lors fu il a seürté
> Qu'il ne pooit mes esgarer.
> Qui que le doie conparer,
> Ne finera tant que il voie
> Le pin, qui la fontainne onbroie,
> Et le perron et la tormante,
> Qui gresle et pluet et tone et vante.
> La nuit ot, ce poez savoir,
> Tel ostel come il vost avoir.

As is evident E has slipped. Clearly *castel* is meant by *chapel* 603, and E wants to say that after following the *sty* Ywain at last has come to the castle of the Hospitable Host. He does not want to say that Ywain can see the chapel from where he stands at that moment. The *wel and þe fayre tre* 602 are so closely associated with the *chapel* that either E or a scribe inadvertently put *chapel* down in the next line instead of *castel*, the proper word to translate Chrétien's *ostel*.

648–50. The manuscript reading, *þaire hauberkes þat men myght ken*, is difficult to make sense of. Lines with similar phraseology occur later in the poem during the combat between Ywain and Gawain (3543–4):

> In many stedes might men ken
> þe blode out of þaire bodies ren;

and (3551–2):

> þaire hauberkes als war al totorn
> Both bihind and als byforn.

On the basis of ll. 3543–4 Schleich emended the line to *At þaire hauberkes men myght ken*, adding *at* and omitting *þat*. A simpler correction is to restore the initial *At* (*Fra*?), leaving the *þat* intact in the interior of the line. In our reading, *hauberkes* is to be syncopated so as to read as a disyllable, as it must a few lines later (653). Lister (*MLR*. xxxv. 57) proposes a more radical solution. He argues that a comparison of the disputed passage with the verses quoted above (3543–4, 3551–2) suggests that 'the scribe has made a mistake in copying and has missed out a whole line and two half-lines. He would probably not be following the meaning of the poem, and on glancing back at his original would mistake the "-es" ending of "stedes" for that of "hauberkes" which he had just written and so continue—"þat men myght ken".' The emendation would then read:

> And feyned þam noght forto fight;
> þaire hauberkes als war al to-torn
> Both bihind and als byforn,
> In many stedes þat men myght ken
> þe blode out of þaire bodyes ren.

This is a trifle too ingenious.

656. Chrétien is more explicit about why the battle *was wele more to prays* (Ch. 855–61):

> Et de ce firent mout que preu,
> Qu'onques lor chevaus an nul leu
> Ne navrerent ne anpirierent;
> Qu'il ne vostrent ne ne deignierent;
> Mes toz jorz a cheval se tindrent,
> Que nule foiz a pié ne vindrent;
> S'an fu la bataille plus bele.

669. E omits Chrétien's long epic simile (Ch. 882–6) in which Yvain's pursuit of the wounded knight is compared to a gerfalcon's pursuit of a crane.

678. In this line and in 1740 the infinitive with *to* is used after *made*. In 1648, 3987 the plain infinitive appears.

691 ff. E is somewhat clearer than Chrétien about where Ywain is imprisoned. Here we find it flatly stated that he is caught *bytwene þa ȝates* (691), that is between the portcullises. In 695 he refers to the place as *þat stall*, and in 710 as *þis halde*. Chrétien, on the other hand, although more lavish with details, is much more vague about the disposition and character of the rooms in the castle. Yvain appears to be a prisoner in the elaborately decorated great hall of the castle (*la sale anclos*). Chrétien also mentions an adjoining *chanbrete* (970) from which Lunete appears. In E Lunet appears much more naturally from a *dore* in the wall of the passageway-prison. E seems to be trying to make his account as simple and realistic as possible. For a fuller discussion of the differences in the two versions, see Introduction, III. E.

708. Except for the terminal curled *r* the first word of this line is completely obliterated by a water stain. Schleich's suggestion, *þare*, does not make sense; *Here* is preferable, meaning 'Here in this castle'. This reading has the advantage of echoing Lunet's words a few lines above (702), '*Here þou has a febil ostell*'.

712. The first *þe* in this line is probably a scribal slip for *þai*, which also occurs in ll. 709, 711, and 712, and which refers in each case to the retainers of the dead lord who are searching the castle for the slayer. Cf. M. Kaluza, *Engl. Stud.* xii (1888), 87.

723. *savese = so avyse* 113. Chrétien is more explicit about Lunete's shortcomings on her embassy to Arthur's court (1004–8):

> Une foiz a la cort le roi
> M'anvoia ma dame an message.
> Espoir si ne fui pas si sage,
> Si cortoise ne de tel estre,
> Come pucele deüst estre.

724. The theme of the discourteous ambassador or messenger is found in the *Morte d'Arthur* where Lynet comes to Arthur's court and is contemptuous of young Gareth; in *The Sickbed of Cuchulainn* where the fairy Liban comes to Cuchulainn in a dream and taunts him; and in *Perlesvaus* where *la Damoisele du Char* arrives suddenly in Arthur's court and complains of his conduct. In each case the damsel's discourtesy at court is markedly similar to Lunete's behaviour in Chrétien's version. See *Arth. Trad.*, pp. 294–300. The fifteenth-century *Der Luneten Mantel* connects Lunet with the messenger in the numerous horn and mantle chastity tests at Arthur's court—F. J. Child, *English and Scottish Popular Ballads* (Boston, 1882–98), i. 261 ff.

731. *I wate, if þou be seldom sene.* A perplexing line contradicted by 1717 f. The corresponding place in Chrétien has (1016–17): *Bien sai, comant vos avez non, / Et reconeü vos ai bien.* French and Hale (*Metrical Romances*, p. 507) suggest that 'possibly the translator mistook *avez* for some form like *savez*, and took the sense to be, "you are not known", and to make the rhyme, gave as a paraphrase, "you are seldom seen".' In any event, E has garbled his source.

737. Chrétien is clearer about how the ring should be used (1030–7):

> Il covient que l'an l'anpoint,
> Si qu'el poing soit la pierre anclose,
> Puis n'a garde de nule chose
> Cil, qui l'anel an son doi a;
> Que ja veoir ne le porra
> Nus hon, tant et les iauz overz,

Ne que le fust, qui est coverz
De l'escorce, qui sor lui nest.

Rings which cause invisibility, invulnerability, forgetfulness, and protection against enchantment are common in romance and folklore—see references assembled in *King Horn*, ed. Joseph Hall (1901), n. to ll. 563–76. Alundyne also gives Ywain a ring which not only protects him against imprisonment, sickness, loss of blood, and capture, but ensures his invincibility as well (1527–40). Cf. Lucy A. Paton, *Studies in the Fairy Mythology of Arthurian Romance* (Boston, 1903), pp. 19, 77 f., 86, 97, 187.

793. *men*, the direct object of *fand*, is the subject of *wald*. See also 2639.

798. *mekil sorow unsoght.* Schleich, who takes the meaning of *unsoght* to be 'frequent', quotes Mätzner, *Altengl. Sprachproben*, i. 362, 97. M. Kaluza (*Engl. Stud.* xii (1888), 87), who offers 'unpunished', is criticized by E. Kölbing (*Engl. Stud.* xxiv (1897), 148) for straining at the obvious. That the meaning is not obvious will appear from what follows. The phrase *sorowe on soght / vnsoght / on-soght* appears three times in the *York Plays*, ed. L. T. Smith (pp. 8/8, 103/44, 316/285), and *vnsoght* is there glossed 'unquiet, untroubled, undisturbed'. In the *Towneley Plays*, ed. G. England (E.E.T.S., e.s. 71, p. 26) *vnsoght* (*In erth I se right noght / Bot syn þat is vnsoght*) is glossed 'unatoned for, irreconciled', as it is also in *The Wakefield Pageants*, ed. A. C. Cawley (Manchester, 1958), and in J. R. R. Tolkien's glossary to *Fourteenth Century Verse and Prose*, ed. Kenneth Sisam (Oxford, 1944), where the word is derived from ON. *ú-sáttr* from older **un-saht*. *OED*. sense 1 b, 'without being sought for, near at hand', is attested by Chaucer, *Complaint unto Pity*, l. 104, and *Ipomedon*, Auchl. 6519, but generally the meaning is 'untold, i.e. uncountable, especially when coupled with sorrow, woe, pain', as in the *York Plays* citations above and in the following: *Sir Tristrem*, ed. G. P. MacNeill, ll. 823–5— *Vn souȝt / Heuede of wild bore / Ichon to present brouȝt*; *Ipomedon*, Auchl. 6658 —*I praye god send him sorowe vnsoght*; *Chester Plays*, ed. H. Deimling (E.E.T.S., e.s. 62, i. 223—(Diabolus speaking) *Endles pains must I have unsought.* The semantic progression would appear to have been: unsought —unexpected—more than expected—innumerable or immeasurable.

799. The door through which Lunet originally came (696) must have been cunningly concealed.

806. *þe maydens hall.* It is clear that E thinks of Lunet's room as distinct from the *halde* enclosed by the portcullises. In E the retainers search the *halde* first, then proceed to Lunet's *hall*. In Chrétien this distinction is not clear. Yvain remains in the *sale anclos* where he was first caught. When the people of the castle enter they see the dead horse (Ch. 1093), but are unable to find Yvain because of Lunete's ring. Shortly afterwards Laudine passes through this room (Ch. 1146) together with the funeral procession and the corpse, whose wounds begin to bleed in the presence of the murderer. Laudine thus passes through the very room where Yvain remains invisible. In E Ywain first sees Alundyne from a window of Lunet's room (850).

819. *A lady folowd white so mylk.* E's comparison is much more homely than Chrétien's courtly *une des plus beles dames, | Qu'onques veist riens teriiene* (1146–7).

829–30. These lines are added by E. The *his* in ll. 830 and 831 apparently refers to Salados, whose horse, armour, and weapons have a place of honour in the funeral procession. The *honoré's* horse and armour commonly preceded the corpse in medieval English obsequies. They are mentioned in records as mortuaries owed to the church where the requiem mass was celebrated—see B. S. Puckle, *Funeral Customs* (1926), p. 114.

836. Schleich suspects a lacuna at this point, corresponding to Ch. 1176–1253, but it is clear that E's omission of Ch. 1070–1 (where Chrétien announces that the body of Esclados will be carried through the room where Yvain is hidden) is a conscious preparation for dropping the scene with the bleeding corpse.

859. *bewte* here refers to general excellence as well as physical attractiveness.

868. The manuscript reading *swownyg* has been emended to *swownyng* rather than Schleich's *swowyng* because it is much more likely that the scribe forgot the abbreviation mark over the *y* (cf. ll. 2237, 3238) than that he transposed the *y* and the *n*. Abbreviated endings in *yg* or *ig* for *yng* (*ing*) are common throughout. For *swownyng* OED. gives Chaucer, *Clerk's Tale*, E. 1086–7 and *Beves of Hamtoun* (E. 4313, 4388); cf. also *swoȝning, King Horn* 444, *swouninge, Joseph of Arimathie* 543, *sowening, Sir Ferumbras* 2585. Schleich's emendation *swowyng* is supported by *swowing* 2064.

870. Schleich also suspects a lacuna after 870. He finds it curious that Lunet should return to Ywain (E. 910–18) without mention having been made that she had ever left the room. But in distilling 279 lines to 39, E could easily have missed the single line (Ch. 1339) in which Lunete leaves the room.

946. *þe Damysel Savage* is a shadowy and indistinct figure in the Arthurian legends. Chrétien mentions her casually (*la Dameisele Sauvage* 1630), without any identification other than that she is in some way connected with the interests of Laudine. In the story of 'Sir Gareth of Orkeney' Malory twice gives the name to Lynet (Lyonett), who presents marked similarities to the Lunet of our story (*Morte d'Arthur*, i. 357–61). However, there is nothing in either Chrétien or E which suggests that Lunet and þe Damysel Savage are identical.

990. *and ȝe kun me [na] mawgre* may be rendered as 'provided you bear me no ill will'. For *mawgre* as a preposition, see 3488.

1003. *He þat has þe bataile*: he who wins the battle.

1048. E omits the point that both Chrétien, the lady, and the courts of love are worried about (Ch. 1809–10):

> 'C'est cele, qui prist
> Celui, qui son seignor ocist.'

1052. E has *come of Adams kynde* for *del ling Abel* (Ch. 1814). It was, of

course, infinitely preferable to be descended from Abel than from Cain;
see note to l. 559.

1056. *kin[g]s son Uryene.* E makes this information part of Lunet's
description of Ywain. In Chrétien Laudine volunteers it on hearing
Yvain's name, indicating that he was widely known.

1090. *out of*: without.

1114. *Medame.* This spelling also occurs in l. 3976.

1142. *OED.* derives *lite* from the verb *lite* (ON. *hlíta*) 'delay', and cites
1620 under this definition; but neither here nor at 1620 does that definition fit easily. We prefer to derive the word from ON. *lýti*, 'vice, flaw,
error', a meaning which suits both appearances in this text. Cf. *Towneley
Plays*, ed. G. England, E.E.T.S., E.S. 71, 85/225, 152/394.

1146. *Salados þe Rouse.* This is the only time this name appears. Loomis
(*Arth. Trad.*, pp. 282–3) asserts that the Storm-Knight is derived from
the ancient Irish hero Curoi.

1175. It is more likely that *kownsail* refers to the advice of Alundyne's
barons (1177) than to the conversation she has just finished. The lines
should probably be transposed.

1211–26. E omits many details from the speech of *li seneschaus* (Ch.
2081–2104) which he considers inessential to his narrative. Most noteworthy is the interesting information that the lady had married seven
years before on the advice of her nobles, and that it had been for sixty
years the custom *an cest chastel* to defend the fountain.

1254–5. The name Alundyne is a mistake. The corresponding lines in
Chrétien are (2151–3): *Prise a Laudine de Landuc | La dame, qui fu
fille au duc | Laudunet, don an note un lai.* Obviously E thought the pre-
position *a* formed part of the proper name. Thus, instead of Laudine, he
read Alaudine, and anglicized it to Alundyne.

Significantly, Chrétien refers to Laudine by this name only once, and
only one (MS. P) of the nine manuscripts which contain this passage
(Ch. 2151–2) uses this form of the name. Another manuscript (MS. V)
has Laudune, while the others merely call her *la dame*, her usual appella-
tion in the rest of the romance. It is possible, therefore, that the name is
merely a corruption of *la dame* and has no other history. However, two
German versions of *Yvain* as well as the English version preserve a form
of the name, a fact which led Foerster to support the reading Laudine.
The name Landuit (Ch. *duc Laudunet*) is possibly a corruption of some
form of Lothian. For a discussion of these names and for an attempt to
connect Laudine with Morgain la Fée and the territory of Lothian, see
Loomis, *Arth. Trad.*, pp. 301–8.

1307. E omits the characterizing detail (Ch. 2230–3) that Kay invariably
went into a pout unless Arthur allowed him to begin a battle first.

1326. *bate.* The verb *bite*, 'bite', is frequently used to describe the

penetration of a sword or lance—see ll. 2070, 2444, *Sir Eglamour*, ed.
A. S. Cook, 1. 488, and Laȝamon's *Brut*, ed. F. Madden, i. 321.

1355. For the use of *half* in similar expressions, cf. 1382, 2914, 3052, 3382.

1368. *purchace* is used in the legal sense of property which one acquires by means other than inheritance, in Ywain's case by his marriage to Alundyne. See ll. 1445–8.

1372. *fowretenyght.* The corresponding passage in Chrétien (2308) mentions *huit jorz toz antiers*, and somewhat later in his own poem E states that Arthur and his knights stayed *aght dayes and aght nyghtes*. Schleich in his note on these lines suggests that *fowretenyght* is a slip for *sevenyght*.

1429. We find no foundation for Schleich's theory of a lengthy lacuna at this point. The transition between 1428 and the next line seems to him so abrupt as to destroy the continuity. The lost passage (Ch. 2395–2442) is an elegantly contrived conceit in which the courtly gallantries of Gauvain and Lunete are described as an encounter between the Sun (Gauvain) and the Moon (Lunete). Much has been made of Chrétien's conceit by those Arthurian mythologists who discover the *numen* of a sun-god in Gawain (see Jessie L. Weston, *The Legend of Sir Gawain* (1897), pp. 12–13, and R. S. Loomis, *Celtic Myth and Arthurian Romance* (1927), pp. 75 ff., 287, 301), but it is just this sort of material that E habitually excises.

1444. *revere.* The sport of hawking, which often took place on the banks of rivers. See *OED.*, s.v. *River sb.*[1] 2.

1461. *endose. MED.* cites this line under *endos* (OF. *a dos*, support) with the conjectural meaning of 'support' or 'backing'. W. Lister (*MLR.* xxxv. 57) derives it from OF. *endosse (en dos)* for which Littré gives: 'toute la peine, toute la responsabilité de quelque chose'. Lister suggests the translation 'great responsibility', or 'great things under his protection'.

1517 f. These lines may be rendered 'And if I could have my desire I would come to you much earlier'.

1527. See note to l. 737.

1560. *he* may be a mistake for *sho*. It is Alundyne after all who has 'set' the day, although E may simply be referring to Ywain's acquiescence to his wife's conditions.

1563. The manuscript reading *Vwayne* is the only occurrence of this form.

1566. E omits time of year, Chrétien mentions *miaost*, 'mid-August' (2679).

1567. *Cester.* Chester was one of the seats of Arthur's peripatetic court.

1591. There is nothing to indicate in either Chrétien or our poem that the *damysele* in question is Lunet.

1592. Characteristically E omits Chrétien's precise descriptive details. E translates *un palefroit noir bauçant* (Ch. 2707) simply as *palfray*.

1604. *of* is also found after *war* 1981.

1661. *bir.* Schleich is undoubtedly right in reading *ful* as an adv. modifying *grim*, and not an adj. *birful*, as does Ritson.

1699. The rhythm here seems to demand the suppression of the first *it*, which may not be genuine.

1713. Schleich does not emend the line but takes *naked* as an adj. used substantively. But the rhythm supports Ritson's emendation *man*, omitted perhaps because the scribe confused *man* with the *me* which follows. The next line does not refute Ritson. *It* suits the indefiniteness (cf. ll. 2107, 2111), for *man* is perhaps used here for a human being regardless of sex— see M. Kaluza, *Engl. Stud.* xii (1888), 87.

1732. Schleich suspects a short lacuna after 1732 on the grounds that E fails to reproduce the lines (Ch. 2915–17) which state that the maiden remounted her horse and returned to her companions. But since one can easily imagine her mounted companions drawing near during her examination of the prostrate figure of Ywain, no violence has been done to the meaning.

1739. *meng a mans blode.* Cf. *þir wordes menged al þe mode* 3701.

1747. Strict scansion demands the suppression of *ilk*.

1755. One suspects a *lapsus* here on the part of E. Clearly *He* refers to *Morgan þe Wise* (1753) and should be *sho*. However, Loomis (*Arth. Trad.*, p. 307) mentions evidence of a tradition that the sex of Morgain was indeterminate. The healing power of Morgan le Fay / Morgain la Fée was famous, and it is quite appropriate that she should here be the source of the magic *unement*. On Morgan see Loomis (*Arth. Trad.*, pp. 179–84, 259–62, 304–7, and *Speculum*, xx [1945], 183 ff.) and Lucy A. Paton (*Fairy Mythology*, pp. 1–166).

1767. *fra* is equivalent to *fro þe tyme þat* 725.

1776. That *hors* is probably pl. here is suggested by ll. 1824–5.

1795. *wher* is equivalent to *wheþer*.

1869. E has *on a day* for Chrétien's more exact *mardi*.

1898. *sese.* The Northern pl. imperative form.

1967. The manuscript clearly has *stedes* here. Both Ritson and Schleich prefer *stede* on the grounds that only one horse is indicated in 1966 and 1972.

1993 f. Note the strong resemblance to a dragon fight in *Beues of Hamtoun*, Auchl. 2878 ff.:

> Er he mi te keuren a wonde
> A hitte him so on þe cholle
> And karf ato þe þrote-bolle.

Cf. Kölbing, *Engl. Stud.* xxiv. 149.

2023–4. For a fuller explanation of the lion's motivation see Ch. 3424 ff.:

> Un petit s'est mis an la trace
> Tant que son seignor a mostré,
> Qu'il a santi et ancontré
> Vant et fler de sauvage beste.
> Lors le regarde, si s'areste;
> Que il le viaut servir an gre;
> Car ancontre sa volanté
> Ne voldroit aler nule part.
> Et cil parçoit a son esgart,
> Qu'il li mostre, que il l'atant.
> Bien l'aparçoit et bien l'antant,
> Que, s'il remaint, il remandra,
> Et, se il le siut, il prandra
> La veneison, qu'il a santie.
> Lors le semont et si l'escrie
> Aussi come uns brachet feïst.
> Et li lions maintenant mist
> Le nes au vant, qu'il ot santi,
> Ne ne li ot de rien manti . . .

2031. *in his nek.* Neck refers to that part of the body on which loads or burdens are carried. See *OED.*, s.v. *Neck, sb.*[1] 1 b.

2040. For manuscript *boght* here instead of *bogh*, cf. 2347 and 3931 where the copyist has carelessly added a *t* to a final *gh*. We follow Ritson and Schleich in emending to *bogh*.

2041. *undone.* Cut up (an animal); cf. *Gawain and the Green Knight* 1327: *Quykly of þe quelled dere a querre þay maked . . . and didden hem derely undo.*

2083. Schleich asks whether *sone* is written for *done*. The manuscript, however, is clear, and *sone* is supported by alliteration.

2090. The French at this point (3528–9) specifies that Ywain overstayed his leave by a year.

2107. Here and in 2111 the neuter *it* is used to indicate that Ywain does not know the identity of the person in the chapel-prison.

2136. As Loomis has pointed out, the theme of the rescue of a lady from fire by the timely intervention of a knight is not of Celtic provenance, but is traceable to a barbaric French law to the effect that a woman who has been accused or who has accused someone is liable to death at the stake if her husband or champion fails the test of battle. For a discussion of punishment by burning alive, and for examples of the common theme in European fiction of timely rescue from the stake, see J. R. Reinhard, *Speculum*, xvi (1941), 186–209, and Loomis, *Arth. Trad.*, pp. 317–19.

2176. The rhythm seems to demand the suppression of the second *na*.

2201 ff. Schleich (p. xlii) finds it curious that Ywain, although he has already assured Lunet of his help (2189 ff.), should once again go out of his way to promise aid (2203 ff.). In Chrétien Lunete had spurned Yvain's aid (Ch. 3732 ff.), making the renewed offer plausible. Schleich infers, therefore, that E originally included an account of Lunet's refusal, and that this account was omitted by the scribe. Schleich ignores, however, the exchange between Ywain and Lunet (2201–4), which would be rendered ineffective if, as Schleich supposes, the episode of Lunet's refusal were inserted.

2222. *at ane mete*, 'in one measure', contextually 'I love him equal to myself'.

2226. *he* is the lord of the castle, as Ch. 3804 ff. makes clear.

2293. *Bot a knyght.* E omits Chrétien's cross-reference to *Lancelot*, where Queen Guenevere is abducted by Meleagant.

2304. *by prime.* The first hour of the day, either six o'clock or sunrise.

2319. *þis knight.* A reference to Ywain. The knight in 2317 obviously refers to the lord of the castle.

2335. In this line *þam* clearly refers to Lunet, and we have retained the manuscript reading *I*, rather than emended to *he* as does Schleich. For a similar use of *þam* with a singular feeling, cf. 3988. This reading has the additional advantage that it makes the reference to Lunet's fate in the next lines perfectly natural, whereas in Schleich's edition these lines (2337–8) seem curiously inappropriate.

2428–9. Between these two lines appears the rubric in the hand of the scribe: *here es þe myddes of þis boke.* The appearance of the rubric at this place, 412 lines past the real middle of the romance, is puzzling. By *þis boke* the scribe is clearly referring not only to his own work, but also to the original of *YG*, since the rubric is not an afterthought but occurs between the lines of the text. We must therefore assume that the scribe is indicating what is the mid-point of his original and what should be the mid-point of his copy. What, then, accounts for the discrepancy? One explanation is that the scribe accurately recorded the mid-point of his original, and then proceeded carelessly to omit some 412 lines from the second half of the romance. In other words there is a possibility that an incomplete copy has come down to us. Schleich ornamented the possibility by proposing a series of lacunae, none of which we are able to accept (see Introduction, III. C). Actually Schleich's theory, far from accounting for the missing 412 lines, merely aggravates the problem, because most of the lacunae which he points out are in the *first half* of the romance. The explanation towards which we lean is that the rubric simply represents the scribe's estimate of the middle of the book. It is reasonable to assume that the lines of his original were not neatly numbered in the modern manner, and that rather than count the 4000-odd lines of the manuscript before him he merely indicated the mid-point very roughly.

2639. The subject of *quit* in this sentence is certainly Ywain.

2661. References to oaths sworn by St. Simon in the romances are collected by Kölbing in *Engl. Stud.* xxiv. 149.

2662. As Ernst Brugger has pointed out ('Yvain and his Lion', *MP.* xxxviii [1941], 277 f.), it was quite usual in the Middle Ages for a fierce and noble knight to be compared to a lion. Thus we find the surnames for King Richard 'Cuer de Lion', King William the Lion of Scotland, and Duke Henry the Lion of Bavaria. In the same way a squire who had distinguished himself for bravery was sometimes called Lionet, Lionel, or Lioncel.

2669 ff. The text as it stands bungles the dramatic irony inherent in the situation (cf. Ch. 4621 ff.). It would be vastly improved if ll. 2675–8 were given to Alundyne and l. 2679 to Ywain. The interjection in 2676 is the stumbling-block. If it were *þe lady said* the passage would come right. (See Kölbing, *Engl. Stud.* xxiv. 149–50.)

2733. This line may be paraphrased: 'No necessities were lacking to him.'

2743 ff. The motif of the disinherited sister does not appear in the Welsh *Owein* and is apparently Chrétien's addition. Loomis suggests (*Arth. Trad.*, pp. 319 f.) that Chrétien, desiring to crown his work with an account of the terrific combat between Yvain and Gauvain, transferred the combat from its original place in the middle of the romance (where it is still found in *Owein*) to the end, where it serves as the high point of Yvain's accomplishment in the romance. To bring about this new combat between the two friends, Chrétien made use of the disinherited-sister theme, the origins of which are obscure, but which is preserved in similar form in *Diu Krone* of Heinrich von dem Türlin and in *La Damoisele à la Mule* (or *La Mule sanz Frain*) of Paien de Maisières. For a discussion of the relation between the three versions of the disinherited-sister theme, see Paien de Maisières, *La Damoisele à la Mule*, ed. Boleslas Orlowski (Paris, 1911), pp. 46–64, and L. L. Boll, *Relation of 'Diu Krone' to 'La Mule sanz Frain'* (Washington, 1929).

2815 ff. In Chrétien (4826–7) the younger daughter falls ill in the castle of a friend (*chies un suen acointe*) who is apparently totally unacquainted with Yvain. Both E and Chrétien agree that a second maiden then takes up the quest for Ywain, but at this point E fails to reproduce Chrétien's account (Ch. 4835–4941) of the night storm in the forest which overtakes the maiden, her distraught prayer to God, the three blasts on the horn which lead her to the white walls of a castle belonging apparently to the husband of Gauvain's sister, his account of Yvain's prowess in killing the giant (presumably Harpin), his hospitality to the maiden, and her journey to the fountain beneath the pine where Yvain and his lion have killed *trois chevaliers*. Here E takes up the story again and the two versions parallel each other in their accounts of the meeting of the second maiden with Lunet, their brief journey together, and their arrival at the castle where Ywain had been healed (E 2878 f. = Ch. 5011 f.). By eliminating the extended account of the journey of the second maiden (Ch. 4832–4938) E has economized by 106 lines, but he has garbled the passage badly, and as a result we are left with several awkward questions. Why does the maiden, who has presumably helped cure Ywain of his *sekenes* and who later takes up the quest for him, deliberately set off in the wrong direction by going to Alundyne's castle where she knows he has fought and received his wounds? Why, also, does she show no sign of recognition when (E 2879) she comes to the castle where Ywain was *helid byforehand*, the castle which is presumably her home and her point of departure? Jessie L. Weston's theory (' "Ywain and Gawain" and "Le Chevalier au Lion"', p. 196) that E's account is an attempt to avoid a discrepancy of time in Chrétien's version does not seem valid. She holds that the castle in which the younger daughter falls ill is not the castle where Ywain has just been cured of his wounds, but the castle of the lady of the ointment (la dame de Noroison) where Ywain recuperated from his madness. She points out that in E 2816 the poet mentions that Ywain has recovered from *sekenes*, not wounds. Unfortunately for this theory, however, Miss Weston fails to account for *þe lord* of the castle mentioned in E 2820, an almost certain indication that the castle under consideration does not belong to the lady of the ointment, who, as we have seen (E 1960 ff.), is unmarried and consequently can have no lord.

In our opinion, E rejected Chrétien's account quite consciously, feeling perhaps that it was a tedious and repetitious impediment to the story. In telescoping Chrétien's leisurely account into a few lines, E, departing from his source, arranged to have the younger daughter fall ill in the castle where Ywain had been healed of his wounds, a castle which E perhaps associated with a mysterious healing power—a castle of health. This solution has the advantage of disposing of the younger daughter easily and naturally during her illness, at the same time that it puts her on the trail of Ywain, a feat accomplished in Chrétien by the visit of the second maiden to the castle of Gauvain's sister. Engaged as he was in a major reduction of Chrétien, E failed to note the inconsistencies in his account and the text comes down to us marred. (Cf. Ritson, iii. 241, and Schleich, note to l. 2827).

2877. This is the only appearance of the form *Luned*.

2922. Although the manuscript clearly has *whare*, Schleich emends to *wher*, a contraction for 'whether', on the grounds that the maiden is asking whether Ywain will *wend* with her, or whether he intends to remain where he is. Such an interpretation is upheld by the corresponding lines in Chrétien (5092-4): '*Or me respondez, s'il vos plest,* | *Se vos venir i oseroiz* | *Ou se vos an reposeroiz!*'

2931-3358. For the kernel of the episode of The Castle of the Heavy Sorrow (*Le Chastel de Pesme Avanture*, Ch. 5107-5809) Chrétien apparently drew on his source *Y*, a version of which episode is also preserved in the Welsh *Owein* (ii. 65 f.). For the development and elaboration of this episode, however, Chrétien seems to be indebted to a lost *conte*, the main features of which are: (1) the arrival of a hero, accompanied by a damsel, at a perilous castle; (2) the traditional figure of the surly porter who admits them, and the inmates of the castle who warn them of danger;

(3) the discovery of a large group of captive gentlewomen who have been sent as tribute to the castle and who are forced to work at silk-weaving under sweatshop conditions; (4) the two ugly and churlish oppressors who fight the hero; (5) the victory of the hero and the liberation of the captive silk-workers. Although no single source has been found for this story, close variations of the theme appear in Pseudo-Wauchier's *Perceval le Gallois* ('Pseudo-Wauchier', *Li Contes del Graal*, ed. Charles Potvin, iv [Mons, 1868], 33–53); Malory's tale of Launcelot in Book VI of the *Morte d'Arthur* (*Morte d'Arthur*, i. 271 f.); and in two episodes of the Vulgate *Lancelot* (*The Vulgate Version of the Arthurian Romances*, ed. H. O. Sommer [Washington, D.C., 1909–16], v. 212–14; iv. 105–7). For a discussion of the relations among these versions, see Loomis (*Arth. Trad.*, pp. 320–6). On Chrétien's handling of the silk-workers, see note to ll. 3047–60.

3019. *Geten of a woman with a ram* translates *Que de fame et de netun furent* (Ch. 5273). *Netun*, 'demon', derives from Neptune by the usual medieval process of making pagan gods into monsters or demons. E has read the French word as *mouton*.

3024. For the unusual use of the plural *yns* here, see *OED.* (s.v. *Inn* 2) which cites *Syr Generides* (Roxb.) 1476: 'Here ynnes ther ful sone thei nam.'

3026. In Chrétien *li rois de l'Isle de Puceles . . . n'avoit pas dis et huit anz* (5276). E makes him younger in order to make him the more defenceless.

3047–60. Chrétien's realistic description (5298–5324) of the enforced silk-weaving operations in *le Chastel de Pesme Avanture* appears to be indebted to Sicilian and Oriental sources, rather than to the existence of similar industrial conditions in northern France of his time. As R. A. Hall has pointed out ('The Silk Factory in Chrestien de Troyes' "Yvain"', *MLN.* lvi [1941], 418–22) there is no evidence during this period of a central workshop large enough to employ 300 women in weaving operations. Moreover, the manufacture of silk on a large scale was unknown in France until 1466, and until that date the bulk of silk and silken goods had to be imported from Sicily and the East. Chrétien's description of the wretched conditions and wages of the workshop is indebted, according to Hall, to actual conditions in Moslem silk-factories where Christian slave girls were sometimes forced to work. Reports of these sweatshops may have reached northern France through traders on their way to the fairs of Champagne, and through returning Crusaders.

3074. *call* is used in the sense of greeting or friendly welcome; cf. 2728. Of course *him* refers to Ywain.

3158. Schleich suggests the addition of *ful* after *a* to rescue the metre.

3264. According to Schleich the first *he* in this line refers to the lion, and *him* to *þat oþer* (*champion*) of the preceding line. The corresponding passage in Chrétien (5659–61) is: *Et maintenant a terre vient | Por l'autre, que li lions tient, | Que rescorre et tolir li viaut.* However, the context strongly supports reading this line so that *he* refers to Ywain, advancing to help dispatch the second champion, and *him* to the lion, who has pinned down his antagonist but as yet has not killed him. The lion, seeing his master approach, quickly dispatches his victim so that he would have some of the honour *to his part*. He acts here in friendly rivalry with Ywain.

3404. Is this the town where Arthur is holding court, or is it, as Schleich suggests, a town between *þe Castel of þe Hevy Sorow* and Arthur's temporary court? Schleich points to the inconsistency between 3404 and 3412, and suggests that *a* be substituted for *þe*. On this question see Introduction, III. F.

3443. On the expression *think (it) long* meaning 'to grow weary with waiting', or 'to be impatient', see *OED*. (s.v. *Think, v.* 9 c).

3481. *elder* is Ritson's emendation for *ȝonger*, which appears in the manuscript written by a later hand over an erasure. Clearly *elder* is correct. The younger sister is indicated by *hyr* in 3481 and by *sho* in 3482.

3509–3674. The incognito combat between Ywain and Gawain belongs properly to that universal folk-motif in which two warriors, closely connected by ties of affection or blood, attempt to kill each other through some misunderstanding. M. A. Potter's study *Sohrab and Rustem* (1902) traces the genesis and development of this theme as it is embodied particularly in the combat between father and son. Chrétien's description of the incognito duel between Yvain and Gauvain is the first example we have of the theme in the Arthurian story, although subsequently it becomes a popular fixture in the romances. For a list of combats between brothers, friends, and close relations in Arthurian romance, see Potter, pp. 207–10.

The striking use of alliteration in the description of the combat (3525 ff.) has been compared with the alliteration in the battle between Arcite and Palamon in Chaucer's *Knight's Tale* and with the description of the Battle of Actium in the *Legend of Good Women*, 635 ff. (see *Works*, ed. Robinson, pp. 680–1).

3614. *might*. Lister (*MLR*. xxxv. 58–59) accepts Ritson's reading *night* and suggests three possible emendations; but the manuscript is clear and the line reads perfectly well as it stands.

3741. *ȝong* probably written for *ȝonger*.

3767–72. This is one of the few instances where E turns from his source and addresses the reader directly.

According to English laws of inheritance during the early Middle Ages the great fiefs into which the land was divided had to descend, if they were inherited at all, in their entirety. This meant that land could not be divided or parted in any way among a landholder's sons, but that it remained a single whole and passed directly into the hands of the eldest son, thus ensuring that only one man, holding the land in fee from his lord, was responsible for the collection of taxes and military levies. The law, however, did not discriminate among daughters of equal rank and showed no preference for the first-born. Generally, co-heiresses divided both land and movables equally, although certain things like castles and the messuage which was the head of a barony were always considered impartible. There were two main feudal schemes for the division of land among co-heiresses. The first of these, tenure in parage, maintains a kind of female primogeniture. In this scheme, when a tenant dies leaving only daughters, the eldest daughter stands out as the representative tenant for the whole property, and her younger sisters hold their land from her. Thus the property remains technically impartible, the eldest heiress being solely responsible for taxes and the military duty. Her sisters will be her tenants and acknowledge her as their head. Gradually, however, as wardships and marriages became of greater importance to the lord than military service, another scheme developed whereby the land was partitioned equally among co-heiresses, each heiress holding her land of the lord. The effect of this scheme was to split the land into as many pieces as there were co-heiresses. The land was then said to be 'parted'.

Of these two schemes, the first seems to answer most nearly to Arthur's solution of the sisters' dispute. The elder sister will be responsible to her lord (apparently Arthur) for the levying of men and taxes. Her younger sister, however, will also have her right according to feudal law. In return for a tenement worth half the value of the property, she will make fealty to her sister and acknowledge herself as her sister's 'man'. Thus the land has been effectively 'parted' in so far as the younger sister has legal possession of one-half the value of the property. Actually, however, her elder sister continues to be the representative of the property in the eyes of her lord and the feudal courts, and the fief remains technically impartible. From a strictly legal view, then, E is not quite accurate when he describes the land as 'parted'. If this were the case, then the younger daughter would hold her land from Arthur and would owe fealty directly to him and not to her elder sister. On the question of partible and impartible lands, see Sir Frederick Pollock and F. W. Maitland, *The History of English Law* (Cambridge, 1911), ii. 260–76.

3838. Ywain's motive for returning to the well is made uncertain by the statement, *þare he thinkes forto dwell*. Surely we are not meant to believe that Ywain intends to atone for his absence by living as a hermit in the vicinity of the well. Why, then, does he pour water on the stone, thus forcing the lady's hand and bring about the denouement? Obviously E has either misunderstood or mistranslated the passage in Chrétien where Yvain's intentions are clearly and logically indicated (Ch. 6517–26):

Et pansa qu'il se partiroit
Toz seus de cort et si iroit
A sa fontainne guerroiier,
Et s'i feroit tant foudroiier
Et tant vanter et tant plovoir,
Que par force et par estovoir
Li covandroit feire a lui pes,
Ou il ne fineroit ja mes
De la fontainne tormanter
Et de plovoir et de vanter.

3980. Note that Lunet violates the pact she had made in l. 3951.

4026. The stark finality of this line is E's addition to his source.

4029–32. The concluding prayer does not occur in Chrétien. Such invocations were a standard feature of minstrel romances, and often echoed the prayer at the beginning. See note to ll. 1–2.

GLOSSARY

THIS glossary is selective: only those words have been included which are (1) obsolete; (2) employed in senses no longer usual in Modern Standard English; or (3) characteristically Northern forms. Nouns and verbs have been entered in the form in which they occur in the text. Unless otherwise indicated, nouns are glossed in the singular when it occurs. Verbs are entered under the form of the infinitive where possible. Otherwise they are entered under the form of the present tense, the past tense, or one of the participles. If no special attention has been drawn to the form of the verb, the reader may assume that the verb has been entered under the form of the infinitive or the present tense. The line numbers are usually the first occurrences of the word or sense.

The letter *y* is glossed as *i*; *ʒ* follows *g*; *þ* follows *t*.

The following abbreviations are used:

absol.	absolute	*poss.*	possessive
adj.	adjective	*pp.*	past participle
adv.	adverb	*pr.*	present
advl.	adverbial	*prep.*	preposition
art.	article	*pron.*	pronoun
attrib.	attributive	*pr. p.*	present participle
cf.	compare	*pt.*	preterite
conj.	conjunction	*sg.*	singular
indef.	indefinite	*trans.*	transitive
interj.	interjection	*v.*	verb
n.	noun	*var.*	variation
pl.	plural	*vbl.*	verbal

a *indef. art.* a, any, some 6, 15, 61, &c.; one, the first 3247; *an(e)* (before vowels) 257.

a *interj.* 3377, 3651.

abayst *pp.* upset, perplexed 846.

aby *v.* suffer, pay for 413; *haby* 1610.

actoune *n.* jerkin 2616.

adrad, adred *pp. adj.* afraid, frightened 718, 771.

agast *pp. adj.* aghast, terrified 3177.

aght *adj.* eight 1438.

aght *pt.* ought 724; 3 sg. pr. *aw* 3668.

ay *adv.* ever, always, continually 72, 100, 128.

ayre *n.* heir 2747, 3093.

al *adv.* *al if, if al,* even if 688, 790, 2006.

alkyn(s) *adj.* of every kind, all kinds of 13, 2088; *on alkins wise* in every way 2579.

als *adv.* also 21, 180; *conj.* as 9, 97; *als fast so* as fast as 630.

alsone *adv.* at once, immediately 281, 495; *alsone als* as soon as 233.

always *adv.* in every way 184.

alweldand *ppl. adj.* almighty, all-ruling 2199.

amerawd *n.* emerald 361.

and *conj.* if 490.

ande *n.* breath 3555.

anely *adv.* only 3744.

anes, anis *adv.* once 292, 811, 1161.

anger *n.* trouble, affliction 1196, 1529.

anikyn(s) *adj.* any kind or manner 3916.

anterd *pt.* risked, imperilled 3809; 3 sg. pr. *antres* 3508.

apertly *adv.* publicly, plainly 517.

are *adv.* formerly, before 224, 374, 610; *compar.* earlier 1061, 1518.

areson *v.* question, examine 1094.

arly *adv.* early 2692.

arow-draght *n.* flight of an arrow 2026.

arsown, *see* **hinder-arsown.**

asay *v.* put to the proof, test the fitness of 551.

ascry *v.* inform upon, give away 3406; *pp.* 584.

aspy *v.* find out, discover 2994.

assise, assyse *adj.* established (as of custom or law) 3148; *n.* custom, practice 3445.

at *prep.* in, on, &c.; from 2798, 2799; of time 3398; of manner or mode 216; by means of, through 4002.

at *adv.* (with infin.) to 132, 703, 812, 1368, 2271.

at *conj.* that 461, 486.

ataynt *n.* exhaustion 3281.

ateyned *pp.* condemned, arraigned 1601.

ath *n.* oath 2264, 3904.

avenant *n.* what is becoming, honourable 3174, 3765.

aventerous *adj.* adventurous, in search of honourable exploits 3399.

avyse *adj.* wise, prudent 113. *See also* **savese.**

aw *n.* power 2411.

aw *v.* control 92; owe 122, 1508.

aw *v.,* *see* **aght.**

awin, awyn *adj.* own 583, 2672, 3754.

bad, *see* **bede.**

bayn *adj.* eager, willing 766, 2097, 2698.

baken *n.* pie, dish baked in pasty 221.

balde *adj.* brave, fearless 70, 290; confident, assured 169, 709.

baldly, baldely *adv.* boldly, fearlessly 3151, 3194; freely, openly 1047.

bale *n.* suffering, misfortune 1588, 1806.

band *n.* stroke (of whip) 2394.

bane *n.* death, doom 709, 816, 1854.

bare *n.* boar 241, 262.

barn *n.* child, youth, man 526, 975.

barnage *n.* body of retainers, nobility 1258.

bate, *see* **bit(e).**

baundoun *n.* power 1944.

bede *v.* offer 953; *pt.* 645; *pt.* *bad* indicated, predicted 482.

bekeand *pr. p.* warming oneself 1459.

belamy *n.* fair friend 278.

belde *v.* comfort, defend 1220.

beleves *imp.* remain (in a certain state) 2674; *pp.* *bylaft* abandoned 35.

berd *n.* beard 783; *mawgre þaire berd* in spite of anything they can do 783.

bere *v.* carry 827; overthrow 421; conduct oneself 449, 1314; *pt.* *bare* 11; *pp.* *born* 827.

bere *n.* bier, coffin 818.

bete *v.* remedy, mend 1588, 1806.

bewtese *n.* beauty 902; courtesy, kindness 3075.

bical *v.* charge, accuse 491, 2133.

bideand *pr. p.* waiting 2550.

bidene, bydene *adv.* entirely, utterly 875, 3546; immediately 513; as a group, one and all 50, 2972.

byfel *pt.* was fitting 14.

big *v.* build, erect 1949.

bihete *v.* assure 158, 1393.

byhove *v.* be physically necessary, needful 600, 2218; be incumbent upon, necessary for (sb.) 2359; pr. *bus* 1085, 1184; *pt.* *bud* 3029.

bylaft, *see* **beleves.**

bilive *adv.* quickly, rapidly 1102, 2546.

bill *n.* mattock, pickaxe 3225.

byn *adv.* within 1214.

bindes *imp.* bind, fetter 3178; *pp.* *bun* 3179, *bunden* 2384, 2511.

bir *n.* armed assault 1661.·

bird, byrd *n.* damsel, lady 2313, 3313.

byswike *v.* betray 2335.

bit *n.* blow with a sword or spear; *toke bit* struck 2444.

bit(e) v. pierce (of a weapon); hurt or
vex 436; pt. *bate* 1326, 2029.
bityde, bytid(e) v. happen, come to
pass 133, 479.
blawand *pr. p.* blowing 340.
blin, blyn v. cease, stop 41, 486; pt.
blan 178, 615.
blist *pt.* gazed, stared 3163.
blith, blyth *adj.* joyful, happy 1315,
1374.
boist, boyst n. box 1761, 1835.
bone n. reward 1075.
borows n. pl. sureties, pledges (of
persons) 1953.
boskage n. wood, wooded country
1671.
bot *conj.* only 426; unless 289, 398;
except 998; *bot if* unless 144.
bote n. avail, use 1971, 3227.
bother *adj.* both (of) 3556, 3759.
boun, bown(e) *adj.* ready, armed
1693, 1852, 3256.
bourd n. amusement, entertainment
1912.
bourding *vbl. n.* trifling, joking
1497.
boure n. inner chamber; esp. a lady's
chamber 2342.
bourewemen n. pl. ladies-in-waiting
1711.
bowsom, bowsum *adj.* willing,
obedient 3101; gracious, kind 1155.
brayd *pt.* wrenched, pulled 3248.
brayded *pt.* roared 2072.
braynwode *adj.* mad 1756.
brand n. sword, blade 1933, 2458.
breke n. undergarment 1770, 3103.
bremly *adv.* fiercely 3163.
brent *pp.* burned 378.
bretise n. parapet, defensive structure 163.
brok n. badger 98.
bud, *see* byhoves.
bun, *see* bindes.
burde, bord n. rectangular sheet of
metal 186, 189. *See also note.*
bus, *see* byhoves.
buskes n. pl. bushes 261.

carped, karped, karpet *pt.* spoke,
talked 25, 467, 498.
case n. incident, occurrence 107.
cete n. town, city 669.

chamberere n. lady-in-waiting, confidante 883.
chavyl n. jowl, cheek 1991.
chere n. state of mind, disposition,
manner, appearance (of person) 214,
631, 2328.
cherel, cherle n. churl, rustic, 268,
612, cf. *karl* 559.
cheverd, *see* shiferd.
choll n. jaw, jowl 1994.
come n. arrival, coming 86, 447, 1378.
conisance n. recognition, acquaintance 3650.
covait v. desire, wish for 3642, 3677.
covenand *pp.* agreed formally 3969.
covenant n. agreement, understanding 2302; *kownand* 3894.
cover v. recover 2141.
craft n. dealings, pursuits 36.
creant adj. ȝelde þe als *creant* sur-
render, acknowledge oneself de-
feated 3173.
croyce n. cross 826.
cropoun n. rump, buttocks 2468.
culpons n. pl. pieces, bits 642.
cumand *pr. p.* coming 629.
cumly, kumly *adj.* noble 2874;
handsome 2886.
cumlyng n. new-comer, new arrival
1627.
cumvay v. convey, accompany as a
guide 1494; pt. *cunvayd* 2687.
cuntre n. country 20; region 1445.
curtayse *adj.* courteous 43, 193.
cutted *pp.* cut short, snub (of a nose)
260.

da n. doe 2027, 2031.
dang *pt.* thumped, struck 3167.
dawes *n.pl.* days 3811; *of ald daw* of
old days 3130.
debonere *adj.* humble, submissive
1160.
ded(e) n. death 380, 425, 714, 4026.
defaut n. want, failure 3650.
dele n. bit, part 3232; division, partition 3583; *everilka dele* the whole,
every part 516; *ilka dele* every bit
960, 1038.
deme v. judge, consider 1186, 3735.
denyd *pt.* refused 80.
depart v. *trans.* divide 3752.
dere v. harm, injure 358; pt. *derid* 3232.

dere *n.* harm, injury 744, 2577.
dere *adj.* of great worth or value 2233.
dere *adv.* dearly, at great cost 1610.
dern *adj.* secret, concealed 2996.
desait *n.* wile, stratagem 3873.
descrive *v.* describe 902.
dese *n.* dais 1207.
despended *pt.* used up, exhausted 1781.
despens *n.* expenditure 1469.
despite *n.* outrage, injury 410, 1327, 2941.
desspytusely *adv.* contemptuously 96.
dight, dyght *v.* prepare, make ready 220, 234; dress, array 404, 593; *pt.* 593; *pp.* 404.
dyke *n.* ditch, moat 165.
dint *n.* stroke, blow 2447, 2454; *pl.* 3232.
do *v.* put 714, 1157; put forth, exert 2438; make, cause 750, 3132; did *pt.* 750; done *pp.* 3131.
doghty *adj.* valiant, worthy 1565, 3065; *adv. dughtily* 1564.
doghtines *n.* valour 29.
dole *n.* grief, sorrow 834, 2091.
doure *v.* endure 2634.
douted, *see* dowt.
downright *adv.* straight down 65.
dowt *v.* fear (hence be in awe of) 1391; be afraid of, apprehensive of 3236; *pt. douted* 3236.
draght, *see* arow-draght.
dreche *v.* vex, torment 480.
dreri, drery *adj.* sad 825, 1976.
dreven *pp.* driven 4026.
drewries *n. pl.* keepsakes, gifts 1406.
dughtily, *see* doghty.
dwergh *n.* dwarf 2390, 2781.

eft *adv.* afterwards, then 780.
encheson, enchesowne *n.* reason 2260, 2946.
endose *n.* support or backing 1461. *See also note.*
enterement *n.* interment 879.
erandes *n. pl.* messages (communicated by word of mouth) 2541.
erel, eryl *n.* earl 1871, 1877; pl. *yrels* 3065.
ese, esse *n.* relief of pain or annoyance 2672, 3759; *at esse* at ease, comfortable 218.

esed *pt.* accommodated 232.
evel *adv.* unfortunately, unhappily 3549.
everilka(ne) *adj.* every, each one 516, 707.

fabil *n.* falsehood, deception 38.
fayn(e), fain *adj.* content, joyous 211, 748, 1346; desirous of, eager for 755; *for fayn* for joy 2086.
fayntise *n.* guile, deceit 79, 3916.
famen *n. pl.* foes 785, 2128.
fande *v.* test strength or skill 316.
fang *v.* grasp, seize 299; receive 2642.
fare *v.* go, travel 99, 2359; happen 506, 519; conduct oneself 911; *pt. ferd* 519; *pp. farn* 911.
fare *n.* adventure, event, course of events 462, 1360.
fase *n. pl.* foes 1534, 1901.
fast *adj.* dense 558; close together 265.
fast *adv.* eagerly, vigorously 25, 769, 1963.
febil *adj.* poor (in quality), wretched 702, 2563.
feyned *pt.* pretended 648, 2239.
fele *adj.* many 3673.
fell *n.* hill, upland waste 2711.
fell *adj.* bold, fierce 3245; villainous, false 101.
fend *v. refl.* defend (oneself) 418, 3040.
fer *adv.* far 1815; compar. *ferr* further 435, 3007; *ferrer* 1813, 2036, 2704.
fere *adj.* healthy, sound 3034.
fere *n.* companion, fellow 1495, 1913; equal, one's match in combat 1318.
ferly *adj.* marvellous, wonderful 462.
ferly, ferli *adv.* wonderfully 1346, 2979.
ferly *n.* astonishment, wonder 3603, 3610.
fest *pt.* held in position 1989.
feste *n.* feast, banquet 15.
fewte *n.* fealty 3762.
flegh *pt.* flew 642.
flyt *n.* strife, quarrelling 93.
flyte *v.* rebuke, reproach 504, 1027.
flogh *pt.* skinned, flayed 1699.
fode *n.* offspring, descendant 1621; person, creature 2262.
fole *n.*[1] foolish or stupid person 461, 2168.

fole *n.*² foal 426.

for *prep.* because of 69, 136, 584; in spite of 714, 1783; with *inf.*: in order to 3045; *for to* in order to, so as to, to 155, 555,601; *for els* otherwise 444.

force n. *mak þou na force (of)* pay no attention to 775.

forfarn *v.* ruin, destroy 976.

forfered *pp.* terrified 1678.

forord *pp.* trimmed or adorned with fur 1104.

forward *n.* agreement, promise 1953, 2572.

found(e) *v.* set out, travel 1495, 3830.

frayn(e) *v.* inquire, ask (a question) 272, 579.

fraisted *pt.* endeavoured, tried 3253.

fre *adj.* gracious, well-mannered 1263, 2228.

fret *pp.* bound, fastened 3160.

fristele *n.* flute, pipe 1396.

frith *n.* forest, woodland 157, 1688, 2207.

fun *pp.* found 3936.

gaynest *adj. superl.* straightest, most direct 1979.

gamin, gamyn, gamen *n.* amusement, mirth, fun 23, 1434, 1440.

gan *pt. auxil.* 163, 405.

gang *v.* go 2915.

gate *n.* way, path 1696, 2984.

gedering, *vbl. n.* assembly, coming together (of people) 3510.

gent *adj.* gracious 1423, 1973.

gentil, gentyl *adj.* noble, courteous, generous 89, 199.

gentry *n.* characteristics of a gentleman; hence, courtesy, generosity, mercy, &c. 980, 3271.

ger *v.* make, do, cause 151, 301; pt. *gert* caused (to do) 1102, 1153.

germayne, jermayne *adj.* germane, closely akin 458, 1275.

gilry *n.* deceit, deception 1604.

gyn *n.* scheme, device 897.

glade *v.* make glad, cause to rejoice 2369.

glotowne *n.* vile, filthy fellow 3247.

goday n. *haves goday* salutation at meeting or parting 2674.

grace n. *faire grace* good fortune, luck 687.

graid, grayd *pp.* prepared, equipped, arrayed 832, 2960.

graithly, graythly *adv.* carefully, properly 1299; promptly, readily 3208.

gram *n.* harm, hurt 3020.

gret *pt.*¹ greeted 2226; *pp.* 1615.

gret *pt.*² wept 1731.

groued *pt.* grew 354.

grunden *pp.* sharpened 676.

ȝalde *pt.* yielded, surrendered 1924.

ȝare *adj.* ready, prepared 2759, 2855.

ȝate *n.* gate 571, 671; *pl.* 691.

ȝe *pron.* you 89, 106, &c.; *ȝow* 109, 119, &c.; poss. adj. *ȝowre* 583, 942, &c.

ȝede *pt.* went 30, 268, 2353; *ȝode* 2390.

ȝeld *v.* yield 3033; *ȝelde* imp. 738; pt. *ȝald(e)* 1924, 2637; pp. *ȝolden* 3653.

ȝelp *n.* boast, mention 2765.

ȝeme *v.* take care of 1185; *imp.* 1544.

ȝere *n.* year 153, 3033; *pl.* 3026, 3091.

ȝern *adv.* eagerly 3220.

ȝerne *v.* desire, long for 1242.

ȝing *adj.* young .722, 1556, 2643; compar. *ȝonger* 3453, 3461.

ȝit *adv.* yet, still 465, 687.

ȝode, *see* **ȝede.**

ȝonder *adv.* at or in that place, yonder 2844.

ȝone *adj.* that, yon 571, 2844.

haby, *see* **aby.**

habide *v. intr.* stay, remain 2935; *trans.* await 3447; *imp.* wait! 2524.

hail n. *ille hail* unfortunately, disastrously 2956.

hailsed *pt.* greeted, saluted 171, 1389, 2882.

halde *n.* fortress 170, 555, confinement 289.

hale *adj.* sound, wholesome 39; whole, entire 118.

halely *adv.* wholly, entirely 507, 881, 2754.

hales *n. pl.* halls 18.

hals *n.* neck, throat 2070, 2468.

hard *adj.* difficult to penetrate 158.

hardy *adj.* bold, daring 962.

hardily *adv.* boldly 277.

hase *adj.* rough, hoarse (of a voice) 3620.

hate *adj.* hot 378.
hauberkes *n. pl.* coats of chain mail 649, 653.
haunt(e), hante *v.* practise habitually, be present at 1470; *haunt armes*, follow arms 1467.
heght *n.* *on heght*, aloft (of position) 363, 3339.
hele *n.* health, sound condition 2397.
helt *pt.* poured 368.
hend *n. pl.* hands 3822; *te hend* accessible, close by 207.
hend(e), hinde *adj.* gentle, courteous, comely 112, 173, 700; *absol.* courteous or gracious one(s) 149, 1952; *als þe hend* courteously 2651; *superl.* 74, 1051.
hend(e)ly *adv.* courteously, graciously 198, 207.
hent *pt.* took hold of; *in armes hent* embraced 1424.
herberd *pp.* lodged, sheltered 609.
heried *pt.* harried, pillaged 2874.
heryn *quasi-n.* *in ilka heryn* in this (lit. 'each') place 3220.
herlotes *n. pl.* rascals, base fellows 2404.
hernpan *n.* skull, cranium 660.
herted *pt.* inspired 1889.
hertly *adv.* heartily 166.
hete *v.* promise 1283.
heþin *adv.* hence 965, 1748.
hevid, hevyd *n.* head 251, 2464.
hy *n.* haste; *in hy*, quickly 433, 1546, 2513.
hy *v.* hasten, speed 1073; *pt. hyed, hied* 407, 604, 2893.
hide *n.* *hide and hew* complexion, colour 886.
hydose *adj.* hideous, frightful 1978.
hight *v.* promise 439, 1077; *intr.* call oneself, be named 59, 2662; *pres. hat* 1053, 2662; *pp. hight* 439.
hilles *3 sg. pr.* guards, protects 741.
hinde, *see* **hende.**
hinder-arsown *n.* the uptilted back of the saddle 681.
hyre *n.* reward, payment 2587.
hone *n.* delay 3669.
honoure *n.* fief, seigniory 3138.
hope *v.* expect, think 382, 1029; *pt. hopid, hoped* 275, 380, 892, 1675.
horde *n.* hoard 147.

hoved *pt.* waited, lingered 3335.
hulde *adj.* faithful, loyal 887.

ilk(a), ylk *adj.* each, every 30, 148; same 323.
ilkane *pron.* each one 23, 815.
ilkane *adj.* each kind of 284; each one of 442.
in, yn *n.* dwelling-place, lodging 445, 565; *pl.* in sg. sense *yns* 3024.
infere *adv.* together, in company 1399, 2315.
inmiddes *prep.* in the middle of 2442.
inogh, ynogh *adj.* enough, sufficient 706, 3463.
insonder *adv.* asunder 3257.
intil *prep.* into, to 3082.
intwyn *adv.* in two, in twain 3587.
yrels, *see* **erel.**
iwis *adv.* certainly, truly 2963.

jermayne, *see* **germayne.**
jewyse *n.* judgement 2127.
jorne, jornay *n.* journey 574, 1066, 1442.

kan *v.* know 1477.
kare *n.* mourning, sorrow 2244.
karl *n.* rustic, low-bred fellow 559; *cf. cherel.*
karped, *see* **carped.**
karping *n.* fault-finding 127.
kene *adj.* bitter, savage, bold 127, 374, 408.
kenely *adv.* daringly, boldly 647.
kepe *v.* take care of 2790; protect, defend 3231; observe a ceremony with due formality 1386, 1387; *pt.* 1387.
kind, kynde *n.* progeny, offspring 1052; nature 2033.
kyndeli *adv.* readily, properly 28.
kyrk *n.* church 2844.
kyth *v.* make known, show 348, 647; *pp. kyd* 530, 647, 658, 3660.
kled *pp. adj.* clad 2383.
kleke *pt.* pulled, snatched 2478.
knawyng *vbl. n.* acquaintance 1342.
knawlageing *vbl. n.* acquaintance 3964.
kouche *n.* couch 2706.
kownand *n.* agreement, contract 3984; *cf. covenant* 2302.

kowth *pt.* could, was able 171; pr. subj. pl. *kun* 990; *kun me na mawgre* bear me no ill will 990; *no wittes kowthe* was witless, stupid 275.

kumly, *see* **cumly.**

kunyng *n.* skill, wit, intelligence 3896.

laght *pt.* received a blow or injury 3230, 3622; took 2025; *pp.* 3622.

laine, layn(e) *v.* conceal, hide, be silent about 580, 2196, 2685; *es noght at laine* it cannot be hidden 703, 1127.

lays *n. pl.* laws 2792.

layt *v.* seek 237.

lang *adj.* tall 2385.

langes *3 sg. pr.* belongs to 3471.

large *adj.* generous, munificent 865.

largely *adv.* greatly, in large measure 423.

lath(e) *adj.* unpleasant, hateful 135, 1863.

lathly *adj.* loathsome, digusting 247.

lathly *adv.* horribly, hideously 2073.

lavedy *n.* lady 2828.

lawnd *n.* glade, open space in woods 245.

lebard *n.* leopard 240.

lechecraft *n.* medical knowledge, art of healing 2736.

lecheing *vbl. n.* medical treatment 2823.

lede n. *in lede,* among people, on earth 865.

lede *v.* lead, guide 1185; treat 1620; pp.*led with lite* treated viciously 1620.

lefe *adj.* agreeable, acceptable 789.

leghed *pt.* charged, accused 2860.

lele *adj.* loyal, faithful 2179, 3986.

lely *adv.* loyally, faithfully 580, 1168.

lely *adj.* white as a lily 2510.

leman *n.* sweetheart, mistress 847, 1474, 1584.

len(e) *v.* give or grant possession of 2676, 2872; lend 1527, 1542.

lend(e) *v.* remain, stay 1449, 1955.

lepes *n. pl.* sudden movements 72.

lere *v.* inform, tell 2990.

lered *pp. adj.* learned 2736.

lese *n. pl.* lies, falsehoods 3696.

lesed *pt.* set free, released 2864.

lesyng, lesing *n.* lie, falsehood 151, 3057.

let, lett *v.*[1] hinder, stand in the way of 108, 554, 916; *intrans.* refrain, check oneself 131, 2995.

let *v.*[2] fail, omit (with infin.) 1515, 1559; pt. *lete wele of* thought highly of 2007; pt. *lete* pretended 1809.

let *n.* hindrance; *withowten let* without doubt 1897.

leþir, *see* **lither.**

leve *v.* accept (a statement) 735.

levening *n.* lightning 377.

levore *n.* bar, pole 2386.

lig *v.* lie (in a recumbent position) 2403, 2606.

light, lyght *adj.* cheerful, merry 366, 781; frivolous 72.

light, lyght *v.* alight, dismount 174; *pp.* 725.

lightli *adv.* easily 554.

lightnes *n.* brightness, light 343.

lyme *n.* lime 1447.

line *n.* linen 269.

lire *n.* flesh 2510.

list *pt.* desired, wanted 3932.

lite *n.* vice, flaw; *withouten lite* without flaw 1142; *led with lite* 1620, *see* **lede.**

lither, leþir *adj.* wicked, base 1602; poor, bad (of things) 599.

loge *n.* temporary lodging-place 2037.

logh *pt.* laughed 1136, 3464.

lorn *pp. adj.* lost 2101, 3408.

lose *n.* praise, renown 45, 1573.

losenjoure *n.* lying, deceiving rascal 1602.

lowe *n.* flame 343.

luf(e) *n.* love 633, 871, 905.

lufsom *adj.* lovable 214; compar. *lufsumer* 197.

ma *adv.,* *see* **mo.**

ma *v.* make 693; 3 sg. pr. *mase* 692, 2683.

may *n.* maiden 446, 3359.

mayne, main *n.* strength, power 3, 658, 663, 2793; adj. *drink of main* strong drink 1865.

maintene *v.* withstand, defend against hostility 1221.

maystres *n.* mistress 936.

maystry, maistri *n.* victory 3708; authority, dominion 4017; superiority in battle 2265.

mall *n.* hammer 189.

mane *n.* complaint, lamentation 942, 2103.

manes *3 sg. pr.* grieves, bothers 93.

manesworn *pp. adj.* forsworn 3938.

mangeri *n.* feast, banquet 1581.

manyfalde, monyfalde *adj.* many and diverse 607, 1534.

manly *adv.* mightily, vigorously 3207.

mare, *see* **mo.**

mate *adj.* dejected, exhausted; *for mate* thoroughly exhausted 427.

mawgre *n.* ill will, displeasure 990, 1137.

mawgre *prep.* in spite of, notwithstanding 783, 3488.

mede *n.* reward, recompense 181, 728, 1965.

mekil, *see* **mikel.**

melle *n.* quarrel, fight 505.

men *indef. pron.* one 36.

menes *3 sg. pr.* remembers, has in mind 945.

meng *v.* stir up, disturb, mix 1739; *pt.* 3701.

menȝe *n.* company of followers, attendants 192, 707, 1215.

ment *pt.* mourned, pitied 2620.

mese *n.* course, serving of food 217.

message *n.* mission 721.

mete *adj.* equal 2114.

mete *n.* measure, dimension; *at ane mete* in one measure 2222.

mete *v.* come together with, embrace 1485.

mydlerde *n.* the earth, the world 3853.

mikel, mykel, mekil, mekyl *adj.* great 22, 58, 161, 798, &c.

mynt *v.* aimed a blow, made a threatening movement 811, 2448; attempted, endeavoured 3437.

misaventure *n.* piece of bad fortune, ill luck 2413.

mischefe *n.* trouble, misfortune 790, 2973.

mysliked *pt.* was displeased 534.

myslikeing *vbl. n.* trouble, unhappiness 388, 537, 2144.

mysprays *v.* dispraise 3308.

myssay *v.* abuse, speak evil of 1017; *pt.* 1041.

mister, mystere *n.* need, necessity 2733, 3205; *have mister* be in want or need of something 762, 1805.

mo, ma, mare *adv.* more 93, 402; *adj.* 307; *absol.* 10.

mode *n.* frame of mind, state of feelings 483, 3701; *main and mode* with strength and spirit 1031.

mold(e) *n.* earth 983, 3048, 3340.

monyfalde, *see* **manyfalde.**

mote *v.* argue 3328.

mountance *n.* amount, distance 2026.

mun, mon *vbl. aux.* shall, will, must 703, 2136, 2258.

murnand *pr. p.* grieving, sorrowing.

murnyng *vbl. n.* grief, sorrowing 2201, 2204.

nakyn *adj.* no kind of, not any 897, 1541.

nanes: *for þe nanes,* a metrical tag having no special meaning 2051.

negh *v.* approach, come close to 2347; *pt.* 596, 632.

nek *n.* the part of the body on which loads are carried 2031.

nerehand *adv.* nearly, almost 1842, 3334.

nete *n.* ox, bullock 252.

nevyns *3 sg. pr.* names, speaks of 1012.

nygromancy *n.* magic, enchantment 803.

nobillay *n.* nobility of nature or rank 3567.

noy *n.* grief, sorrow 885; cf. *anoy* 2677.

nome *pt.* took 1377, 1483; pp. *nomen* taken, captured 3664.

of *prep.* from 411, 739; off 592, 689.

ogain *adv.* in answer 279.

ogayne, ogains *prep.* against 342; opposite 1198.

olyfant *n.* elephant 257.

omang *prep.* among 34, 64, 98, &c.

omell *adv.* in the interval 119; *prep.* among, amid 1428.

onane, onone *adv.* at once, straightway 313, 367.

or *adv.* before 66, 178, 1523.

ordain *v.* prepare, make ready 1546; *pt.* 1867, 3386; pp. *ordand* prepared 2731; arranged, planned 3123.

oste n.[1] host 222, 234, 440.
oste n.[2] host, army 956.
ostell n. lodging 702.
outbrast pt. burst or broke out 644, 721.
outtak v. except, exclude 1524.
owþer adv. either 402.

pay n. satisfaction, contentment 2568.
paid, payd pp. adj. pleased, contented; hald us paid consider ourselves pleased 1228, 1232, 1246.
payned pt. refl. took pains, trouble 3109.
palfra(y) n. saddle horse 568, 575.
palis n. fence of pales, a palisade 2964.
pane n. lining of a garment 204.
panele n. cloth or pad placed under saddle 473.
par aventure adv. by chance, perchance 3348.
parage n. lineage, rank 1239, 3036.
parcayved, parsayved pt. perceived, observed 2034, 2463.
parfay interj. by (my) faith 294, 2150.
parred pp. enclosed, hemmed in 3228.
party n. a party in part, somewhat 3169.
pase n. gait, speed 619; playn pase at full speed 3082; gude pase at a brisk pace 619.
pawm n. paw 2615.
pece n.[1] cup, drinking-vessel 760.
pece n.[2] piece, fragment 3202.
perry n. gems, precious stones 1106.
pete n. pity 2077, 2371.
pine n. torment, suffering 489.
playn adj. full, entire; in playn batayl in full battle 712; playn pase at full speed 3082.
plevyne n. pledge, warrant 1253.
pover adj. poor 2968.
presand pt. presented to 1330.
present n. in þaire present, in their presence 1252.
prest adv. quickly 2441.
preve adj. secret, hidden 854.
preveli adv. secretly 3835.
prevete n. secret design or matter 578, 997.

prime n. first hour of the day (six o'clock) or sunrise 2304.
pryse n. value, anything worth striving for 22; bare þe pryse was the most distinguished 11.
prow n. advantage, profit 1154.
purchace n. property obtained by means other than inheritance 1368.
purpure n. purple cloth or clothing 203, 1403.
purst pp. withdrawn (of a boast) 1277.

quert n. health, sound condition 1488, 1614, 1741.
quick adj. alive 668.
quyn n. whin, furze, gorse 159.
quisteroun n. scullion, base-born fellow 2400.
quit(e) v. set free, acquit 730, 2639; repay, requite 3568; pp. 3808.
quite adj. free, clear 685, 3295, 3304.
quoke pt. shook, trembled 3849.

rad adj. frightened, alarmed 481, 844.
rafe pt. tore, pulled away 2467.
rare v. roar 242.
rase pt. pulled, plucked, 3267.
rath adv. quickly, swiftly 1101, 1177, 3728.
raw n. row 1227.
real adj. royal 3089.
really adv. royally 1569, 3112.
recreant adj. admitting defeat in battle, surrendering 3281, 3710.
rede n. scheme, plan, counsel 662, 1090, 2161; will of rede at a loss for a plan 379.
rede v.[1] advise 477, 3305; pt. red advised 589; so God me rede so God guide me 713.
rede v.[2] discern, make out 2153.
reherced pt. related, recounted 142.
remu v. depart, go 297.
renable adj. eloquent, ready of speech 209.
rerde pt. reared up, rose to hind feet 2073.
rese n. rush 3245.
reve v. rob, deprive forcibly 2906, 3434.
reven pp. adj. torn, split 653.
revere n. sport of hawking 1444.

reverence *n.* deep respect, deference 1322.

rewes *3 sg. pr.* distresses, affects with regret 1040.

rewfully *adv.* dolefully, sorrowfully 242.

rewth *n.* compassion, pity 2388.

ryg *n.* back (of an animal) 1833.

rike, ryke *n.* kingdom, realm 142, 2336.

rinand *pr. p. adj.* running 1067.

ryve *v.* split, cleave; pp. *reven* 653.

roght *pt.* took care, heeded 969.

rope *v.* cry out 242.

rouse *adj.* red-haired 1146.

rowncy *n.* riding-horse, saddle-horse 252.

rowt *n.* retinue 1024.

sagh, *see* **se.**

saght *adj.* in agreement, free from strife 3898.

saghtel *v.* reconcile 3917; *pp.* 3952.

saghteling *vbl. n.* reconciliation, agreement 2644, 3682.

sayne *v.* say 2849.

sayned *pt.* made the sign of the cross 614.

saint *n.* girdle 1772.

sakles *adj.* innocent 2526.

samin, samyn, samen *adv.* together 24, 1417, 2223.

sare *n.* wound, injury 2655.

sarily *adv.* sorrily, wretchedly 431.

savese (= **so avyse**) so wise, prudent 723.

savore *n.* smell, scent 2019.

saw *n.* speech, discourse, sententious saying 83, 131, 1228.

sawnfayle *adv.* without fail, doubtless 1004.

sawter *n.* psalter 888.

scarlet *n.* rich cloth, often bright red 1103.

scath *n.* injury, harm 3684.

schare *pt.* cut 683.

schilde, shilde *v.* shield, protect 2, 3354.

se *v.* see 163, 191; pt. *saw, sagh* 51, 152; pp. *sene* 34.

seignory *n.* territory under domination of a lord, a feudal domain 2121.

seker *adj.* certain, sure 601; secure, safe (esp. of defensive armour) 1301.

sekerly *adv.* certainly, assuredly 457, 1219.

sekernes *n.* assurance, certainty 991.

selly *adj.* strange, marvellous 107, 3513.

selly *n.* marvel, wonder 3521.

sembland, semblant *n.* person's outward appearance; demeanour, countenance 210, 448, 631.

semely, semeli *adj.* pleasant, fair, pleasing 97, 365; *superl.* 196.

sen *conj.* since the time that 354, 896; seeing that 101.

sere *adj.* various, divers 1443, 2919.

serk *n.* shirt, garment worn next to the skin 1770, 3103.

sertayne *adj.* secure 929.

sertes *adv.* of a truth, assuredly 135, 488, 3696.

servandes *n. pl.* servants (of the Lord) 2.

sese *v.*[1] stop, cease 3591, 3695; pt. *sesed* 384, 625.

sese *v.*[2] put in legal possession of a feudal holding 3760.

sesowne *n.* period of time 903; due or appointed time 3425.

seth *pt.* boiled 1699; pp. adj. *sothen* 1701.

seþin, seþen, *adv.* afterwards 2356, 2644, 2799.

shende *v.* injure, harm, shame 487; *pt.* 1586.

shever *n.* splinter, chip 3234.

shiferd, cheverd *pp.* splintered 637, 3539.

simpil, simepel *adj.* artless, straightforward 1638, 2107.

sith(e)(s) *n. pl.* times, occasions 178, 615, 1092.

skalde *n.* person of ribald speech, scold 69.

skath *n.* matter for sorrow or regret 1859.

skill, scill *n.* cause, reason 293, 2129; that which is proper or reasonable 968; statement made by way of argument 3451.

slik(e) *adj.* such 141, 341.

slogh *pt.* struck (a fire) from flint 2039.

smertly, smertli, *adv.* quickly, promptly 471, 512, 961; sharply, curtly 117, 466, 1308.

soght *pt. on* . . . *soght* attacked, assailed 2445.

solace, solase *n.* pleasure, entertainment 24, 108; consolation, comfort 388, 2176.

solers *n. pl.* upper rooms or apartments in a dwelling 808.

sone *adv.* quickly, straightway 472, 544.

soth n. *þe soth to say* to tell the truth 15, 614.

sothen, *see* **seth.**

span *n.* distance from tip of thumb to tip of little finger when hand is extended 256.

spell *n.* tale or narrative 149, 4028; speech, discourse 867.

spend *v.* expend, consume 1766.

sperd, sperred *pt.* fastened (door or gate) with a bar or lock 1677, 2979.

speres-hord *n.* point of a spear 45.

spy *v.* seek an opportunity for, look out for 3013.

spill *v.* destroy, kill, shed blood; pp. *spilt* 2152, 2540.

spir *v.* make inquiries, inquire, ask 2829, 3013.

squier, swier *n.* squire, personal attendant 533, 567, 588.

stabil(e) *adj.* trustworthy, steadfast 37, 210.

stage *n.* period of time 1068, 2501.

stak *pt.* shut up, enclosed, locked 699; pp. *stoken* 695, 3186.

stark *adv.* absolutely, utterly 1880.

sted, stad *pp.* situated, placed 717, 843, 903, 3196.

stedes *n. pl.* places 1718.

steppes *n. pl.* hoofprints 2889.

sterin *adj.* inflicting severe pain or injury 3219.

sty *n.* narrow path or way 599, 1977.

stif *adj.* stout, strong 31, 654.

stifly *adv.* steadfastly, stoutly 655, 3186.

stighteld *pt.* fought, contended, strove 3241.

styk *n.* stitch 3053.

styr v. *styr of* leave, move from 646; pt. *stird* bestirred, acted energetically 1883.

stody *n.* state of mental perplexity 909, 972, 975.

stonayd *pp.* stunned, stupefied 428.

store *adj.* violent, fierce 373.

store *adv.* violently, fiercely 1297.

stoure, stowre *n.* fight, armed combat 31, 61, 3559.

stownde *n.* time, while, short time, short space 6, 384, 428.

stowtlyk *adv.* resolutely, valiantly 667.

straytly, straitly *adv.* narrowly 674; *straytly stad* sore beset 717, 3196.

strete *n.* road, way, path 552, 611.

swyke *n.* snare, trap 677.

swilk *dem. adj.* such 14, 45, 83.

swith *adv.* quickly, swiftly 527, 568.

swogh *n.* swoon 824.

swowing *vbl. n.* swooning 2064.

swownyg 868 (*see note*).

ta, *see* **take.**

take *v.* take 454; 1 sg. pr. *ta* 3504; 3 sg. pr. *tase* 841; pt. *toke* 890; pp. *tane* 2558; imp. *takes, takes to* interpret as 88.

talvace *n.* shield or buckler, often of wood 3158.

tane *pron.* the one (of two); sometimes opposed to *toþer* 2142, 2145.

target *n.* shield 832.

tel *v.* declare, announce 3438.

telde *n.* tent or covering; hence, dwelling-place 2053.

tene *n.* anger, wrath 3756.

tent *n.* attention, care 890, 951; *tak tent* take heed 1225.

tent *v.* pay attention 2305.

thar *v.* need 1140.

the *v.* thrive, prosper; *so (als) mot I the* as I may prosper 1015, 3141.

think *3 sg. pr.* seems 285.

thole *v.* suffer, undergo 425; pt. *tholed* 383.

thra *adj.* stubborn, reluctant to give way 3570.

thrall *n.* servant, serf, slave 2416.

thraw, throw *n.* space of time, while, short time 849, 2361.

thriswald *n.* threshold 3222.

throte-boll *n.* Adam's apple; hence, larynx 1993.

throw *n.,* *see* **thraw.**

thwang *n.* thong, narrow strip of hide 3160.

tide *n.* space of time, season 3388.

tyght *pp.* intended, proposed 111.

tint, tynt *pt.* lost, wasted 2599, 3438.

tite, tyte *adv.* quickly, immediately 105, 409, 1328; *comp.* 1852.

tythand *pl.* **tithandes** *n.* news of an event, reports, intelligence 140, 2774, 2808; event 336.

tiþ(y)ng *n.* piece of news, information 1057.

tobreke *v.* break into pieces, burst asunder 964.

todrogh *pt.* pulled to pieces 823.

torent *pp.* torn to pieces 309; *pp. adj.* 2619.

toreven *pp.* split asunder, splintered 3632.

toþer *pron.* the other (of two) 686.

towches *3 sg. pr.* touches, affects 115.

towhils *adv.* during the time that, meanwhile 1079.

traystes *3 sg. pr.* trusts, has confidence in 2908.

tre *n.* wood 187.

trindeld *pt.* revolved, rolled 3259.

trispase *n.* transgression, wrong, breach of duty 4002.

trist *adj.* confident, sure 3888.

trofels *n. pl.* false, foolish, or trivial tales 150.

trow *v.* believe, trust 981, 2591.

trowage *n.* tribute 3035.

twyn *v.* go asunder (of two persons or things), part 2220.

þeder *adv.* to or towards that place (with verb of motion) 453, 604.

þederward *adv.* thither, in that direction 164.

þeþin *adv.* from that place, thence 382, 524, 2745.

þore *adv.* there 56.

þusgate *adv.* in this way, thus 3777.

umage *n.* act of homage, formal acknowledgement of allegiance 1952.

umbithoght *pt.* called to mind 1583.

umstrade *pt.* bestrode 1302.

unement *n.* ointment 1752, 1755.

unhende *adj.* discourteous, impolite 488, 502.

unkowth, unkouth *adj.* unknown, strange 501, 2944.

unkunand *adj.* ignorant, unsophisticated 76.

unnethes, unnese *adv.* with difficulty, hardly, barely 342, 344, 376.

unsely *adj.* bad, unfortunate, unlucky 2939, 3129.

unshet *pp.* opened 63.

unsought *adj.* untold, uncountable 798. *See also note.*

untill *prep.* to 138.

vasselage, vassage *n.* action befitting a good vassal, prowess in battle 1240, 2502, 2915.

velany *n.* insult, injury 88.

veneri *n.* venery, hunting 26.

verraiment, verrayment *adv.* in truth, truly, 1491, 2317.

vetale *n.* military stores, provisions 1873.

wa *n.* woe 432, 822, 1643.

wan *pt.* succeeded in doing, managed 1803; *refl.* betook oneself 3412; pp. *wonnen*, obtained, acquired 3435.

wane *n.*[1] dwelling; *wil of wane* homeless 1643, 2115.

wane *n.*[2] abundance; (*ful*) *gude wane* a good number, a great amount 1429, 1665, 1685.

war *adj.* sagacious, cunning 12, 21.

warand *n.* defender, champion 2583.

warand *v.* give warranty, guarantee 1049.

warisowne *n.* wealth, reward 918, 3586; *gif to warisowne* give as prize 2399.

warist *pp.* healed 2654.

warned *pt.* refused, forbade 2261.

wate *v.* know 423, 2836.

wate *v.* wait, watch 311.

wede *n.* clothing, garments 2724.

wede *v.* become mad 2632, 3647.

welde *v.* rule, command 3025.

wele *v.* choose, pick out 2507.

welefare *n.* good fortune, success (in living) 1354.

welk *3 sg. pt.* walked 1653.

wende *v.* go away, betake oneself, journey 477, 527, 921; pp. *went* gone 536, 1561.

wene *v.* think 73; pt. *wend* 378, 685.

were *n.* danger, peril 1212.

were *v.* protect, guard against 1743, 2578.

werr *compar. adv.* worse 436.

wharesum *adv.* wherever 30.

whas *pron.* whose 2841.

whederward *adv.* to what place 2837.

wheþen *adv.* whence 1044.

wheþer *pron.* which of the two 1002.

whideware *adv.* far and wide 3782.

wight *n.* creature, human being 212, 245, 2111.

wight *adj.* strong, courageous, powerful 830, 1219.

wightly *adv.* boldly, swiftly, rapidly 932, 965.

wike *n.* week 3058.

wil, will *adv.* straying, wandering; *will of rede* at a loss for a plan 379; *wil of wane* homeless 1643, 2115.

wyn *v.* obtain by effort 898; rescue, deliver 3198.

wyn *n.* joy, bliss, delight 1113, 1121, 2219; *als have þou wyn* as you expect to have bliss 1113.

wirships *n. pl.* honours, distinctions 1572.

wis *v.* give information, direct, guide 1046, 1826.

wise, wyse *n.* manner, fashion 455, 837; *on al wise* in all ways, in every way 130, 227, 1233; *on alkyn wyse*, see **alkyn**.

wit *v.* know 578, 998; 1 sg. pr. *wote* 2585; 3 pl. pr. *wote* 2585; pt. *wist* 86, 661.

wite *v.* accuse, blame 895, 1028.

withset *pt.* blocked, beset a way to prevent passage 1921.

Witsononday *n.* Whitsunday 16.

wittes *n. pl.* faculty of thinking, understanding 275; *see also* **kowth**.

wode *adj.* insane, mad 484, 822, 2378.

wogh *n.* evil, wrong; *with wogh* wrongfully 895.

won *v.* live, dwell 863, 2249; pp. *woned* 212.

wonder *n.* wonder 2938; *have wonder* be greatly surprised, astonished 617, 2241.

wonder *adj.* wonderful, wondrous; in compounds: *wonder-mace* 250, *wonder-wede* 267.

wonder *adv.* wonderfully, wondrously; in compounds: *wonder-wele* 218, *wonder-blak* 269, *wonder-fayne* 386.

wonderly *adv.* to a wonderful degree 1456.

wonyng *n.* dwelling 1065.

wonnen *pp.* of *winnen*, to win.

worth *v.* become; *worth of* become of, happen to 546, 924.

worthly *adv.* elegantly, nobly 184.

wote *v.* know 82, 915.

wrath *adj.* wrathful, irate 136.

wreche *adj.* miserable, unfortunate person 2939.

wreghed *pp.* accused, charged 2859.

wreke *v.* avenge 587, 2206; pp. *wroke(n)* 1319, 2437.

wreth *v.* grow angry 995.

INDEX OF PERSONS AND PLACES